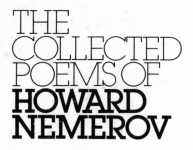

# THE COLLECTED POEMS OF HOWARD NEMEROV

Joan L Ceale
738 Wolcott Dr.
Phila. PA 19118

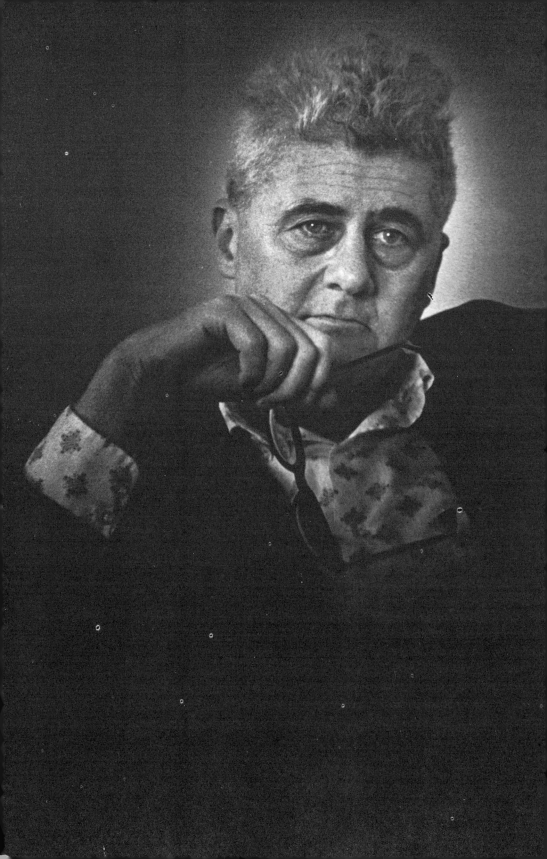

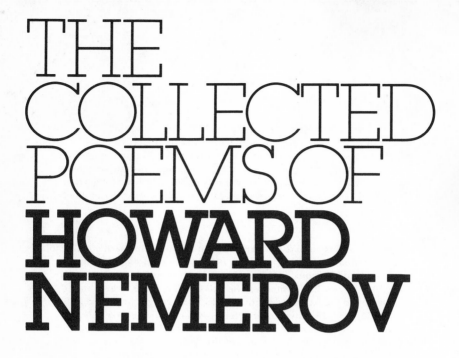

# THE COLLECTED POEMS OF HOWARD NEMEROV

THE UNIVERSITY OF CHICAGO PRESS · CHICAGO & LONDON

HOWARD NEMEROV is the Edward Mallinckrodt Distinguished University Professor of English at Washington University in St. Louis. He was associate editor of *Furioso* magazine from 1946 to 1951 and consultant in poetry to the Library of Congress from 1963 to 1964. Mr. Nemerov has won many notable literary awards, the most recent being the Levinson Prize from *Poetry* magazine and the Fellowship of the Academy of American Poets in 1971.

The poems in this volume have appeared in the following earlier collections: *The Image and the Law*, copyright © 1947 by Henry Holt and Company, Inc.; *Guide to the Ruins*, Random House, 1950, copyright © 1947, 1948, 1949, 1950 by Howard Nemerov; *The Salt Garden*, Little, Brown and Company and the Atlantic Monthly Press, 1955, copyright © 1950, 1951, 1952, 1953, 1954, 1955 by Howard Nemerov; and *Mirrors & Windows: Poems*, © 1958 by Howard Nemerov; *New & Selected Poems*, © 1960 by Howard Nemerov; *The Next Room of the Dream*, © 1962 by Howard Nemerov; *The Blue Swallows*, © 1967 by Howard Nemerov; *Gnomes & Occasions*, © 1973 by Howard Nemerov; *The Western Approaches: Poems 1973–75*, © 1975 by Howard Nemerov, all by the University of Chicago Press

The University of Chicago Press, Chicago 60637
The University of Chicago Press, Ltd., London
© 1977 by Howard Nemerov
All rights reserved. Published 1977
Printed in the United States of America

81 80 79 78 77    54321

**Library of Congress Cataloging in Publication Data**
Nemerov, Howard.
   The collected poems of Howard Nemerov.
   Includes index.
PS3527.E5A17   1977         811'.5'4         77–544
ISBN 0–226–57258–7

Frontispiece by Scott C. Dine
Courtesy of *St. Louis Post-Dispatch*

# Contents

GUIDE TO THE RUINS (1950)

THE SALT GARDEN (1955)

1

# MIRRORS AND WINDOWS (1958)

## 1

## 2

## 3

NEW POEMS (1960)

# THE NEXT ROOM OF THE DREAM (1962)

### 1 Effigies

### 2 Emblems

### 3 Vaudeville & Critique

## THE BLUE SWALLOWS (1967)

### 1 Legends

xiii

GNOMES & OCCASIONS (1973)

1

4

## THE WESTERN APPROACHES (1975)

### 1 The Way

xvii

# THE
# IMAGE AND
# THE LAW
# (1947)

*For John Pauker and W. R. Johnson*

1

EUROPE

Saint and demon blindly stare
From the risen stone;
Brought to a common character
Neither can stand alone.

Saint and demon both look down
Upon the public square:
*Iubilate,* says the one,
The other says despair.

The people knit Assyrian brows
Like statues on the rack;
They all have eaten up their cows
And drink their coffee black.

Nothing in Heaven is of stone
And nothing dusts away.
Of the blood of redemption
The angels drink alway.

No stony powder scores their throats
Who have this saving cup,
But saints and beasts are beams and motes
To silt our voices up.

Else should we Alleluia sing
Across the withered gut,
As fiddles over hollows sing
To make the air sound out.

New eucharists we must call down
To fill our empty rooms:

New heroes stagger into town
Under their heavy tombs.


## THE FROZEN CITY

1   Visionary and not believed
   Is no longer the position
   Nor the prerogative of
   Saints, mystics, and the holy poor.
   Rather on reefers and coke
   I expound to the multitude
   Traumatic aggrandizements
   Of my person in triplicate
   At least; for this receiving
   The indifference of belief
   From those who love the miracle
   And let the doctrine go.

   I enter upon my song and dance:

2   I saw by moonlight New York
   Which was called in my dream
   The Island of God, and achieved
   In the paralysis of distance
   A splendid fixity, as though
   The parable of a town.
   Cold space parted me from
   The marvelous towers
   Towards which I strained.
   With every appearance of
   Solidity the city yet
   Possessed the radiant dead
   Purity of ice, glass, reflecting
   Clearly the multitudinous stars.
   Under the constellation of
   A sword, Blake and Augustine
   Swam the middle air

Extending their perpetually
Protecting benediction
Over the silver port.
All bridges were down, and ships
Sharply broke up in the frozen rivers.
My eyes, from the abysmal
Heaven of the dream's stance,
Detected no commerce or action,
And the snow lay undisturbed
By wheel or step and flashed
With sidereal brilliance the
Respeculation of Heaven.

This was, as the dream understood,
The artifice of eternity
Produced by efficient suffering
And the total wish for death.
How the committees had worked,
Organizations of ladies begged
The people to refrain from eating:
The assault on Heaven's justice
(Scorning mercy) had been conducted
By many the most eminent
Citizens and public men;
The rape of God's attention
Employed the methods commended
By the superior saints, with only
A hint of economic condescension
And the irony of the best people.

Descending and moving closer
I saw the sad patience of
The people awaiting death
(They crossed their bony 'legs,
Their eyes stared, hostile and
Bright as broken glass). The dream said:
You must know that the period
Of partial damage is complete:
Nothing now will defray the costly

Agonies of the sempiternal.
Understand that these are dying
Into grace by an act of the will;
And if some still stare at the harbor
And mutter of nipples or ten per cent
This ghostly quality of lust retains
No understanding of itself: for as
All words are prayer, all words
Are meaningless, by the last fiat
Of the last secular council.

This was true. Moving, I saw
The murderer staring at his knife,
Unable to understand, and a banker
Regarding a dollar bill with fixed
Incomprehension. Queerest of all,
Children rolled skulls in the street,
The sound of their light laughter
Contrasting strangely with their
Gangrenous flesh and the
Convulsive motions of their limbs.
Parents looked on from doorways
And were alert with approval
For the quickest among the children:
But more than once I saw envy in
Their shining eyes.
                              Some, while
I watched, died (their heads
Rolled off, this signifying
An abdication of the will)
But the cold preserved them in
Their charnel integrity.
As from a distance, down
Halls of column and arch, I heard
Meanwhile many voices singing:

*Tuba mirum spargens sonum*
*Per sepulcra regionum,*
*Coget omnes ante thronum.*

Looking skyward then, I heard
The mighty guardians reply
To the city's qualified despair.
Tears spun from their eyes
Like suns, and wheeled glittering
Out to space, new planets of
Compassionate experiment:

*William*
*Blake*  Jerusalem, desiring the vine
Blindly we have built the machine:
For the eye altering alters all.

*Saint*
*Augustine*  *Quomodo ardebam, deus meus,*
*Revolare a terrenis ad te,*
*Et nesciebam quid ageres mecum.*

Then in my dream the blind
Mercy of the Lamb was loosed
Upon the moral world: the sun
Burned Heaven from the town,
Flowers grew with monstrous
Innocent speed. The dead arose,
And began with spastic hands
To gather money from the streets:
As though ravaged by intolerable
Heat of life, people ran to the cool
Marble vaults of bank and tomb
And threw themselves upon the cold
Gold or earth, it seemed for
Sovereign unredeeming solace.

I found myself leaving the city
And fading from my own dream.
From a distance the scene
Showed no unusual activity.
My last sight was of Blake
And Augustine, in whose glacial
Eyes, frozen by their last tears,
City and dream were locked together.

3        Waking, close to midnight and
By irony in the same city,
I listened to the usual noises:
The argument of two women, the drunk
Singing in the back yard, and
Various metal, rubber, wooden
Sounds that spoke of the normal.

The healthy man, waking at
Midnight, turns over to sleep
Again. What sound began and
Ended at once his dream, in time
Immeasurable by clocks or
Time for meals, was his only
Warning from the metaphysical,
Suspected not even by his sleep.


## FROM A RECORD OF DISAPPOINTMENT

It is the hour of indecision,
Decembers of Tuesday pass.
Now consider the high
Ridges and ridings where
The wind blows the cold snow.

Here, the stove has gone out
And we reach a metropolitan
Genteel conclusion, as the snow
Freezes the windows open or shut.

Look outside. The relevant
Is everywhere, and like the snow
(Though blown by the wind in unmanned spaces)
Locks and latches the tall
Shiplike city and ourselves
In the chaste paralysis
Of decided history.

# THE TRUTH OF THE MATTER

The Sunday papers are on the streets.
Several people starved in Bucharest.
Read (because the truth is black and white)
The truth. When one reads it is
As much the black as the white that
One reads, construing the letters.

Here the human faces are gray as
Old bread, where the camera has
Stopped two or three on a gray day
In a sky that seems to be raining.
Words show that these faces have shuddered
Instantaneously from, say, Madrid.

The citizen reads the Sunday papers.
He thanks his God he is not
In Posnan or Allenstein or Belgrade.
He is, for example, in Chicago.
The world situation is terrible,
The famine a terrible thing.

The head of a great sugar refinery
Has died of diabetes. That sounds right:
The citizen considers divine justice,
Reads further of the Ministers at Paris:
A person with a flaming sword has been
Arrested in the rain, in Schenectady.

On Monday morning the truth comes
In smaller packages, neat and pale
With a brand of words over the brow.
On Monday the wisdom of Sunday
Drifts on the gutter tides. The pale,
The staring faces, twirl around and go down.

TWO POEMS

I

The house is named of night. Pale maidens sing
The satisfactions of the night. We lie
In the round of the egg, and cannot be conceived
By drummers throbbing at the hollow round.

In Africa, whole tribes with painted rumps
Circle their fires, beating out no code
Of civil overtures, but humping up
A savage erudition to the sun.

Yet here (already) we have invented tools
For clawing nervously the beard or hair,
And limbs of artifice that can outline
Featly the spastic motions of despair.

Seductive music all the same: a band
Of black men with their drums and horns askew.
Now sound, black man, your oboe's lowest O,
That syllable eclipsed behind the sun:

Reverberate the problems of the egg
That was before the world; of that black king
Or shaman that was naked principal
Begetter of the world upon the sun.

And here white girls reply: our genesis
Was on a satin bed. Pythagoras
Drummed us to being on a whore, we are
Ladies who have intelligence of love.

White scientists at corner tables frown,
And isolate corruptions of the sun
Which will, in capsules for the innocent,
Make everglades of these pale continents

And increase aged lust with light's increase.
The jungle roars with carnal artifice
And swollen creepers choke the former trails:
Pallid spinsters sing love's pale empire.

II

Cases of light and shadow on Times Square
Are facts, lucid and black. But in the jungle
The torn and divided shadow falls as it may
In green lightning, and on this leaf or that.

Ideas of the jungle define the man, define
His dream: the fragmentation of his shades
Produces wilderness enough, in which
All single light, refractory, cracks up.

The jungle nights, too, with their snowy moons,
Bring generation from carnality:
He realizes his romantic lust
In the erratic angles of his dream.

Yet history begins at home. The lights
Of fancy stain his shadow on the stone:
It follows him through crowds, runs up the thighs
And breasts of his impracticable wives.

Thus affianced, divorced, he does not turn
But paces jungle paths, a hot patrol
Past ruined images, dishonored styles.
Thick grasses overgrow his yielding heart.

Also in Angkor Vat, he thinks, the sun
And moon beat blackest rhythms from the stone.
The spirit, the idea, the politic
Left volumes, records, empty offices.

What is it that he lacks? The bright machine
With gold connecting rods is dead. He has

Legend and image, divine relations,
Knows of Thermopylae and Bunker Hill.

Their insufficiency appalls. He will
Design a history to himself: himself
The hero, the comic and the tragic man,
Honor himself in Marathons and studs.

Here he begins. In Times Square, at the same
Time in the jungle. In precise blue air
He stands, a solitaire, and drags to begin
His broken shadow through the green debris.


## THE STARE OF THE MAN FROM THE PROVINCES

In the metropolis of hooligans
Sweet May reigneth forever. Do you hear
The pale chitter of china wings in windows?
Glass parakeets preen and silently shrill.

The perfumes of hooligan ladies spill
An old delight upon the ground, their shadows
Couple inconsequentially everywhere.
Peacocks in windows spread up their proud fans.

Indeed the city coruscates with eyes
Both bold and proud, of dames and gentlemen,
That flowerlike upon their haughty stalks
Bulge at the perfect springtime of the streets.

Only at night, between the snowy sheets
Resting infected feet from pleasant walks,
All eyelids close, confine the citizen
Within the echoing caverns of his eyes.

At night all hooligans in lonely bed
Must suffer cry of birds they had thought dead.

And diamond beak, unfashionable nails
Tear at the eyes until in sleep sight fails.


## PORTRAIT OF THREE CONSPIRATORS

They sit in a room. Outside the world revolves,
And the tired despotic seasons succeed
Each other forever. They sit there forever.

A venomous, fanged one. One delicate
And velvet. And a bitter man between
Who no longer believes the world a stage.
He arbitrates. These are the conspirators.

Among imaginations of the world
A room, four walls, a table and three chairs;
Strong light and language to misunderstand.

They plan the overthrow of something,
Maybe by bomb, or gun, or spoken word.
That something exists. It modifies the words
Of the conspirators, which break against
Implacable existence. Life, a diamond:
I know how it is. And once I had thought
Of diamond self with diamond life, a true
Tension and irony; but now I know
This life, these lives, will break.

It is night, and it is the season of winter.
It is in time, and time passes, and
The world is not a stage. I thought of these
Conspirators: the snake, the Machiavell,
The bitter man between; and composed
Their portraits with the clear impotence
Of judgment. Now season and element
Resolve, combine, distract me with their change.

I say to my assassins, Look: the mind
That made you cannot discompose you nor
Rouse you to life, but you sit in the mind
Revolving schemes referring to the real.
You are not real, the splendor of your words
Falls coldly on the seasons as they go
Like disappointed kings to burial.

I say to them, I must die, because the world
Is not a stage. And you are growing old,
You are not diamond that might scratch the glass
Of Heaven or the mind: you are the shadows
Of posturing desire, and you effect no change
In the position of things as they are.

Nothing can change them. They sit there as if
Immortal, and mutter, like actors on a stage,
Of art and wisdom, and a change of life.


## THE TRIUMPH OF EDUCATION

The children's eyes were like lakes of the sea
And baffling with their false serenity
When they were told, and given all the cause,
"There is no Santa Claus."

The children's eyes did not become more bright
Or curious of sexual delight
When someone said, "Man couples like the beast,
The Stork does not exist."

The children's eyes, like smoke or drifted snow,
White shifted over white, refused to show
They suffered loss: "At first it may seem odd—
There isn't any God."

The children, not perturbed or comforted,
Heard silently the news of their last bed:

"For moral care you need not stint your breath,
There's no Life after Death."

The children's eyes grew hot, they glowed like stoves.
Ambitious, and equipped with all our proofs,
They ran forth little women, little men,
And were not children then.


IN THE GLASS OF FASHION

I am asked why I do not
Stop writing about death
And do something worth while.
To write about what would be
Not to write about death?

Let me hypothesize an
Invasion of El Morocco by
Armed insurgents, probably
Mongol; and describe the
Muscular economies of the
Human face, where terror
Would continue to smile:
Is this funny enough?

In the same way, one
Goes on dealing in a set
Of manners that do not
Perhaps apply to the local
Situation: with verity
Chilled to the page: but
There is no help for this.

The virtuous express their
Virtue by laughing at the
Distant catastrophe: when
Shanhaikwan was taken there
Were enough people at dinner

Who found it amusing, since
"Whenever one laughs, a man
Is dying."
                Admitted: and yet
Their open faces have the look
Of faces paralyzed during the
Performance of an indecent act.
Which is to say: the laugh
That was appropriate for Spain
Will do for Shanhaikwan
If one is able to repeat
Exact equivocations of the mask.

But the verities, I say again,
Continue to repeat themselves in
Precisely the same manner; and the
Resemblance to death is inescapable.


## WHO DID NOT DIE IN VAIN

The voyager returned, but much perplexed:
For several years himself had sacrificed
But carried still that self-same incubus,
Unfriendly and persistent as a wound.

The high heroic, with its mud and blood,
That made a virtue of a dirty face—
He was reputed to have left it there,
Sloughed it in meadows where the corpses lay

Of others who, more fortunate or less,
Had fluted in the grass final designs:
For death, he thought, can no man take away
From the dead, who are precisely what they are.

Who whether mournful, reverent or proud,
Or deprecating, supercilious,

Have no man's message in their open mouth:
Whose silence will support no politic.

However it had been, here he came back
Tired, to drag the gangrene—all his past—
Along familiar ways, to carry home
Whatever viciousness he learned to breathe.

And his acquaintance-dead, that never left
Bastogne, or sank beneath the China Sea,
Their death the death of movies, amplified
Beyond his power or belief to share—

Their silence was by politicians used,
Their teeth opened with phrase, their puppet heads
Voided comic balloons: their speaking death
Supposed his debt, and gave him much advice.


## THE PLACE OF VALUE

The way MacLane died, they set
His feet in a bucket of drying
Cement and let him off the bridge
Late one night. He screamed once,
An adequate criticism and his best
Epigram. It was a private fight.

What shall I say? That the world
Is set in its hardening history
Like MacLane, to scream going down?
Or that MacLane was like
MacLane and no one else, and he
Is dead and there is no other,
Unique and unimportant?

The white moon breaks to dust
On the river where he sank;

The Septentrion shines high
In cold temporal distance.
Let everyone go home: MacLane
Is no longer known by that name.

The "place of value in
A world of fact" is to supply
Cohesiveness, weight, stability,
And to give reason and point
To the particular screams
Which otherwise merely would
Echo between empty buildings
Or make bubbles in the water.
As it is, irrelevance
Already surrounds us, and
I have known people to die
By the failure of a cotter pin
Who believed they were fighting for truth.

Consider the position: the light-
Minded faces met on every street,
The vacant expressions of
The habitually wary, the snide
Incredulous stares of the
Proprietors of contemporary thought,
Are facts: their screams are facts
And their silences also scream.
The parietal structure (bone
Or cement), in order to operate
At all, must act at a level
Common to all, the level of
Eating and defecation, of sex
And sleeping, and the careful
Conveyance away of waste products
(On which nightmares are known
To feed). The history of
These faces, whose death-masks,
Already taken, are wrapped
In wet newspaper and kept on file,
Is of necessity disregarded:

MacLane is his own business,
Who dealt by night in surrogates—
Money, cigars, amniotic beer—
For unreckoned satisfactions.

Even the greatest state subsists
By necrocytosis and the nightly
Secession of its smallest unit
Into the unexampled lechery
And soft gluttony of dreams:
MacLane made concrete equivalence
And died of relevance and justice
By his lights. The rest of us,
Amazed mice, face the neurosis
Of the continual choice on which
All depends; or play the hopeless
Shell game against the cheerful
Healthy statistician, who knows
"Pretty well" the final result.

Numberless stars, like snow
In Heaven, shine on the black
Water, so dancing and so still:
Reflect inextricable confusions
Of value in fact. The singular
Angel of each event protects
That event from being perfectly seen.

In a bucket of cement
Cohesiveness, weight, stability.
It is a private fight.


UNDER THE BELL JAR

*For the Eye Altering Alters All*

Number, said the skull Pythagoras,
Their transfixed eyes design the world.

Sprung by sun and moon their bones
Lattice and net the light in number.

The beaches of the world are full,
The rivers are silted with the dead.
At Thebes and Antibes taking the sun,
In the sand and salt of eternal life
They turn in season to the sun.

By the moon will they escape?
In terrified cold virginity
Their falling forms reject us
By unspeakable accident of stance?
Abstracts of night they would not know
God and Son and guarding Ghost
Out of the writings of the cold saints.

Who are the dead, and what do they ask?
Holy Diana, Aquinas, Lord Lord.
They act to the suffossion of life, their graves
Undercut the foundations of cities:
Powerless they gain the ascendancy.
We maintain life on old battlegrounds,
Where death fattens the seed for death.


## THE MASTER AT A MEDITERRANEAN PORT

*In Memoriam: Paul Valéry*

What, Amicus, constitutes mastery?
The perdurable fire of a style?
A rock that the incessant sea
Thunders against for fifteen hundred years?
Or maybe, manners that can speak
Of excrement without offense.

Here even the ocean relaxes its incessant
Organic shudders, finds an evident
Repose where keel to keel the brilliant vessels

Elide the shadow and the real, gliding
Between the clearest elements of glass.

And man, geometer, construes his arcs
And angles to cathedral poise, of which
Sunday's massive reserve composes still
Continuous limits of the possible.

But yonder in white foam Poseidon rises:
It is a disputed field, it changes sides,
Is turbulent, is unreflecting, deep
And deep and deep, and boils at interruption
Of wind or keel.
                    O valuable glass,
Clear harbor, floor not altogether false:
Respect the doubleness of these laws.
Mastery, the master, his image and his stance,
His way of seeing, his eloquent speech:
Amicus, these are no perdurable fire,
No steadfast rock. They are
The manners of a time, an age perhaps
Ready to die, a classical notation
For the harbor glass, the law against the truth.


PARAPHRASE FROM NOTEBOOKS

Well, the brilliance is gone,
Change in the weather chills.
Sometimes you feel you are alone
On a planet tilting from the sun.

Like the fall of nations in the mind
Soundless each leaf falls
Disturbing to some certain end
The leaves in patterns on the ground.

Is it the end? In a failing light
Engines begin to pulse:

Will the great searchlights go out,
Or history gutter in the night?

Forget all this, forgive the time
Your birth, and other faults
Or combinations of the game:
The time one day will lose its name.

On God and the Egg then speculate:
All meditation else
Would be to this a counterfeit:
What put the fire in the fat?


THE SITUATION DOES NOT CHANGE

Only the dead have an enduring city,
Whose stone saints look coldly on a cold world
With the compassion of pure form not flesh.
They look upon the signatures of things
Where clarity and singular radiance
Display beholder and beheld. They see
Only the clear reduplicated forms.

Who travels, nomad, on the face of things,
Pitching his city like a tent, must pray
But not for clarity. His images
Are wax, his candles before any saint
Melt in their unregenerating heat.
In his inconstant travel he cannot
Achieve a proper motion or be still.

Yet this relates to the desires of
The saints, whose lines of pity show that they
Too burned or melted once, in pilgrimage
Not endless if to our uncertain end.
And all of these in stone are still consumed
In untold fires, only now as image
To show the mind unspoken piety.

O Lord, we may not pray for permanence:
Not for death, nor for destruction of cities.
Neither moving nor still, lost in the vast
Desert or tundra, our Atlantic time
Coastless and without depth or place to hide
Lord from thy sun. Like melting wax we change,
Waiting the last shape of death at thy hand.

# 2

## OBSERVATION OF OCTOBER

An old desperation of the flesh.
Mortification and revivification
Of the spirit. There are those
Who work outdoors, and others
Who pull down blinds against the sun.

A cold October day I find
Fear of death in the weather, for
Those in the streets are hurrying,
And those at home take hot baths
Or pace the floor and refuse to go out.

And many, winter approaching,
Go early to bed at night, refuse
To admit their friends or read the papers,
And sleep curled up. There are, I think,
Simplicities in every life.

## METROPOLITAN SUNDAY

Newspapers cover the floor,
A slight headache is the only
Proof of the world's existence.
Outside, black smoke ascends
Directly to Heaven and is lost,
The Chrysler building points
With obscene derision at the bland
Submissive sky, where a blimp
And a toy balloon swim about

Unreal and nonchalant as
An instruction in geometry.

A day of the portly but
Amiable music of Handel.
Could not one be
Elsewhere, or in Boston?
Aimless and important, the
Newspapers freeze life
To the floor, the advancing
Ice-cap of every Sunday.

Sleep is the only remedy for such
A day: but always I am dragged
Back to amazement by the sight
Of the man at the window opposite,
Who resembles Laval and is always eating.


WARNING: CHILDREN AT PLAY

The children in the street play hard.
By hopscotch, ball, and circle they
Design the mental maze.
They play by rule and stretch the cord
Unworried by their elders' praise.

The elders' games are not so good.
For the jump-rope that caught the neck
Incriminates desire:
Too old for games, they play for blood,
A sullen chess beside the fire.

The arguments of play will come,
Children, to virtue in the end.
The rope that hangs by rule
Will mind you then to play the game
That keeps you in long after school.

## TWO SIDES TO AN OUTSIDE:
## MEDITATION FROM EMPSON

*Matter includes what must matter enclose.*
*It is Styx coerces and not Hell controls.*

The universe of course is infinite,
Said Epicurus, throwing a javelin
Off from the outer edges of assumption:
For if the spear rebound there's more outside,
And more outside if it go on in flight.

Repeat the experiment at every stage,
He said, but lacked the energy of proof.
He thought that reason was for mind enough,
And he concluded there; he was no drudge:
I doubt he ever would have reached the edge.

We've gone alone into the sky with spears
To stalk upon that ancient game preserve,
But always at the throw have lacked the nerve:
So big a flank no tinder matchstick scares—
And we return to boasting over beers.

The mind includes what must the mind enclose:
The universal skin has pins for hair,
And on each point the angels dance an air.
We wear this turncoat on the mind like clothes
See how our gilt-red doublet bravely shows!

Reversible coats are all our rage this year.
Both sides the same they never keep us warm:
The trick's to turn the sleeve upon the arm
For comfort when it's rain or storm you fear;
Wear metaphysic when the sky is clear.

# A MORALITY

*Mentre che il vento, come fa, si tace.*

They all were spared to tell their stories,
Seemed not to mind the burning and the pain:
For while they spoke, the wind, fire, and furies
Rested attent, reasoned with them their stain.

As though they had some doubt of the great decree
They sat, sullen perhaps, but leashed to words:
It was the joke, too, with Orpheus, that he
Disordered all created things with chords.

    Good folk all, may ye take from this to sing
    And tell your stories round, that for short time
    The interest of Heaven should each one bring
    Small cess from pain, excuse his silly crime.


# EPITAPH ON A PHILOSOPHER THE REPORTS OF WHOSE DEATH HAVE BEEN GROSSLY MINIMIZED

You have denied hard fact, or never tried
To verify that stone from which you cut
Your gods who would not trouble to exist.

Something remains: in its unholy pride
The fictive bone, like a disease of light,
Sheds an old sack of shadow on the ground.

If you are this, you are beyond reproach,
Have passed the scandal of a rebel heart
With heresy no longer possible.

I think of caves of shadow where the thing
Is mourned, adored, and all its thingness gone:
For of your grave the undeluding dark

Makes further shadow: relative to this
You have become a subject for belief,
Cold fact that grieving heretics deny.


## THE BARON BAEDEKER BLEW HIS NOSE AND, SIGHING, DEPARTED

Hector (for example) is dead. So also
Joseph of Arimathea and Arthur Rimbaud.
Over the multitudinous dead

The eleven heavens of the eleven
Desirable civilizations
Lie in tumultuous decay.

Empyrean Paris lies in ruins,
London town is tumbling down:
Ah ciel, ah ciel, said Mrs. St. Cloud,
Where shall I go to die?

The Ritz remains. There they build
Of rock and glass the last
Fashionable tomb; and there sweet girls
With lipsticks paint reluctantly
Shy, filthy limericks.

Contempt for death, desire to the world:
Compulsive ironies of "our time."


## CROCODILE AT THE ANCIENT TOMBS

The Pharaohs were sealed up in their own dust
And filed away beneath their heavy stones,
Waiting the future reference of the sands
Which in a slow search covered and discovered.

But Mr. Crocodile, the traveler,
Went through the pyramids like a strong purge.
The sunshine of his smile may yet be seen
at Karnak, or on camels near the Sphinx.

He made the slow hotels vicious with life,
The past departed at his near approach.
Embarrassed strangers still have photographs
Of Crocodile astride a sacred cat.

He desecrated temples with good will
And photographed the gods. His name is cut
In the stones of sacred places; once at Thebes
A tomb collapsed where his scout knife went too deep.

O dark the latter end of Crocodile,
Whose suitcase was discovered full of sand.
The labels shone like battle honors, but
Of Crocodile was only his panama hat.

The Pharaohs long ago were wound in shroud
And immunized against eternity;
But Crocodile, a paler dust, has left
His hat, his smile, his memorable name.


## GLASS DIALECTIC

*For Dunstan Thompson*

A. Look in this mirror, tell me what you see.
B. Briefly, the good hypostasis of me.
A. A Glass from time and space to set you free.
B. And safely: mirrors have no memory.

Do not delude yourself, you are enthralled.
Magic in glass, your eyes reverse the world
And powerless, you cannot be recalled.

Dead men have been seen, whose eyes retained
A glassy charm: it may be, boy, you stand
In very hell, which cannot be explained.

Midnight, among the cabalistic books,
Old Faustus fell. The means were orthodox:
Red tights, a beard, and operatic spooks.

Faustus was saved, some claim, in his last hour:
You might not have his luck, might fall before
The contract drawn in pale reflection's power.

Narcissus too, reflected on the pool,
Was caught in simile and drowned; or fell
Right through, like Alice: Freud would call him fool,

His name indeed in books on vanity
Often occurs; but, every child's idea,
Alice has gained an awkward sanctity.

The lesson is, you are your metaphor,
Reflecting a light pallid and unsure
From substance that no mirror ever bore.

This ghost will speculate in glass, is cold,
But answers to your name when it is called.
Sometimes, at night, you feel you have been sold.

But you pretend there's time, you are enthralled:
You have changed sides and cannot be recalled,
From very hell your eyes reverse the world.


REFUSAL OF A KINDNESS OFFERED

Rump-Trumpet, the Critic
(Whose pseudonym was bestowed
After thought from a maidenly

Transliteration of Dante),
Graciously offered, poems,
To look you over, and give me
A sound opinion.
                    I dread
The test. How long will you live?
Must you be sent to the mountains?
What will the X-rays show?

In any case, what a thumping
There will be of chests, and
Humping about the room to a
Latinate tune; and then, the
Ahemming and Hrumph! Hrumph!
That will weigh acquaintanceship
Against that "critical reputation."

No! we will refuse his offer.
Not the poking and prodding that
We deprecate at his hands,
But to listen, afterwards, to the
Tedious, gloomy lecture of one
Who would have to rise above himself
In order to talk through his hat.

## A CHROMIUM-PLATED HAT: INLAID
## WITH SCENES FROM SIEGFRIED

*Choreography by the* New York Times Book Review

Greatness. Warmth, and human insight. Music.
But greatness. The greatness of Socrates
And Dante and Alexander Woollcott, and the
True charm of Horatio Alger, Jr. Also,
The greatness of eighteen-year-old girls,
The warmth of retired corporation lawyers,
The impossibility of having enough books

About truth. The important thing is
The relation of truth to our time to Kitty Foyle.
In addition, music. It is good to have music,
But not at the expense of greatness:
Better to be truly great and unmusical.
If you are merely musical you are probably
Not one of the great authors. The place
Of the glorious few is in that case
Not for you, but for Thomas B. Costain,
Who is welcome here almost any time.

To sum up, the truth of the matter is,
Quoting William Lyon Phelps, "There is
No masterpiece like *Lohengrin*, that
Masterpiece," and it may be better anyhow
To have human warmth than greatness:
Like Grandpa, who sat by the fire all
Winter long, in a buffalo rug with fleas.


## HISTORY OF A LITERARY MOVEMENT

After Margrave died, nothing
Seemed worth while. I said as much
To Grumbach, who replied:
"The oscillations of fashion
Do not amuse me. There have been
Great men before, there will be
Other great men. Only man
Is important, man is ultimate."
I can still see him sitting there,
Sipping level by level his
Pousse-café. He was a fat man.
Fat men are seldom the best
Creative writers.

                    The rest of us
Slowly dispersed, hardly

Ever saw each other again,
And did not correspond, for
There was little enough to say.
Only Impli and I
Hung on, feeling as we did
That the last word had not
Finally been said. Sometimes
I feel, I might say, cheated.
Life here at Bad Grandstein
Is dull, is dull, what with
The eternal rocks and the river;
And Impli, though one of my
Dearest friends, can never,
I have decided, become great.

# 3

AUTUMNAL

October: the falling leaves resume the earth,
Recording time upon the sodden floor;
All energies and foreign heats retract

And luminous at night, in rain, the mold
Decays. It is a timely paradox
To be considered by who works in stone.

Fading the flesh delineates the bone,
Indicts your face, a precious artifact,
That so your legal beauty may be known.

Mortal and inconclusive every fall
By repetition further unredeemed
Tears at the rotting fabric of this world

And falls away: in the destructive hour
False permanence of stone can speculate
In splendid light, illumination and

Reconnaissance of always failing time.
How should we be the emblem of our tomb?
Always we fail with time to fall: and yet

Love might construct a form so true, so tense
As to survive its own antithesis,
Achieving an ironic permanence

With, for a pulse, repetitive despair.
Fading, the flesh delineates the bone
As surely, certainly, as autumn leaves

Describe a tree when they resume the earth.
Then do not fear your beauty will be known
Only by fever, attempted by decay:

Love is the form of stone, statue and law
As far locked from corruption of the sun
As Buddha smiling in the seamless rock.

*. . . for my wife*

## FOR THE SQUADRON

*236th Coastal, Royal Air Force*

A salt weather on the East River
Where it runs with bristling spine
Between the towns.
               An ocean day,
And they are taking the guns
Off the ships.
             We fought the war
From places called North Coates and
Skegness, and saw the Danish coast
And Heligoland like a gunboat
On the shallow sea. That time
Is gone, they repaint the ships
Gay colors.
            Yet here the sea
Floods in among us, black, silent,
Moving ever its continual cover.

The water in every ocean, like
The blood in one body, ever
Equalizing pressure and level.

Of Middlemas and Prince, then . . .

Resting forever behind their
Four smashed and rusting guns.

In this same water.


## FOR W_____, WHO COMMANDED WELL

You try to fix your mind upon his death,
Which seemed it might, somehow, be relevant
To something you once thought, or did, or might
Imagine yourself thinking, doing. When?

It was, once, the most possible of dreams:
The hero acted it, philosophers
Could safely recommend it to the young;
It was acceptable, a theme for song.

And it was wrong? Daily the press commends
A rationed greed, the radio denies
That war is right, or wrong, or serious:
And money is being made, and the wheels go round,
And death is paying for itself: and so
It does not seem that anything was lost.


## SEPTEMBER SHOOTING

Now is the season for dry smell of powder,
The blue smoke inciting wood and fen
To silence after the gun's report.

Life has been long. But death comes quickly
And is not famous nor even identified
In the quiet marches where our bones remain.
The anonymous bullet flies out of
An irrelevant necessity, and knows no evil.

But we, while wearing other mask, have heard
The voices, moved with injudicious heat,
Incite to hate from the world's various heart,
Whose license rules the citizen no season.

Have seen the cities to the bomber's view,
Outlined in red on maps, like mental wounds:
Or like the wounds in majesty to second sight
Some weeks before the act, while still
Assassins group and choose their knives.

How should we know, what time or chance decides?

Living this fall, and maybe living next
Is little, or is much, depending on
Casual causes far beyond control:
The autonomous voices of the air
Echo reasoning and prayer; and death,
Standing as always, never moves unless
Somehow advised.

        The gray goose flying south
Consider: fix this central in your sight
And keep it, hold your breath and fire, once.


## THE SOLDIER WHO LIVED THROUGH THE WAR

I

Deliberate motion and the blue sound.
In plagal periods I hear the politics
Of the sea. It is the holiday speech

Made by the gloomiest orator, the orator
Whose words are the blue resonance of
Final defeat. His tongue savors salt.

Here is an audience
Of voluptuary innocence:
The panther girls on the sand
And the dead men grinning by.

## II

The men in helmets and final steel
Machine the seashore with their tread.
This is the parade of the ultimate will.

The last organism in the world
Flashes in final steel. This is
At liberty to hate or love.

As if risen from the sea
Rejecting the blue foam
Comes the great plated turtle
Whose back, they thought, would bear the world.

## III

And now the sunshine like the blessed rose
Sweetened the climate of lust, so that
The tawny-hided girls could seem to please.

This was the world, a select
Club for orgiastic rites, to which
Your entrance fee and dues are paid.

And if the blue sea spoke
Without a peroration to
Its flourishings, you would not blame
The dead men that they seemed to grin.


ACCORDING TO HIS SEASONS

You watch the night for images of death,
Which sleep in camera prints upon the eye.

Fires go out, and power fails, and breath
Goes coldly out: dawn is a time to die.
It ends. The heart and mind, untenanted
Of lust alike with logic and main chance,
Speak in the cold idiom of the dead,
Inelegant, compared beyond your sense.

The sun must raise you from this bed to play
At other dreams, these true or false to be.
So Jesus did to Lazarus, who then
Could neither live nor die like other men.
Night kills you; and you live unwillingly
By power pitiless and good as day.



TO THE MEMORY OF JOHN WHEELWRIGHT

There is no drug can shock you into pain.
Pain is a drug that makes the sleeping clear.
There is no hope or torment but you fear
These things the sleepers set in train.

There is a cup you old ones always find:
You must believe to see. It was not grief
Made dreaming Christ expect reprieve.

How should he fall through sleep so soon? Not blind:
It is the pain that makes the sleeping clear;
You should be blessed for holding sleep so dear,
That drugged and dreaming always kind.

The love is pain that is a sleeping draught.
The emptiness under sleep is all you fear,
The dead directionless winds that blow there.
It is a hunger you have fought.

It is the cup you old ones always take.
You must believe to see, on this waste shore,

That fury makes us, makes our fury more:
Few men drink of this bottomless lake.

The emptiness under sleep makes sleeping clear.
Dream comes down like the shadow of a cloud:
The worst pain you're damned to is old and cold;
Cold wind beneath the sleep you fear.

It is the drink you old ones always take.
You must believe to see.
                              But I had thought
These great racked and rudderless to be caught
In the dead winds that blow under death,
That made their dreaming seem so strange.
I see that dreams do not so much derange
The dreamer as the world he dreams:
You dared to keep that emptiness so near,
Emptiness made sleep so clear and dear.

I understand there was this certain faith
And that the dying was no change.


ANNIVERSARY

Time in the seed that grief put down, return
Reflective and seasonal beneath
All accidents. Centrique spring, we mourn
Not half enough. Insufficient breath

All life offers adequate, and we
Plow under harvest here, we sheaf
The bundle of our virtues up to be
Provender to the winter of a grief.

Time then proves grief on this reflection
The cancer of a glass, the catch
In all the smooth canals. Grief, being done,
Grows tall again in any glass you watch.

40

I live then, grow, by plagues of green that end
Now never, riotous glass: you, first dead friend.

## LOT'S WIFE

I have become a gate
To the ruined city, dry,
Indestructible by fire.
A pillar of salt, a white
Salt boundary stone
On the edge of destruction.

A hard lesson to learn,
A swift punishment; and many
Now seek to escape
But look back, or to escape
By looking back: and they
Too become monuments.

Remember me, Lot's wife,
Standing at the furthest
Commark of lust's county.
Unwilling to enjoy,
Unable to escape, I make
Salt the rain of the world.

## AN OLD PHOTOGRAPH

No one escapes the perjury of time:
This permanence that light and shade have struck
So brave in attitude, I would believe

Essential, and innocent of change.
I hold your head here, on a paper platter,
The eyes unswerving in dead constancy.

Then are you honest? Your smile is still and strange
(Your ignorance still able to deceive),
For, smoothed out, polished, and entirely plane,

Still you remain a subject for belief,
A frozen image in a wilderness
Where change officiously denies your life.

Call me the first of your idolaters:
As the prerequisite of sanctity
Is death or absence, you shall be adored;

Your eyes, that stare dimension from this flat,
Shall fix me to conceive your solid ghost.
Only do not come back, for if you do

And change, I'll hold this image to the sun
And watch the lines dissolve as light denies
Your eyes unswerving in dead constancy.


## THE PHOTOGRAPH OF A GIRL

I have your likeness here: you were like this.
Light swears by shadow here, that on a day
And in a place (but tells not where it is
Or when) you are to be supposed this way.

Or as some king, to whose golden use the sun
Must stamp new images to sanction trade,
Would you enrich me with a single coin
Where others, with many, have much commerce made?

Or do you tend me some security
For time, that when I come to you, we'll stay
Alone for just such time as this (though he
That took it, stands but twenty feet away?)

I doubt it is a parable of time:
How love can make an angle with the sun
To trap time on a page, forcing the same
To other time, and without running, run.

But I alone, and you in this flat land
Remain. That time and place you have abstracted
Will turn and die upon my turning hand:
With twice dying, time has some price exacted.


## ON READING "THE LOVE AND DEATH OF CORNET CHRISTOPHER RILKE"

Between death and the celebration of death
They intervene, the ancestors, with their
Extremes of calm create a larger space.
And you had thought that gaudy sweat of death
Great doings. Boy, a thousand of the fair
There fell, fought there on that calm tapestry.
Ancestors, fathers, progenitors, in death
Willess, you warp us on the looms of place:
We, threads and lines, we fall there, grow to be
These shields, these helmets, raveled out of death.


## SESTINA I

Thickness of paint or flesh cannot deface
The honor of the bone, no metaphor
Can name or claim that tempest of clear form.
Look through the eyes, conceive the fret and lace
Of place and age. Acid will only grave
Deeper love's lines that limit form's desire.

The painter's hand establishes the form
In volume, space; so that the painted face

43

Deepens the flat. Deep, deeper than the grave
The brush stroke cuts, involving a fine lace
Of blood and bone and vein, a metaphor
For what, speaking loosely, we call desire.

From chaos, dark night and, desolate, the grave,
From winter's rotten branch, essential form
Advances like a season. The metaphor
Of time extends itself to show your face;
And in this parable, time and desire
May meet as on a cross, or crossed in lace.

Consumed in time, you are a metaphor
Decided on dark ground. Space is the grave,
But this is borne out, perfect, by desire.
Fire in shape, consumption of clear form,
Elected light within the bone, can lace
What seems the constant bearing of your face.

And like a needle to its north, desire
Continually creates a metaphor
Of truth in falsity. Paint will unlace,
And flesh; and faithful time, maybe, deface
Even the honor of the bone, deform
Even the sense of eyes, serene and grave.

And all this light, reverting from your face,
Will be in parable a metaphor,
No more, for death. The moment of your form
Exerts a force on time, a constant lace
Endures on your dark ground that will but grave
Deeper with looking, limits of desire.

No matter to deface that metaphor
Now clear and formal, caught and crossed in lace:
The echo of the grave perfects desire.

# SESTINA II

A   No waste is trackless: all terrain the lost
    Discovers. Stones take footprints, bear the witness
    Of his being. Flight, the wanderer's end
    And only limit, teases, gives him leave
    At a rope's end, returns him to the city
    Where shadow fears know him and know his tracks.

B   Yet barrens there must be, that bear no witness:
    Some town of neutral mutes, or stranger city
    Fears cannot follow in, at warrant's end.
    There, in that air, no earth would take his tracks—
    No stone so tender, nor no record to leave
    At inns and shelters. That would please the lost.

A   O small chance, fellow! How could there be a city
    So strange those wardens of the blood would leave
    It unmolested? Cities are the end,
    The final snare set to beguile the lost.
    Why, every street would register his tracks
    And every peering cobbler bear him witness.

B   Now tell me, for what cause and by whose leave
    Are these spies set to smell about his tracks
    So that his fears can neither rest nor end?
    Who is it makes the journeyman bear witness
    To the telltale smoke and pleasure of the lost?
    Who sets against him all stones in the city?

A   I cannot tell, fellow. He leaves no tracks,
    That one, where's grievous pursuits affright the lost.
    I think he rules us in a world without end.
    It is to be his snares we build our city.
    He suffers each to bear his ghostly witness,
    His breath in us, we breathe but by his leave.

B   Stranger, let us pray for all the lost.
A   Fellow, you may not pray, but only witness.

B   Stranger, has this silly game no end?
A   Fellow, beware! You play it by his leave.

B   If I were lost I'd hide out in the city.
A   Hide where you will. But look: here are your tracks.


## THE FORTUNE TELLER

The fortune teller, certainly a fake,
Quite rightly holds you in contempt, for she
(Though she take your hand before she speak,
Nor can you question her sincerity)
Suspects the wisdom of your lucky break:
She knows the dark man and the ocean passage
For envoys of uncertain embassage
That may be evil (but their fortunes rise)
Or may be good, until they equalize.

She understands the fate you seek must bear
What fate's already given, or will give;
And views you with an intimate despair
That chuckles mournfully, but cannot grieve.
She prophesies, without asking to share,
Portals to fortune that can swing both ways
And boodle independent of your essays.
When you have gone she may, remotely, weep
At vague ambitions quartered on her sleep:

But not for you, whom she has sent away
With fortune of a sort, sentenced to wait,
Piously turning corners every day,
Computing and interpreting your fate:
Regretting departure but afraid to stay.
She cries, quietly in her mind, for reason
Unwise as that you cry for, under question
In constant session of another's lust,
Which she may bear some after you are dust.

46

# ADVICE FROM THE HOLY TOMB

Noon casts no shadow. Any other time,
A prophet's memory, darkens the land:
But shade is night, to cover any crime.

To walk in the sun at noon is for the bland
Eyes of those virgins, too young for any thought,
Whose haloes, parasols, your loves command.

The lover, though, the sinner, let him watch out,
And stare from any center of his sense:
Noon's doom is innocence.

Now it is noon, gather your daughters hence;
This one, that's none; that one, whose all at noon
Enfolds her all, exploring further continence.

I tell you it is too bad. These daughters, soon,
These curled and scented ornaments, will be
Sisters of light, antic ghosts of the sun.

Pity them, then, whose useless artistry
Serves to conceal shadow beneath the foot:
Their doom, and their prophetic memory.

Trust not clocks, division. Noon is not,
Like your days, numbered. Nor can the watching hand,
Radiant on the earth's face, be your root.

But glass, we are glass. Wherever we would stand
High noon will magnify light to a fault:
Doom will consume the land.

And your transparent heat will call a halt
Too late. Melting, your art cannot sublime
Fire to gold or spice, or decent salt.

Noon is your trial; and not put off on time.
Your life must serve, the earth and you aflame:
Whose suffering all the same
Brings shadow that will cover any crime.


## UNSCIENTIFIC POSTSCRIPT

There is the world, the dream, and the one law.
The wish, the wisdom, and things as they are.

Inside the cave the burning sunlight showed
A shade and forms between the light and shade,

Neither real nor false nor subject to belief:
If unfleshed, boneless also, not for life

Or death or clear idea. But as in life
Reflexive, multiple, with the brilliance of

The shining surface, an orchestral flare.
It is not to believe, the love or fear

Or their profoundest definition, death;
But fully as orchestra to accept,

Making an answer, even if lament,
In measured dance, with the whole instrument.

# GUIDE TO THE RUINS
# (1950)

*The living man who finds spirit, finds truth.*
*But if he fail, he falls among fouler shapes.*
Kena Upanishad

*To Reed Whittemore*

## GUIDE TO THE RUINS

One lives by commerce, said the guide.
One sells the available thing, time
And again: the ruins, the temple grove,
The gods with their noses knocked off.
One profits by the view.

It is a difficult trade, he said,
To give to the dishonored dead
Their stature and their stony eyes.
The vulgar paint has flaked away
Leaving the color of time,

The unimpassioned grey which is
Not now in commodious demand.
One gives, with broken Herakles,
A premium of legend, a pamphlet
To certify the chill.

What is it that one sells, the self?
I think not. One sells always time
Dissembled in heroic stone: such eyes
As look like cloud-reflecting lakes
In the old mountains of time.

## THE SECOND-BEST BED

Consider now that Troy has burned
—Priam is dead, and Hector dead,
And great Aeneas long since turned

Away seaward with his gods
To find, found or founder, against frightful odds.

And figure to yourselves the clown
Who comes with educated word
To illustrate in mask and gown
King Priam's most illustrious son
And figure forth his figure with many another one

Of that most ceremented time
In times have been or are to be
Inhearsed in military rime;
And will recite of royal fates
Until, infamonized among those potentates

By a messenger from nearer home,
His comedy is compromised
And he must leave both Greece and Rome
Abuilding but not half begun,
To play the honest Troyan to a girl far gone.

The wench lived on, if the son died—
All Denmark wounded in one bed
Cried vengeance on the lusty bride,
Who could not care that there would follow,
After the words of Mercury, songs of Apollo.


A POEM OF MARGERY KEMPE

I creature being mad
They locked me in my room,
Where, bound upon the bed
With smiling Satan there,
I would have broke my side
And given the heart to God.
Men said it was pride
Brought me to that despair.

> *Alas! that ever I did sin,*
> *It is full merry in heaven.*

The priest so angered me
That I would not confess.
I suffered his reproof
Scornfully, for my God
(I said) has mercy enough.
His kingdom I see
And Lucifer His rod
In my wretchedness.

> *Alas! that ever I did sin,*
> *It is full merry in heaven.*

When I recovered reason
I would have lived chaste,
And mocking my husband's right
I for a little season
Kept me for the sweet Christ,
Who said to me, "Dear Bride,
Rather the good man's lust
Than this dry pride."

> *Alas! that ever I did sin,*
> *It is full merry in heaven.*

But I, except in bed,
Wore hair-cloth next the skin,
And nursed more than my child
That grudge against my side.
Now, spirit and flesh assoil'd,
Against the wild world
I lace my pride in,
Crying out odd and even,

> *Alas! that ever I did sin,*
> *It is full merry in heaven.*

## A SONG OF DEGREES

Though the road lead nowhere
I have followed the road
In its blind turnings, its descents
And the long levels where the emptiness ahead
Is inescapably seen.

I have cried for justice, I have cried
For mercy, now I desire neither.
A man may grow strong in his wandering,
His foot strong as a wheel
Turning the endless road.

Foot and hand hardened to horn,
Nose but a hook of bone, and eyes
Not liquid now but stone—I
To myself violent, fiercely exult
In Zion everywhere.


## ON A TEXT: JONAH IV, xi

The Lord might have spared us the harsh joke;
Many that live in Nineveh these days
Cannot discern their ass from a hot rock.
Perhaps the word "cattle" refers to these?


## NICODEMUS

I

I went under cover of night
By back streets and alleyways,
Not as one secret and ashamed
But with a natural discretion.

I passed by a boy and a girl
Embraced against the white wall
In parts of shadow, parts of light,
But though I turned my eyes away, my mind shook
Whether with dryness or their driving blood;
And a dog howled once in a stone corner.

II

Rabbi, I said,
How is a man born, being old?
From the torn sea into the world
A man may be forced only the one time
To suffer the indignation of the child,
His childish distempers and illnesses.
I would not, if I could, be born again
To suffer the miseries of the child,
The perpetual nearness to tears,
The book studied through burning eyes,
The particular malady of being always ruled
To ends he does not see or understand.

A man may be forced only the one time
To the slow perception of what is meant
That is neither final nor sufficient,
To the slow establishment of a self
Adequate to the ceremony and respect
Of other men's eyes; and to the last
Knowledge that nothing has been done,
The bitter bewilderment of his age,
A master in Israel and still a child.

III

Rabbi, all things in the springtime
Flower again, but a man may not
Flower again. I regret
The sweet smell of lilacs and the new grass
And the shoots put forth of the cedar
When we are done with the long winter.

Rabbi, sorrow has mothered me
And humiliation been my father,
But neither the ways of the flesh
Nor the pride of the spirit took me,
And I am exalted in Israel
For all that I know I do not know.

Now the end of my desire is death
For my hour is almost come.
I shall not say with Sarah
That God hath made me to laugh,
Nor the new word shall not be born
Out of the dryness of my mouth.

Rabbi, let me go up from Egypt
With Moses to the wilderness of Sinai
And to the country of the old Canaan
Where, sweeter than honey, Sarah's blood
Darkens the cold cave in the field
And the wild seed of Abraham is cold.

## TO THE BABYLONIANS

*If I forget thee, O Jerusalem . . .*

Driven out of Paradise,
Shame and knowledge in their eyes,
My first parents in the dust
Taught the generations lust.

All, because Abel was slain,
Pass the narrow straits of Cain—
Children of the Land of Nod
Driven to freedom by their God.

*The spider spun, and the gull cried:*
*For all that, the world was wide.*

Brother against his brother fought,
Slavery was sweetly bought.
Up from Egypt then did come
All the chosen and then some.

When Saul's kingdom came to wreck
Over Agag of Amalek,
Samuel, before he died,
Made the future out of pride.

> The spider spins, and the gull cries:
> Doubtless man is always wise.

Out of pride it still is made,
Place is hollowed with the spade
For the Jew whose wicked guile
Finds no other safe exile.

Thus the planetary Jew
Bears the old law with the new,
And must suffer Israel
As stranger nations suffer hell.

> The spider may spin, the gull cry:
> The mighty of the earth ride high.


## VIRGIN AND MARTYR

I saw the sailor dead at sea,
The soldier smashed upon the earth.
I heard the angry sergeant cry
That the fighters must go forth
Only to die. "Lord, let me too," I said,
"Lie worthless with the damaged and dead."

I saw the mad in canvas bound,
The sick, with sores biting the back,

And nurse and keeper with iron hand
Busied about the human wreck—
"Let me in turn," I prayed, "be put away
Out of the clear light and the Lord's day."

I saw old women scrub the floors
In early morning, and compared
The knees of girls in subway cars,
And I cried, "Let my knees, O Lord,
Also be broken in the marble ways,
But to Thy pleasure, Lord, pleasure and praise."

In place of pain why should I see
The sunlight on the bleeding wound?
Or hear the wounded man's outcry
Bless the Creation with bright sound?
I stretch myself on joy as on the rack,
And bear the hunch of glory on my back.


MARS

When I came from my mother's womb,
My brow already creased with doom,
I was thought a blessed child.
They tell me that I always smiled.

   *Blood of the Lamb*
   *A little dram*

When my teeth began to grow
That first opinion had to go.
They say my smile became a grin
And my baby lips were thin.

   *Smile of the ape*
   *Biting the nape*

When I showed a serious mind,
To all but study deaf and blind,
Uncles and aunts, their pride increased,
Predicted I'd become a priest.

*Mouth of the lion*
*Singing of Sion*

With these there wanted one thing more
That I might rule this threshing-floor—
Love, which does as well as hate,
Brought me to the mighty state.

*Lust of the goat*
*And a thing of note*


## PEACE IN OUR TIME

Honor is saved by the national will,
The burgher throws up his cap.
Gone is the soldier, over the hill,
And the rat has defended his trap.


## SONG

Provide your friend with almanacs
And cast him up a horoscope
Suggest the future that he lacks
Would have supplied his hopes

Give him beer and several wives
Good books and blankets for the trip
With stuff enough for fifty lives
Flatter his mortalship

Lay his weapons by his side
His address book and telephone
Try to convince him of the pride
Felt by the folks back home

And write him letters now and then
Be sure to put them in the post
Sound as cheerful as you can
Care of the holy ghost

Like anyone gone overseas
He'll take kindly to your talk
There in the camp beneath the trees
Where the sentry worms walk


THE BACTERIAL WAR

Above all, not by violence—
We fought without brutality
And only test-tubes could incense
Heroes to their mortality.
The public and obedient saints,
The right to serve their single pride,
Lined up with all their documents,
Enlisted and inhaled and died.

Encounters with the enemy
Were frowned upon by adjutants;
Soldiers instead would fight to be
Strangled by simple ambience,
And breath was all the bravery
Of those without the uniform
Who did not hold Thermopylae
Against the microscopic worm.

Not guilt but total innocence
The outcome of this holy war—

Not so much man's was the offense
But it was nature's so much more.
The sons of man with perfect sense
Thereon attacked both time and space,
And sought to kill the present tense
And square the round world's grievous face.


REDEPLOYMENT

They say the war is over. But water still
Comes bloody from the taps, and my pet cat
In his disorder vomits worms which crawl
Swiftly away. Maybe they leave the house.
These worms are white, and flecked with the cat's blood.

The war may be over. I know a man
Who keeps a pleasant souvenir, he keeps
A soldier's dead blue eyeballs that he found
Somewhere—hard as chalk, and blue as slate.
He clicks them in his pocket while he talks.

And now there are cockroaches in the house,
They get slightly drunk on DDT,
Are fast, hard, shifty—can be drowned but not
Without you hold them under quite some time.
People say the Mexican kind can fly.

The end of the war. I took it quietly
Enough. I tried to wash the dirt out of
My hair and from under my fingernails,
I dressed in clean white clothes and went to bed.
I heard the dust falling between the walls.

## TO A FRIEND

*gone to fight for the Kuomintang*

Not that, of course, you couldn't stick it out
—the cigarettes turned brown in coffee cups
And all suchlike our civil disciplines—

But that pity and hate overcame you
Where you slept in this wilderness of mind
So that wrestling, in the fixed match, seemed vain.

You be my conscience, then, and with my love
Fight what entrenched savagery you find—
Blest, if not by the angel, then by man,

Or if not by all men, yet blest of those
Who, undeceived in the strange Orient,
Would know the Harvard Club through all disguise.

But this, I see, is also vain. You know
In me a mind cancered (as you say) by
The worm I worship in the mystic rose,

Where, according to me, the blessed sit
In great humility, scratching their heads,
And pondering, according again to you,

The fathomless dialectic of the tide
But never speaking of the stinking fish
That the wave drives up but does not pull back

—*Quae mundi plaga*, dear man? China? Rome?
No matter. As between the golden mean
And the meanness of gold, there is no matter.

Or has the argument somewhere gone wrong?
Might I be forced to conclude, you to doubt?
In the violent life, you know where you are.

You have permission, then, to use my name
And die under it for all the difference—
And that's enough. I'll keep your name alive

And teach school under it, or write a book;
But when things get hard on this backward front
And all of us redeem your dollar life,

Write to me. When the engines resonate
On the cold drome, and you hear their huge strength,
The strength is not yours, neither is the will;

But write to me anyhow. Let me know,
Are there yet heroes? Do they wish to kill?
What is the will of the dead we dying do?


## GRAND CENTRAL, WITH SOLDIERS, IN EARLY MORNING

These secretly are going to some place,
Packing their belted, serviceable hearts.
It is the earnest wish of this command
That they may go in stealth and leave no trace,
In early morning before business starts.


## A FABLE OF THE WAR

The full moon is partly hidden by cloud,
The snow that fell when we came off the boat
Has stopped by now, and it is turning colder.
I pace the platform under the blue lights,
Under a frame of glass and emptiness
In a station whose name I do not know.

Suddenly, passing the known and unknown
Bowed faces of my company, the sad

And potent outfit of the armed, I see
That we are dead. By stormless Acheron
We stand easy, and the occasional moon
Strikes terribly from steel and bone alike.

Our flesh, I see, was too corruptible
For the huge work of death. Only the blind
Crater of the eye can suffer well
The midnight cold of stations in no place,
And hold the tears of pity frozen that
They will implacably reflect on war.

But I have read that God let Solomon
Stand upright, although dead, until the temple
Should be raised up, that demons forced to the work
Might not revolt before the thing was done.
And the king stood, until a little worm
Had eaten through the stick he leaned upon.

So, gentlemen—by greatcoat, cartridge belt
And helmet held together for the time—
In honorably enduring here we seek
The second death. Until the worm shall bite
To betray us, lean each man on his gun
That the great work not falter but go on.


THE HERO COMES HOME IN HIS HAMPER, AND
IS EXHIBITED AT THE WORLD'S FAIR

I exhibit here the well-known failure of
Communication, nerve and power of love.
A miracle of godly medicine,
I am without facilities for sin,
Being a lump of undistinguished skin
Sans this and that after the mine went off,
Beneath my feet, with an unhealthy cough.

My flesh, a protoplastic epigram,
Suggests, without asserting, that I am;
And of my little life because I reap
The pain of waking in conclusive sleep,
I may grieve, in my basket, but not weep
Over what things, what mortal touches more,
My humble mind remaining has tears for.

Gape as you please, but keep your sympathy;
I have become my own sufficiency.
Though I was broken by the mighty fist,
By healing Nature all my wounds were kissed
And I was made the utter solipsist.
My happy state! These thoughts, within their bound,
Although they go not out, go round and round.


THE BRIEF JOURNEY WEST

By the dry road the fathers cough and spit,
This is their room. They are the ones who hung
That bloody sun upon the southern wall
And crushed the armored beetle to the floor.

The father's skin is seamed and dry, the map
Of that wild region where they drained the swamp
And set provision out that they might sit,
Of history the cracked precipitate,

Until the glass be shattered and the sun
Descend to burn the prosperous flesh away
Of the filthy world, so vilely fathered on
The fathers, such black cinders, sitting there.

Old pioneers, what lecheries remain?
When schoolgirls pass, what whispers of their skirts,
Cold gleams of flesh, solicit in your veined
And gemlike eyes the custom of desire?

None now. Their eyes are sunk in ancient flesh,
And the sarcastic triumph of the mind
They now enjoy, letting their lust alone
Who may have kin but have no longer kind.

Neither tomorrow's monstrous tumor nor
The reformation of the past they wish,
Who hold in silent colloquy the world
A shrivelled apple in the hand of God.

They hang at night their somber flags aloft,
And through the amorous dark pursue their theme
Of common images, that sleep may show
Them done with all disasters but the one.


SUCCESSION

Furnished and clean, this room does not betray
The traces of another tenancy,
Discourages what charges you might lay
Against its suspect calm. But lingering by
The door the woman hints a history—
The priest, your predecessor, "went away"
(So much you might have gathered; did he die?
Was it a year ago or yesterday?)

Left alone with the horrible brass bedstead,
Imagine the Father to come in at night,
Undo his collar, lie upon the bed
(His naked feet incongruously white)
And close his eyes against the icy light
For half-an-hour's nap, his dreaming head
Reworking all the daytime in a rite.
Rising, he dines on onion soup and bread.

So much you see, but cannot see his face,
And have no further wish to follow him

Where he has gone, for now the room awaits
The thud of your belongings and your name—
How easily it will encompass them!
Behind the door the sycophantic glass
Already would reflect you in a frame
That memorizes nothing but its place.

Hypocrisy! you'll get to know them well,
Wallpaper, closet, bureau and the bed,
Their repetitions in the glass, that tell
A ceaseless inventory of the bled
Stuff of your life. While in your lonely head
The poor gone priest cries vanity and hell.
O murderous usurper! Is he dead?
Has any man late heard the passing bell?

Like kings of Egypt, dreaming death a dream
In which their men and women still would come
To minister as always to a whim,
You may make of this place a kind of home:
Straighten the wrinkled window blind, make dumb
The dripping tap, let neither drop nor dram
Derange the composition of the room,
The furnished room, the garment without seam.


## FRAGMENT FROM CORRESPONDENCE

                    . . . is superficially
The same as a hotel, grand and de luxe,
And bears its gold-encrusted coronets
On bills and menus with the usual air.

In the mornings, from the wide balconies
Where we breakfast in sunlight, I can see
The Marientor rising from silent waters,
Footed in fog but crowned with snowy light,

So arrogant and still. At ten the bus
Takes us to the baths, and calls for us again
At noon; the solemn porter tips his hat
As we pass through the doors, and we tip him.

But then, who is there whom we do not tip?
Even the chambermaids, who smooth the sheets
Our wretched bodies twisted, estimate
Exactly what our patience will endure,

And secretly I sometimes think this is
An Auschwitz for the very old and rich,
Whose money does for blood, until their blood
Leaves dry the drained purses of their flesh.

As I look up, I see the walk below,
Where Baron Kraft and Mrs Tenedine
Are walking arm in arm, her parasol
Patching a flowered shade on his parched head

—How they seem courtly, frivolous and vain!
I can't help thinking how, perhaps tonight,
Tensed on the white table stained with blood,
The Baron or the lady, like a dog

Bleeding to death in the hot New Jersey street,
Might iterate the scandal of our flesh
So loud that this firm masonry would shake
And from the cellars give its secrets up

To indignation. Though they do these things
Quietly, though I have been told nothing
Nor heard the soft tires that by night
Bear failure to the furnace and the urn,

I know these men, with their white coats, their smiles;
Their rubber and moist fingers sometimes in dreams
Press tentatively against my naked heart,
Over their masks the eyes are pitiless. . . .

# FABLES OF THE MOSCOW SUBWAY

The earthly doctor fiddled with his beard,
Considered the spiders Svidrigailov saw
Climbing the bath-house of eternity.
Man lives, he said, only by parricide.

Madame la Mothe had lovers one two three
Moonlit among the Dresden figurines.
And her brocaded dress was thumbed aside
Silently, and her heavy hair caressed.

The displaced persons wandered all this while
Through everglades where the loud-shrieking worm
Struggled in fragile webs; or came beyond
The tragic scene, to temples which were tombs.

The doctor, in an illustrated tome,
Saw mitred bishops creeping from a cave.
In gowns heavy with gold they went haughtily,
He thought, between the knees of Babylon.

Madame la Mothe, after the last man left,
Lifted Venetian blinds upon the town.
The lights were necklaces, and at her feet,
She thought, the world lay flat as a five-pound note.

And when she had coiled up her hair in nets
And nakedly had sunk into pale sleep,
She was as ocean, alone and deep and mute
(The moon being lost now outside the clouds).

But the doctor, with smoldering cigar,
Waked, and went patiently among the dead;
Inquired how their parents were, and when
They last had wet the bed or dreamed of God.

He read in the *Timaeus* once again
That the good old days were gone beneath the sea.

He seemed to understand, coughed once, and slept.
And then it was revealed to him in dream:

*That Martin Luther shrieked aloud, Thou Pope!*
*And fled to England, and created the Boy Scouts,*
*Who were encamped above Lake Titicaca*
*And might invade the Rhineland if they wished.*


## THE OLD COUNTRY

Cold in cathedral the old women pray;
Outside, soldiers at ease sweat out the day.
Of Lord or Priest not much good is got
When love is cold as stone, and hate as hot.

Hate should be frozen, and most rigorous,
A soldier must be rather bone than pus;
And in the craters of his eyes must shine
The heavenly night-light of his design.

Old lovers should, that they may be well done,
Pray to be petrified by too much sun.
But such old trees are raised by burning pride
And when they fall they lie on this world's side.

All, veterans not implacable but weak,
Turn first the raw and then the roasted cheek
To the dry ice and then to the strong sun.
The God they love, the God they obey, is One.


## TRIAL AND DEATH, A DOUBLE FEATURE

*for Allen Tate*

A panorama of ruined houses, walls,
A broken aircraft, bundles of the dead

Lying powdered in snow. We live in our
Resentful eyes, fixed to the shifting front,
And there interpret moving shadows while
Our violated will screams from the screen.

Poor Platonists, we huddle paralyzed
To watch the black complicity of dreams
That dextrous and sinister shuffle past
So plausibly the Japanese the Jew
The housewife in Berlin, any grey face
Caught in the sunlight of a public court.

Under the automatic rifles now
They die crowded, and a good death is one
Well in the foreground and by the green flare
Given a candid gloss; photographers
May pick and choose at will, their dirty thumbs
Rifle the white eyes of the negatives.

Maybe the proper virtue of our minds
Teaches a mute respect in two dimensions
For what we might find merely base in three,
Or neutral at the least—the radar screen,
The gun, the whispering committeemen.
For even heroes have been scared of ghosts,

Those stuffed sheets that parade against a wall
And, light-struck by some weak exploding star
That catches in them radical character,
Will delegate from their dead mouths revenge
On mother or usurping uncle; so
The youngster may embrace his proper crime.

But vex not the matter with our sentiment.
Not many, ever, were five acts at dying,
Neither commanded of the Erinyes
The unbaited revengefulness, nor were
So richly by many lords and ladies danced
Attendance to anciently vulgar death,

71

Which if it have ten thousand several doors,
Has none of them significant of choice.
Value is something else again, as those
Know who have died for this and lived for that,
Whose languid hell exists *in vacuo*
Within the breathless center of the will.

Soon we, not violent, may go out among
The Chinese faces on the windy airdrome
Under the white sky snowing; and meanwhile
In this theater of the world's going war
We cannot but reflect their images
Who shadow blood upon our sheer cave wall.

Whether the violence dies in the idea,
Whether violence and idea die together,
Whether idea drowns in particular
Confusions, or survives in the violent man
As singular weakness and a forbidding face,
These shadow murders gain a mortal weight,

Our shrouding screen will shatter under wounds,
And horror drill the eyes in every head
So deep the dry Platonic mind must bleed.
So we attend the agon of our star
That burns, on the dusty and tarnished air,
The helpless light that is its only speech.


SONNET

A form of Christ cut from dark wood, the pale
Paint rude on his cracked face—blood as red
As blood ran from the crown upon his head
(A hot day but cold in the cathedral,
On your own brow you felt the sweat grow cold)
To where his mouth a wound opened the sweet

Grained wood which in the forest had grown straight
Until the face was hacked out wry and old.

Where is the cup in which this blood was light
(With vinegar and sweat the natural part)?
And when the Germans bled the babies white
Where was the *skepsis* of the sculptor's art?
The question is of science not to doubt
The point of faith is that you sweat it out.


CAROL

Now is the world withdrawn all
*In silence and night*
To beweeping Adam's fall
That this biography began
Of vile man.

Now the serpent smiles on sin
*In silence and night*
And sees the tumor swell within—
The heavy fruit that was the heart
Beat apart.

The spider's spittle weaves the shroud
*In silence and night*
Wide enough for all the proud;
Gapes the grave in pompous black
At our back.

Christ the King is born again
*In silence and night*
Bringing mercy to all men
Whose separate pride full is beguiled
By this child.

From Eden's Tree the Cross is made
*In silence and night*
Where Adam's bondman now is nailed
While the wild multitude
Cries for blood.

The great grave stone is rolled away
*In silence and night*
And He arose on the third day
That Adam might, free of the chains,
Choose his pains

And follow Him upon the Cross
*In silence and night*
And disdain all worldly loss
And to the compassionate King
Pray and sing.

Therefore do we cross this hour
*In silence and night*
Our grief and joy, weakness and power,
Whereto Christ's glory and His pain
Both constrain.

For there was born at Bethlehem
*In silence and night*
The world's and heaven's single stem
That to both kingdoms we might then
Say Amen.


SONNET AT EASTER

You splice together two broomsticks, then reef
A tie (a Christmas present) at the throat.
A hat must rattle on the knob, a coat
Keep warm the chest (for he has little beef).
You set this person up disguised as you

And let him flap. He hangs lonely as grief.
His wraithless hull, no blood and no belief,
Your children don't despise but your crows do.

He is a habit now, perennial,
One of your pieties. You plant him deep,
And though you have no earthly use for him
You dress him in your father's coat, and call
Good Evening sometimes when the light is dim,
Seeing he stands for you in upright sleep.


## ELEGY OF LAST RESORT

The boardwalks are empty, the cafés closed,
The bathchairs in mute squadrons face the sea.
Grey cloud goes over, the baffled involved brain
Of the old god over the vacant waters:
The proprietors of the world have gone home.

The girls, the senators, the priests, are gone,
Whose gowns the summer wind billowed no less
Than this of autumn does the scarecrow's coat;
And are not otherwise remembered than
As ideas of death in the dry sand blowing.

Aschenbach is dead, and other invalids
Have coughed their poems and died in bed.
The sea wind salts the rotting timbers,
Sand rattles against the empty windows,
Last week's newspapers crumple at the wall.

These visitors of smoke in sallow light
Curl, drift, dissolve to seaward in the wind.
They were the piteous shapes of accident
Whose winter substance ate and drank elsewhere
Time's rigors: a harder bread, more acid wine.

And some doubtless with sullen breath do praise
Autumnal pieties: the speech against
Nothing, and meaning nothing; the pain of prayer
That time's corrupted body will not hear;
The unfriendly marriage in the stranger's house.

We enter again November, and the last
Steep fall of time into the deep of time,
Atlantic and defeated, and to die
In the perplexity of a sour world
Whose mighty dispensations all are done.

This shoulder of the earth turns from the sun
Into the great darkness, into the steep
Valley of the stars, into the pit
Of frozen Cocytus, where Satan stands
Wielding the world upon his pain and pride.

We enter again November: cold late light
Glazes the field. A little fever of love,
Held in numbed hands, admires the false gods;
While lonely on this coast the sea bids us
Farewell, and the salt crust hardens toward winter.


STILL LIFE I

The eunuch is a silly fat
Man wearing silk pajamas and
Armed with a kind of yataghan:
He guards the technicolor wives.

Within this frame, though, there are only
Three bulging oysters on a plate
Together with a white carafe
And a long loaf, all on green baize.

A marble wall and panelling
Appear behind, the marble grained

With what look like trypanosomes
Flirting in grey magnification.

Not Artemis could be more chaste
Than oysters and this alabaster
That heaves a torso from the waist;
It is cold in this public room

Of the outmoded Hotel Nord.
Even in summer icebergs float
Past where the guests sit on the porch
Knitting their sweaters too late too late.

It is as though all man had been
Castrated with a single knife.
We shudder on the porch, and hear
The foghorns weeping in the sound.


STILL LIFE II

Dishes are apples are guitars
Floating in pools of their own flesh,
But chastity of coupled jars
Rebukes the riot of the sense.

These things upon the tilted table
Grow tense with only standing still,
While shadows patched of slate and sable
Seek to make all matter spill.

By the just rigors of an art
That hung relation on the void,
The natural man, for his poor part,
Is half-embarrassed, half-annoyed,

And in the slight migraine of form,
Holding together every side
Against the old atomic storm,
His eye grows dull, and lets things slide.

## STILL LIFE III

The décor of the darkened room
Is bleak, Victorian-ascetic.
In the scrolled and golden frame
Grey wash of light is anesthetic.

The proposition of the place,
That shadow is what light is not,
Stands abstracted on the table
By a candle and a coffee-pot,

While next to these, in grey and white
As bony as a China moon,
Are posed in agonized design
A cup, a saucer and a spoon.

Outside the cities are alight
And money talks and things make sense
And we know where we want to go
And what's to do at what expense.

Here, nothing has happened, but
Maybe to such a starving air
A young man will come in alone
And sit down in the ornate chair

And pour the coffee in the cup
To drink it though it is not hot;
Then standing, reach a careful hand
Nicely to pinch the candle out.


## THE LIVES OF GULLS AND CHILDREN

Around the headland, at the end
Where they had not been before,

Paced by the white and the grey gull
With loud shrieking, and by the neat
Black-hooded tern, they found the place of death.
When they looked back along their way they saw
The footprints lonely and loud on the sand.

Few bones at first their feet kicked up,
Then more, a flat thicket of bone
And tangled cartilage, dry white and clean,
Tasting of salt when the children licked them.
Further on were feathers, then flesh
Strung on the bone ragged and rotting,
With still red tendons curled. Twice they saw
The whole delicate skeletons with the hard
Hornlike feet peacefully displayed, and there
A loud few flies buzzed on the torn meat
And dishevelled feathers; a sick and wrong
Smell mingled with the heat of the salt wind.

Silence strangely was twisted there
By the voices of the children, by
The outcries of the living gulls aloft
Swinging over the wash and rush of the sea
Between the heat of the sand and the blind sun of noon.

They saw there a great gull dying,
Huddled in the sun and shuddering out
Now and again a heavy wing in cold
Effortful motion; he stared at them
Out of a steady and majestic eye
Like a sun part baffled in cloud,
So rheumed over with the morning of death.

They would have reached out hands to him
To comfort him in that human kind
They just were learning—how anything alive,
They thought, hated loneliness most; but he,
A grim great-uncle with a cane, struck out,
Sullen and weakly fierce, with hooked beak and a claw.

He would have flown, but had not strength to rise,
Could not even, ridiculous, waddle away.

The children watched him for a moment more;
But at a distance, and did not see him die;
For he, making his death, would out-endure
What interest they had, who, being humankind,
Had homes to go to, and a bed this side of death.

But they knew the Atlantic kind he was,
And for this moment saw him swaying
In the grey dark above the cold sea miles,
Wingtips ticking the spray of the slow waves,
Leaning on the unhavening air the dangerous
Sustaining of his own breastbone; they knew
The indifference of time dragging him down.
And when after silence they turned away,
"No one has ever been here before,"
They cried, "no one, no one, no one."
Their mournful word went out, no one,
Along the shore, now that they turned for home
Bearing the lonely pride of those who die,
And paced by the sweet shrieking of the quick.


THE EARTHQUAKE IN THE WEST

*"At seashore resorts mothers ran*
*screaming down the beaches, searching*
*for their children, who, they feared,*
*might be caught up in tidal waves*
*that failed to materialize."*
The *New York Times*, Thursday, April 14, 1949

The art of writing an honest prose
Is no very difficult one, and may
Be mastered in little time by persons
Willing to obey such simple rules

As are to be found in almost any
Comprehensive handbook of the subject.

Beyond this, as a general thing,
One should learn to keep demeanor
In trying situations, at times
Of public crisis and disaster.
The attitude should be remote
A little, possibly a little amused;
Being a spectator requires its own
Peculiar and somewhat cold patience.

This is, admittedly, not simple.
When the familiar world shatters,
When the flat walls begin to bulge
And mothers run screaming on the shore,
It is difficult not to become
Too personally involved for the pure
And detached vision to be possible.
But then the subterranean dread
Will heave and turn in the flawed syntax
Both of the world and of the word,
Until the mothers, the children, all,
Be whelmed in the one wave together.


PRAISING THE POETS OF THAT COUNTRY

Many poems may be composed upon the same theme.
The differences between them may be slight
—a comma, or the tilt of an eyebrow—but not
Superficial. Whole traditions existed
For which the strict imitation of the predecessors
And not originality, was the matter of pride.
The poet then is seen as bearing a priestly part
In the ritual, confirming the continuance
Of this that and the other thing, humbly
Refreshing the hearer with his ceremony.

The place of the poet was often hereditary:
Thus, G_____ was a learned man, but his grandson,
Left to himself, could not have written a line;
That was no matter. In conversation, however,
Such poets often displayed wit and extravagance
Which they would have thought unworthy
Of the strenuous character of their art.
It was not, that is, a question of "talent,"
But rather of a fanatic and ascetic practice
Of willed submission to the poem existing.
R_____'s epitaph read, "The man who placed
The adjective 'calm' in its proper context."
This, a matter of pride, in forty years of work.

Then the beloved face was known to the whole people.
The complexion *white,* the eyes *dark,* and *like*
*Twin suns,* the lips *like cherries* or
*Of the color of rubies,* the hair *glorious*
*And shiningmost mystery,* the shoulders *like cream*
And then the Sestos and the Abydos of it.
These things were well-known, and each man with his doxy
Might make what he might out of the whole business
Nightlong, and daylong if he liked and was able.
Under the cadence the beat of the common meter
Sustained the matter, and the exact rime
Measured the moment with a considered force.

These not eccentric men were held in honor
Wilder than the expectations of despair;
No valorous excess could mar those characters
That guarded times to time on the baffled drum,
Holding in secret the still-beating victim heart,
While elsewhere the profane crowds would walk
Unthinking their free and many ways to death.

# MADRIGAL

She is the darkness where I wander
Who was the light that found my way.
What time and choice have torn asunder
Come together in no day.

Blackness her great beauty bringeth
Upon me, and I go my way
Singing as one lonely, that singeth
Unregarding and astray.

Night time on her also is fallen,
Shadow clouds her perfect way.
For her the winter sun rides sullen
And shines not on the dark day.

To such a year no springtime riseth,
Nor is no excellence in May,
But darkness in the sky abideth
Where the world wanders astray.


# FOUR SONNETS

1

Earth orbits on the sun and has no sign
But her fidelity must be her ruin,
Yet serpentwise on the consuming line
She flies from darkness into noon
Seeking to burn; while on the shadow side
Where dreams are plotted at the speed of light
The brain-cold sleepers lie in lonesome pride
Staring with glacial and ecstatic sight.
I circle so, contracted to your sun
Which reins me, though my wintry mind's desire
Elsewhere would spend that force by which I run
Through death to landfall in your centrique fire;

Only to show what quality of lust
Enters the composition of this dust.

2

You too will cool, though from your distance light
Cold and denatured still may seem to flow
Which space not yet annihilates, nor night
Proves a divorce, and mortuary show.
The imposition of your eye's regard
Even in cause of death deceives me still
After that love that lived without reward
Is burnt aether to earth despite your will.
Yet you in your own deceit own coldness kills,
And when your latest light is in my eyes
Drowned and entombed, when by disordered wheels
Beyond the sun you wander through blind skies,
    Remember him your fire chilled with fever
    Sometimes to shake him, but to warm him never.

3

Of fire and of lust proceeds the world
And not of your cold liking, nor the chaste
Glass to your mind, the moon aged and scarred
By the huge and master light in which you waste.
Scanning your distant heaven I may see
Your too nebulous light but not your flame,
Not sacred rage but pale astronomy
Still spinsterish with a too ancient fame.
Think, if the sun should waste in your delay
And sink down bleeding from the bloodied sky,
Your pale reflexion, at his final day,
Ends with his lustiness, and you must die.
    Then thinking of that outer night you know
    This darkness where you make me wander now.

4

Your beauty once the profit of your scorn
Blinded almost the burning eye of time,

Which from the head of heaven being torn
Had left the world lit by your lonely prime;
But having burned your days to brilliant light,
Feeding expression on your own cold blood,
The waste of this is reckoned up to night
And that you cannot keep which kept you proud.
So to the blackness of an unloved day
Your mortal flare condemns the world and you,
Which locked in mutual contempt display
The scars of married rage, bound to be true
    With neither love nor pride nor beauty won
    From your proud pacing of the lonely sun.


## THE ECSTASIES OF DIALECTIC

Her laughter was infectious; so, some found,
Her love. Several young men reasonably
Regret inciting her to gratitude
And learning of her ardent facility.

She has gone, back it may be to the world,
To ply her silken exercise elsewhere.
Now is occasion for the medication
(As possible) of ills not all of the heart,

And certain hints, conveyed in sermon or
By private word, are reasoning the weight
Of pleasures, pains. Thus her capable joys
Are debased by her ignominious communications.

"The flesh, the rouged cheekbones of Babylon,
The unclean loins, the thief of legal delight,
O ye generations!" "The spider that eats up
Her mate!" "The test-tube of iniquity!"

Despite the wisdom of Christian Epicures
Many of the affected more regret

Her going than her legacy. They huddle
At street corners, before drugstores, and moon

Over the hour of pestilent delight,
The yellow taste good times will always have.
"The proof of the apple is in the worm," they say,
And hug their new knowledge of life and death.


ANTIGONE

I

Under the moon my brother's body lay,
Beyond the city, on the vacant plain,
In the pale light his face untimely grey
With blowing dust over the dry bloodstain.

Keeping the intervals of Creon's guard
I scratched the shallow grave, and buried him
With my own hands bloodied on the hard
Clay soil. His cold eyes for the last time

Stared up, as though he tried to lift his head
And speak through choking death, or his cold hand
To touch my shoulder and so to his poor bed
Beckon me down. And as I understand,

No form or ceremony of the state
So drew me, breathless, to my brother's side,
But my blind will, having all life in hate,
Gave me to kingly death to be his bride.

II

There followed capture; tears, threats, high talk
By both parties, myself as obstinate
As Creon could be; neither one would balk
At the last fence whether of will or fate.

For I desired the locked and choking tomb
Which all my light desires had but veiled.
Deathward dreaming, the mind wants little room,
Its own room in darkness, and that room sealed.

I know now that it had to be this way
Always (and the young Haemon too is dead).
The bride is dressed and goes forth from the day
To the dark hour of her desire and dread.


## SONNET

*"The one complete book for serious players . . . how
to be a consistent winner . . . full information on
all forms of cheating . . . how to avoid being a
'sucker' . . . the all-inclusive guidebook for all who
play for money."*
Advertisement

It seems to be the trouble, everyone
Is not the one always who wins, though he
Be never so serious, and never see
On next to nothing only for the fun.
Maybe no guide, when the great wheel is spun,
Can balance man against peripety,
Or keep him upright that he may not be
By forms of cheating done if not undone.

It is a sin against the life to come
If Mistress Fortune falsely implicate
Equality and grace, for wise or dumb
They win not always in their playing state,
   But suckers and the guileless, at this game,
   Come out as well, or so some guidebooks claim.

## A LEAN AND HUNGRY LOOK

It is cold in my refrigerator.
Salami, liverwurst and beef
Are frozen there and frozen well,
With pickled herring, lettuce leaf
And consommé I left to jell.

It is warm in my refrigerator.
Steady blue flame, to my belief,
Signifies that I live well—
Incessant whining is the chief
Complaint I have about my cell.

It tells me my refrigerator
Suffers the European grief,
Its stout heart's oily tears expel
Remorse but offer no relief,
Freezing the hard eyeballs of hell.



## THE PHOENIX

The Phoenix comes of flame and dust
He bundles up his sire in myrrh
A solar and unholy lust
Makes a cradle of his bier

In the City of the Sun
He dies and rises all divine
There is never more than one
Genuine

By incest, murder, suicide
Survives the sacred purple bird
Himself his father, son and bride
And his own Word

# THE
# SALT
# GARDEN
# (1955)

*For S. E. H.*

# 1

FALL SONG

Darkly against the winter's white
   The bundled lovers go,
And do, unless indoors at night,
   No more than show
      Delight.

The first beginning of the spring
   Bids lovers to the lawn;
Chameleonlike against the thing
   That sets them on
      They cling.

Summer, in the disguise of green,
   Deceives me least of all;
An undiscriminating screen
   Where lovers sprawl
      Unseen.

The bridled bloodshed of the fall
   Reveals how to my spleen
Discamouflaged the naked crawl
   Where the leaves grow lean
      And fall.


THE WINTER LIGHTNING

*for Paul*

Over the snow at night,
And while the snow still fell,

91

A sky torn to the bone
Shattered the ghostly world with light;
As though this were the moon's hell,
A world hard as a stone,
   Cold, and blue-white.

As if the storming sea
Should sunder to its floor,
And all things hidden there
Gleam in the moment silently,
So does the meadow at the door
To split and sudden air
   Show stone and tree.

From the drowned world of dark
The sleeping innocence
Surrenders all its seeming;
Under the high, charged carbon arc
Light of the world, a guilty sense
Stiffens the secret dreaming
   Animal park.

So in the camera's glare
The fortunate and famed,
For all their crooked smiles,
Reveal through their regarded stare
How all that's publicly acclaimed
One brutal flash reviles
   For cold despair.

So is the murderer caught
When his lost victim rises
Glaring through dream and light
With icy eyes. That which was thought
In secret, and after wore disguises,
Silts up the drowning sight
   Mind inwrought.

So may the poem dispart
The mirror from the light
Where none can see a seam;
The poet, from his wintry heart
And in the lightning second's sight,
Illuminate this dream
    With a cold art.


## ZALMOXIS

The way spring comes this time, with a soft
Suddenness: after the robin-snow a rain,
After the rain the sun in a ragged cloud
Making a mild mist on the cold meadows,
On stone walls veined with ice, on blind windows
Burnt red beneath the southward slate of houses.

From the pale, yellow and peeled branches of willow
And alder the globes of water grow and fall
In ripenings of light; and a crystal thread,
Enlaced with the needles of the pine, silvers
The earliest sketches of the spider, softens
Coldly to life the leaves of pupal sleep.

Warm in the house, at the bright window's edge,
A fly crawls on the dry, leathery spines
Of the sleeping dramatists; the speckled dust,
In the long light's line between the blinds,
Dances until the scholar's ancient eye
Lights between sleep and waking. He leaves his book,

And, rising, he throws open the window wide,
Watches cigar smoke swaying in the room
Till smoke and dream dissolve in air together;
Then stares down the field to the wild hill,
Where on this day the sullen and powerful bear,
Drunken with deathlessness, lurches from sleep.

## DANDELIONS

These golden heads, these common suns
Only less multitudinous
Than grass itself that gluts
The market of the world with green,
They shine as lovely as they're mean,
Fine as the daughters of the poor
Who go proudly in spangles of brass;
Light-headed, then headless, stalked for a salad.

Inside a week they will be seen
Stricken and old, ghosts in the field
To be picked up at the lightest breath,
With brazen tops all shrunken in
And swollen green gone withered white.
You'll say it's nature's price for beauty
That goes cheap; that being light
Is justly what makes girls grow heavy;
And that the wind, bearing their death,
Whispers the second kingdom come.
—You'll say, the fool of piety,
By resignations hanging on
Until, still justified, you drop.
But surely the thing is sorrowful,
At evening, when the light goes out
Slowly, to see those ruined spinsters,
All down the field their ghostly hair,
Dry sinners waiting in the valley
For the last word and the next life
And the liberation from the lion's mouth.


## MIDSUMMER'S DAY

*for my son*

A misty heat, now that the spring has gone,
Glitters out on this hillside and the meadow,

94

Over the bend where the slow river turns
To be lost among willows. Hardly a shadow
But the high sun seems to see through, who burns
As from within, till the green world goes brown
Under the skin, and the heights of summer lie
Parched with life at the lid of the mind's eye.

This ruinous garden an old woman made
And fertilized with tea leaves and coffee grounds,
Is wild grass mostly, climbed up to the thigh;
The multitude of dandelion surrounds
Enclaves of iris and opening peony;
While at the wall, the handle of a spade
Is toughly fastened in a climbing vine
That's crawled among blue flowers, serpentine.

I have looked out and seen the summer grow
Day after day between the cracked flags
Of the terrace where no one wishes to sit,
And thought of fortune and family, the fine rags
Brutal desire, poor patience, or a nice wit
Had made to be stitched together in a show
For everyone to marvel at, a pride
That must have been already withered inside.

This place belonged to farming people once—
Maybe a pity that it doesn't now;
For any mind, even on the summer's side,
Will let it go, cabbage chicken and cow,
From piety of sorts, or for the ride
Downhill on history, seeing that fate runs
Wild as the summer—Babylon and Rome,
As ruin remains, brought in a sense home.

Ruin remains, and nature pays no mind.
This mind, that flesh is and will go like grass
In the brief stubble burnt at harvest or
In the sun's long stare, sees as though sealed in glass
The high and silent wave over the floor

Of summer come, casting up seed and rind;
And, held upon this hill, among the trees
Hears the loud forage of the honey bees.


## THE FIRST LEAF

Here is one leaf already gone from green
To edged red and gold, a Byzantine
Illumination of the summer's page
Of common text, and capital presage
For chapters yet to fall. An old story,
How youth may go from glory into glory
Changing his green for a stiff robe of dry
Magnificence, taking the brilliant dye
From steeped oblivion; going, near a ghost,
Become a lord and captain of the host;
Or cardinal, in priestly full career,
Preach abstinence or at the most small beer.

Success is doubtful, you may be perplexed,
Reaching it rich, and old, and apoplexed
To bloody innocence, teaching the green
One of the things at least that life must mean,
And standing in the book of days a splen-
did summary, rubric, index of the end,
Commerced with time to great advantage, high
And singular with instruction how to die—
And immortality, though life be cheap,
For the early turncoat and the Judas sheep.


## SUNDAY AT THE END OF SUMMER

Last night the cold wind and the rain blew
Hard from the west, all night, until the creek

Flooded, tearing the end of a wooden bridge
Down to hang, trembling, in the violent water.

This morning, with the weather still in rage,
I watched workmen already at repairs.
Some hundred of us came around to watch,
With collars turned against the rain and wind.

Down the wild water, where men stood to the knees,
We saw come flooding hollyhock and vine,
Sunflowers tall and broken, thorny bramble
And pale lilies cracked along the stalk.

Ours was the Sunday's perfect idleness
To watch those others working; who fought, swore,
Being threshed at hip and thigh, against that trash
Of pale wild flowers and their drifting legs.


A HARVEST HOME

To stand on the long field in fall,
To feel the silence of the sun
Bending the earth toward afternoon—
So hot and mute the human will
As though the angry wheel stood still
That hub and spoke and iron rim
Might fall, might burn away in air
And rot in earth before the ear
Had lost the last, grinding scream;
So much the moment was a snare
For time to pull from and be torn
Screaming against the rusty brake—
Until four crows arise and shake
Their heavy wings across the way,
Four shadows dragging on the shorn
Beard of the field, on the baled hay.

So afternoon resumes its slow
And ancient ceremonious bow
Down to the field and so beyond
The gate, the houses and the pond,
Out where the tracks run west and trains
Cry out, leaning in the long curve
Away, away. The owl complains
In darkness, and at dawn the jay
Proclaims the colors of the day.
All tendrils of the lonely nerve
Stand out in sunlight, and will serve.


## THE CUCKOO KING

My head made wilderness, crowned of weed
And marigold, the world my witching bride
And the half of my kingdom lying in the seed,
I reap the great root of a planted pride.

All earth broken under the harrow's heel,
I through my comely kingdom went a-riding
Out where the bearded grass climbed to rebel
And the tall stalking flower fired from hiding.

The world, O my daughter in the crooked nest,
Bridles with lust, that you by force betray
Me, weed and marigold, to the naked crest
Where castles fall; but I will make this hay
In husbandry beneath the rebel's height,
Though all the hairs of my head stand upright.


## THE POND

At the long meadow's end, where the road runs
High on a bank, making a kind of wall,

The rains of last October slowly built
Us up this pond some hundred yards across
And deep maybe to the height of a man's thigh
At the deepest place. It was surprising how
Slowly the water gained across the land
All autumn, no one noticing, until
We had the pond where none had been before
To any memory—most surprising in
This country where we think of contours as
Fixed on a map and named and permanent,
Where even if a stream runs dry in summer
You have the stream-bed still to go by and
The chartered name—Red Branch, and Henry's Creek,
And Anthony's Race—for reassurance, though
The reason of those names be sunken with
The men who named them so, in the natural past
Before our history began to be
Written in book or map; our history,
Or the settled story that we give the world
Out of the mouths of crones and poachers
Remembering or making up our kinship
In the overgrown swamplands of the mind;
And precious little reassurance, if
You think of it, but enough about that.
Here was, at any rate, surprisingly,
This piece of water covering the ground:
Clear blue, and pale, and crisping up to black
Squalls when the north wind moved across its face;
The question whether it would go or stay
Never came up, and no one gave it a name—
Only the water-birds on their way south
Accepted it, and rested there at night,
Coming at dusk down the meadow on wide wings
And splashing up on beating wings at dawn.

By Christmastime the pond was frozen solid
Under a foot of snow, level and white
Across the meadow so you couldn't say
Except from memory where the water was

And where the land; and maybe no grown-up
Would have remembered, but the children did
And brought their skates, and someone's father patched
Together a plough from plank and two-by-four
That half-a-dozen kids could lean against
And clear the snow down to the glittering ice.
They skated all the darkening afternoons
Until the sun burnt level on the ice,
And built their fires all along the shore
To warm their hands and feet, and skated nights
Under the full moon or the dark; the ice
Mirrored the moon's light, or the fire's, cold.
There was a tragedy, if that is what
One calls it, the newspapers called it that:
"Pond Claims First Victim" (it still had no name),
As though a monster underneath the ice
Had been in wait to capture the little boy
Skating in darkness all alone, away
From the firelight—the others heard his cry
But he was gone before they found the place—,
Or else as though, a tribe of savages,
We sanctified our sports with sacrifice.
At any rate, the skating didn't stop
Despite the funeral and motherly gloom
And editorials; what happened was
The pond took the boy's name of Christopher,
And this was voted properly in meeting
For a memorial and would be so
On the next map, when the next map was drawn:
Christopher Pond: if the pond should still be there.

The winter set its teeth; near Eastertide
Before the pond was free of ice all night;
And by that time the birds were coming back
Leisurely, staying a day or so before
They rose and vanished in the northward sky;
Their lonely cries across the open water
Played on the cold, sweet virginal of spring
A chaste, beginning tune carried along

With a wind out of the east. Killdeer and plover
Came and were gone; grackle, starling and flicker
Settled to stay; and the sparrowhawk would stand
In the height of noon, a stillness on beating wings,
While close over the water swallows would trace
A music nearly visible in air,
Snapping at newborn flies. Slowly the pond
Warmed into life: cocoon and bud and egg,
All winter's seed and shroud, unfolded being
In the pond named for Christopher, who drowned.
By day the birds, and then the frogs at night,
Kept up a music there, part requiem,
Part hunting-song; among the growing reeds
The water boatman worked his oar, the strider
Walked between air and water, dragonfly
Climbed to be born, and dazzled on clear wings.
Then day by day, in the heat of June, the green
World raised itself to natural arrogance,
And the air sang with summer soon to come.

In sullen August, under the massy heat
Of the sun towering in the height, I sat
At the pond's edge, the indeterminate
Soft border of what no longer was a pond
But a swamp, a marsh, with here and there a stretch
Of open water, even that half spread
With lily pads and the rich flesh of lilies.
And elsewhere life was choking on itself
As though, in spite of all the feeding there,
Death could not keep the pace and had to let
Life curb itself: pondweed and pickerel-weed
And bladderwort, eel-grass and delicate
Sundew and milfoil, peopled thick the city
Of themselves; and dragonfly and damselfly
By hundreds darted among the clustering leaves,
Striders by hundreds skated among the stalks
Of pitcher-plant and catkin; breathless the air
Under the intense quiet whining of
All things striving to breathe; the gift of life

Turning its inward heat upon itself.
So, Christopher, I thought, this is the end
Of dedication, and of the small death
We sought to make a name and sacrifice.
The long year has turned away, and the pond
Is drying up, while its remaining life
Grasps at its own throat: the proud lilies wilt,
The milfoil withers, catkins crack and fall,
The dragonfly glitters over it all;
All that your body and your given name
Could do in accidental consecrations
Against nature, returns to nature now,
And so, Christopher, goodbye.

                                 But with these thoughts
There came a dragonfly and settled down
On a stem before my eyes, and made me think
How in nature too there is a history,
And that this winged animal of light,
Before it could delight the eye, had been
In a small way a dragon of the deep,
A killer and meat-eater on the floor
Beneath the April surface of the pond;
And that it rose and cast its kind in May
As though putting away costume and mask
In the bitter play, and taking a lighter part.
And thinking so, I saw with a new eye
How nothing given us to keep is lost
Till we are lost, and immortality
Is ours until we have no use for it
And live anonymous in nature's name
Though named in human memory and art.
Not consolation, Christopher, though rain
Fill up the pond again and keep your name
Bright as the glittering water in the spring;
Not consolation, but our acquiescence.
And I made this song for a memorial
Of yourself, boy, and the dragonfly together.

# 2

## THE SCALES OF THE EYES

*a poem in the form of a text and variations*

I

To fleece the Fleece from golden sheep,
Or prey, or get—is it not lewd
That we be eaten by our food
And slept by sleepers in our sleep?

II

Sleep in the zero, sleep in the spore
Beyond the fires of Orion's hair,
Hard by the spiral burning dust;
Time being Always going west,
Let it be your dream.

Sleep sound in the spaceless lost
Curve running a blind coast;
Number and name, stretch the line
Out on the liquid of the brain,
Begin a falling dream.

The eye will flower in your night
A monstrous bulb, the broth of light
Stew in the marshes of a star;
Death is the wages of what you are,
Life is your long dream.

III

Around the city where I live
Dead men in their stone towns

Wait out the weather lying down,
And spread widely underground
The salt vines of blood.

Trains run a roaming sound
Under the wired shine of sun and rain.
Black sticks stand up in the sky
Where the wild rails cross and sprawl
Fast and still.

Out there beyond the island
The sea pounds a free way through,
Her wide tides spread on the sand
Stick and brine and rolling stone
The long weather long.


IV

Beneath my foot the secret beast
Whispers, and its stone sinews
Tremble with strength. In the dark earth
Iron winds its tangled nerves,
And the worm eats of the rock
There by the old waters.

Down in dark the rich comb
Gathers wrath out of the light,
The dead ploughed down in their graves
Record the canceled seed its doom.
City, white lion among waters,
Who settest thy claw upon the time,

Measure the tape, wind the clock,
Keep track of weather, watch water
And the work of trains. The bees hum
The honeyed doom of time and time
Again, and riddle this underground
How sweetness comes from the great strength.

V

(a can of Dutch Cleanser)

The blind maid shaking a stick,
Chasing dirt endlessly around
A yellow wall, was the very she
To violate my oldest nights;
I frighten of her still.

Her faceless bonnet flaps in wind
I cannot feel, she rages on,
The mad Margery of my sleep;
The socks wrinkle about her shoes
As she drats a maiden dream.

So shines her bleached virginity
On underground conveniences
That roar at once in porcelain hunger;
Her anger leaves me without stain
And white grits in the tub.

VI

The angry voice has sought me out,
Loud-speakers shout among the trees.
What use to hide? He made it all,
Already old when I began.

He held it all upon his knee
And spoke it soft in a big voice
Not so much loud as everywhere,
And all things had to answer him.

This world is not my oyster, nor
No slow socratic pearl grows here.
But the blind valves are closing
On only one grain of sand.

VII

The low sky was mute and white
And the sun a white hole in the sky
That morning when it came on to snow;
The hushed flakes fell all day.

The hills were hidden in a white air
And every bearing went away,
Landmarks being but white and white
For anyone going anywhere.

All lines were lost, a noon bell
I heard sunk in a sullen pool
Miles off. And yet this patient snow,
When later I walked out in it,

Had lodged itself in tips of grass
And made its mantle bridging so
It lay upon the air and not the earth
So light it hardly bent a blade.


VIII

From the road looking to the hill I saw
One hollow house hunched in the shoulder.
Windows blinded in a level sun
Stared with not random malice,
Though I had not been in that place.

But I have seen, at the white shore,
The crab eaten in the house of self
And the torn dog shark gutted in sand;
The whole sky goes white with silence
And bears on a few brazen flies.

As though the ground sighed under the foot
And the heart refused its blood; there is
No place I do not taste again

When I choke back the deeper sleep
Beneath the mined world I walk.

## IX

Striding and turning, the caged sea
Knocks at the stone and falls away,
Will not rest night or day
Pacing to be free.

The spiral shell, held at the ear,
Hums the ocean or the blood
A distant cry, misunderstood
Of the mind in the coiled air.

## X

Roads lead to the sea, and then?
The signs drown in the blowing sand,
The breathing and smoothing tide.
It has been a long journey so far.
Gull, where do I go now?

No matter what girls have been laid
In this sand, or far-wandering birds
Died here, I think I will not know
What no galling road has told,
Why to be here or how.

Question the crab, the wasted moon,
The spume blown of the smashed wave,
Ask Polaris about the fish.
No good. I could go home, but there is
No way to go but back.

## XI

Plunged the tunnel with the wet wall
Through, sounding with sea space
And the shaken earth, I fell below

The shark diving and the wry worm.
Blindly I nudged a gasping sky.

Against drowning to be born in a caul
Is well. But all free engines
Race to burn themselves out, tear up
The earth and the air and choke on a mouth
Of dirt, throwing their oil.

In long halls of hospital, the white
Eye peeled beneath the pool of light;
Then the blinded, masked and stifled sky
Screamed silver when it grated bone
Beaching a stained keel.

But at last the moon swung dark and away
And waters withered to a salt.
Parched and shaken on a weaned world
I was in wonder burning cold
And in darkness did rest.


XII

In the water cave, below the root,
The blind fish knew my veins.
I heard ticking the water drop,
The sighing where the wind fell,
When the bat laddered the black air.

Chalk and bone and salt and stone.
Let mother water begin me again,
For I am blackened with burning, gone
From the vain fire of the air,
The one salamander weather.

Slow cold salt, weeds washed
Under crumbling rock ledges
In the water cave below the root,
Quiet the crystal in the dark,
Let the blind way shine out.

## XIII

Gone the armies on the white roads,
The priests blessing and denouncing,
Gone the aircraft speaking power
Through the ruined and echoing air;
And life and death are here.

The quiet pool, if you will listen,
Hisses with your blood, winds
Together vine and vein and thorn,
The thin twisted threads red
With the rust of breath.

Now is the hour in the wild garden
Grown blessed. Tears blinding the eyes,
The martyr's wound and the hurt heart
Seal and are dumb, the ram waits
In the thicket of nerves.

## XIV

In the last hour of the dream
The eye turned upon itself
And stood at bay, peering among
The salt fibers of its blood.

String of the cradle and the kite,
Vine twisted against the bone,
Salt tears washing the sinews,
The spider strangled in her web.

I stood in the last wilderness
Watching the grass at the sea's edge
Bend as to the breathing touch
Of a blind slither at the stalk.

String of the navel and the net,
Vein threading the still pool,
Dumb fingers in the wet sand
Where the heart bled its secret food.

Salt of the flesh, I knew the world
For the white veil over the eye,
The eye for the caged water of light;
The beast asleep in the bleeding snare.

XV

And the rabbis have said the last word
And the iron gates they have slammed shut
Closing my body from the world.
Around me all Long Island lies
Smouldering and still.

Cold winter, the roller coasters
Stand in the swamps by the sea, and bend
The lizards of their bones alone,
August of lust and the hot dog
Frozen in their fat.

But the sea goes her own way,
Around and down her barren green
Sliding and sucking the cold flesh
Of the wrinkled world, with no bone
To such mother-makings.

I have sept through the wide seine.
From Coney Island to Phlegethon
Is no great way by ferris wheel,
And we informal liquors may
Easily despise your bones.

XVI

Snow on the beaches, briny ice,
Grass white and cracking with the cold.
The light is from the ocean moon
Hanging in the dead height.

Gull rises in the snowy marsh
A shale of light flaked from a star,
The white hair of the breaking wave
Splashes in night sky.

Down at the root, in the warm dream,
The lily bows among the ruins.
Kingdoms rise and are blown down
While the summer fly hums.

## XVII

When black water breaks the ice
The moon is milk and chalk of tooth.
The star is bleeding in the still pool
And the horny skin is left behind
When journey must be new-begun.

Teiresias watching in the wood
A wheel of snakes, gave his sight
To know the coupled work of time,
How pale woman and fiery man
Married their disguise away.

Then all was the self, but self was none;
Knowing itself in the fiery dark
The blind pool of the eye became
The sailing of the moon and sun
Through brightness melted into sky.

## XVIII

Of leaf and branch and rain and light,
The spider's web glistered with wet,
The robin's breast washed red in sun
After the rapid storm goes on;

Of long light level on the lake
And white on the side of lonely houses,
The thunder going toward the hill,
The last lightning cracking the sky;

New happiness of everything!
The blind worm lifts up his head
And the sparrow shakes a wet wing
In the home of little while.

# 3

THE SALT GARDEN

*for S. M. S.*

I

A good house, and ground whereon
With an amateur's toil
Both lawn and garden have been won
From a difficult, shallow soil
That, now inland, was once the shore
And once, maybe, the ocean floor.
Much patience, and some sweat,
Have made the garden green,
An even green the lawn.
Turnip and bean and violet
In a decent order set,
Grow, flourish and are gone;
Even the ruins of stalk and shell,
The vine when it goes brown,
Look civil and die well.
Sometimes in the late afternoon
I sit out with my wife,
Watching the work that we have done
Bend in the salt wind,
And think that here our life
Might be a long and happy one;
Though restless over the sand
The ocean's wrinkled green
Maneuvers in its sleep,
And I despise what I had planned,
Every work of the hand,
For what can man keep?

## II

Restless, rising at dawn,
I saw the great gull come from the mist
To stand upon the lawn.
And there he shook his savage wing
To quiet, and stood like a high priest
Bird-masked, mantled in grey.
Before his fierce austerity
My thought bowed down, imagining
The wild sea lanes he wandered by
And the wild waters where he slept
Still as a candle in the crypt.
Noble, and not courteous,
He stared upon my green concerns,
Then, like a merchant prince
Come to some poor province,
Who, looking all about, discerns
No spice, no treasure house,
Nothing that can be made
Delightful to his haughty trade,
And so spreads out his sail,
Leaving to savage men
Their miserable regimen;
So did he rise, making a gale
About him by his wings,
And fought his huge freight into air
And vanished seaward with a cry—
A strange tongue but the tone clear.
He faded from my troubled eye
There where the ghostly sun
Came from the mist.
               When he was gone
I turned back to the house
And thought of wife, of child,
And of my garden and my lawn
Serene in the wet dawn;
And thought that image of the wild
Wave where it beats the air

Had come, brutal, mysterious,
To teach the tenant gardener,
Green fellow of this paradise,
Where his salt dream lies.


## THE SANCTUARY

Over the ground of slate and light gravel,
Clear water, so shallow that one can see
The numerous springs moving their mouths of sand;
And the dark trout are clearly to be seen,
Swimming this water which is color of air
So that the fish appear suspended nowhere and
In nothing. With a delicate bend and reflex
Of their tails the trout slowly glide
From the shadowy side into the light, so clear,
And back again into the shadows; slow
And so definite, like thoughts emerging
Into a clear place in the mind, then going back,
Exchanging shape for shade. Now and again
One fish slides into the center of the pool
And hangs between the surface and the slate
For several minutes without moving, like
A silence in a dream; and when I stand
At such a time, observing this, my life
Seems to have been suddenly moved a great
Distance away on every side, as though
The quietest thought of all stood in the pale
Watery light alone, and was no more
My own than the speckled trout I stare upon
All but unseeing. Even at such times
The mind goes on transposing and revising
The elements of its long allegory
In which the anagoge is always death;
And while this vision blurs with empty tears,
I visit, in the cold pool of the skull,
A sanctuary where the slender trout

Feed on my drowned eyes. . . . Until this trout
Pokes through the fabric of the surface to
Snap up a fly. As if a man's own eyes
Raised welts upon the mirror whence they stared,
I find this world again in focus, and
This fish, a shadow dammed in artifice,
Swims to the furthest shadows out of sight
Though not, in time's ruining stream, out of mind.


## THE GULLS

I know them at their worst, when by the shore
They raise the screaming practice of their peace,
Disputing fish and floating garbage or
Scraps of stale bread thrown by a child. In this,
Even, they flash with senseless beauty more
Than I believed—sweet are their bitter cries,
As their fierce eyes are sweet; in their mere greed
Is grace, as they fall splendidly to feed.

And sometimes I have seen them as they glide
Mysterious upon a morning sea
Ghostly with mist, or when they ride
White water or the shattered wind, while we
Work at a wooden oar and huddle inside
Our shallow hull against the sea-torn spray;
And there they brutally are emblems of
Soul's courage, summoners to a broken love.

Courage is always brutal, for it is
The bitter tooth fastens the soul to God
Unknowing and unwilling, but as a vise
Not to be torn away. In the great crowd,
Because it gathers from such empty skies,
Each eye is arrogant and each voice loud
With angry lust; while alone each bird must be
Dispassionate above a hollow sea.

White wanderers, sky-bearers from the wide
Rage of the waters! so may your moving wings
Defend you from the kingdom of the tide
Whose sullen sway beneath your journeyings
Wrinkles like death, so may your flying pride
Keep you in danger—bless the song that sings
Of mortal courage; bless it with your form
Compassed in calm amid the cloud-white storm.


## I ONLY AM ESCAPED ALONE TO TELL THEE

I tell you that I see her still
At the dark entrance of the hall.
One gas lamp burning near her shoulder
Shone also from her other side
Where hung the long inaccurate glass
Whose pictures were as troubled water.
An immense shadow had its hand
Between us on the floor, and seemed
To hump the knuckles nervously,
A giant crab readying to walk,
Or a blanket moving in its sleep.

You will remember, with a smile
Instructed by movies to reminisce,
How strict her corsets must have been,
How the huge arrangements of her hair
Would certainly betray the least
Impassionate displacement there.
It was no rig for dallying,
And maybe only marriage could
Derange that queenly scaffolding—
As when a great ship, coming home,
Coasts in the harbor, dropping sail
And loosing all the tackle that had laced
Her in the long lanes. . . .
                              I know

We need not draw this figure out.
But all that whalebone came from whales.
And all the whales lived in the sea,
In calm beneath the troubled glass,
Until the needle drew their blood.

I see her standing in the hall,
Where the mirror's lashed to blood and foam,
And the black flukes of agony
Beat at the air till the light blows out.


## THE GOOSE FISH

On the long shore, lit by the moon
To show them properly alone,
Two lovers suddenly embraced
So that their shadows were as one.
The ordinary night was graced
For them by the swift tide of blood
That silently they took at flood,
And for a little time they prized
    Themselves emparadised.

Then, as if shaken by stage-fright
Beneath the hard moon's bony light,
They stood together on the sand
Embarrassed in each other's sight
But still conspiring hand in hand,
Until they saw, there underfoot,
As though the world had found them out,
The goose fish turning up, though dead,
    His hugely grinning head.

There in the china light he lay,
Most ancient and corrupt and grey.
They hesitated at his smile,
Wondering what it seemed to say

117

To lovers who a little while
Before had thought to understand,
By violence upon the sand,
The only way that could be known
   To make a world their own.

It was a wide and moony grin
Together peaceful and obscene;
They knew not what he would express,
So finished a comedian
He might mean failure or success,
But took it for an emblem of
Their sudden, new and guilty love
To be observed by, when they kissed,
   That rigid optimist.

So he became their patriarch,
Dreadfully mild in the half-dark.
His throat that the sand seemed to choke,
His picket teeth, these left their mark
But never did explain the joke
That so amused him, lying there
While the moon went down to disappear
Along the still and tilted track
   That bears the zodiac.

# 4

DIALECTICAL SONGS

I

Let sin be preordained
To match the world's desires,
The undying but stained
Soul walk in ancient fires.
If sanctity is wit
I will have none of it.

These fires are something shrewd
And courteous to a fault
That of the snide and lewd
Sublime essential salt,
Making the saint begin
Right in the teeth of sin.

How can the good bourgeois,
Though his virtues speak loud,
Ever consent with Yah?
The camel's neck is proud,
His hump to him is all,
And the needle's eye is small.

II

*Lucifer*

The wind created by his fall
Became the breath of life in all.
By hollowing his dreaded cup
He raised the holy mountain up,
Till at the apex of his crater
A home was made for our first nature;

And landing in the frozen lake
He was enslaved for our sake,
And beat six wings in vain until
We made our center in the Will.

Then was his majesty made known
When the footstool became the throne.
So fast the holy circles turn
That the Intelligences burn
In the wild grinding of the spheres.
So pride, stripping our worldly gears,
May make sole heaven of this hell
And set some fire in heaven as well.


III

Now that the salt has lost its savor,
Wherewith again shall it be salted?
I, when I first began to waver,
That white hot purity defaulted;
When my lust for the seasoned sky
Deliquesced, and was not dry.

The ancient demon of the moist
Destroyed in me the salty dry,
Left me eternally despiced
Of any flavor, although I
To get it back equally bolted
Martini and the chocolate malted.

The liquid bed where I was borne
Might dampen better men's desire
So to exalt their mortal horn
As make such smoke from little fire:
I cannot longer praise the maker
For what poured from the old salt-shaker.

The visions given me at night
Are nameless, not to guarantee.

Though both kinds shed a holy light,
Of sandy shore or salty sea,
I, the world's gull, remain between,
And north or south am peregrine.


## RETURNING TO EUROPE

Before their journeys men have dreams,
And in my dream I am always lost
In ruined streets, in roofless houses
Under a sky splintered with rafters.
It tells me nothing, yet I know
That place is old, mean with the sly
Innocent secrecy of old men
Who rock in the corner, mouthing the thing
The world has given them to keep.

This dream forgot to wake me once,
And told me this one thing. There is
A room in one of those ruined houses
I must not enter. Any door
Might be the one, and I keep on
Opening every door I see
Although I know I am afraid.
Soldiers are sleeping in those rooms,
Shapeless in rags, but they are not
The one I fear to find, the self,
The image of the lost war
Secret and pale with long denial,
Who will embrace me brotherly
And put his greedy mouth on mine.

## ARMISTICE

His name is Legion, and with a red eye
Gay as a gander's he offers me
The paper opiate of this poppy
Twisted on a green wire stem.

Remember who died for you. They sleep
In Flanders, in the poppy beds,
The real, narcotic and forbidden
Beds of huddled buddies dead.

The man is drunk—on poppy seed?
Who bought my freedom holds it dear.
Before this great fairy's budding glare
I weep my green and paper blood.


## THE VACUUM

The house is so quiet now
The vacuum cleaner sulks in the corner closet,
Its bag limp as a stopped lung, its mouth
Grinning into the floor, maybe at my
Slovenly life, my dog-dead youth.

I've lived this way long enough,
But when my old woman died her soul
Went into that vacuum cleaner, and I can't bear
To see the bag swell like a belly, eating the dust
And the woolen mice, and begin to howl

Because there is old filth everywhere
She used to crawl, in the corner and under the stair.
I know now how life is cheap as dirt,
And still the hungry, angry heart
Hangs on and howls, biting at air.

## YOUNG WOMAN

Naked before the glass she said,
"I see my body as no man has,
Nor any shall unless I wed
And naked in a stranger's house
Stand timid beside his bed.
There is no pity in the flesh."

"Or else I shall grow old," she said,
"Alone, and change my likeliness
For a vile, slack shape, a head
Shriveled with thinking wickedness
Against the day I must be dead
And eaten by my crabbed wish."

"One or the other way," she said,
"How shall I know the difference,
When wrinkles come, to spinster or bride?
Whether to marry or burn is bless-
ed best, O stranger to my bed,
There is no pity in the flesh."


## INSTRUCTIONS FOR USE OF THIS TOY

*For in the lond ther nas no crafty man,*
*That geometrie or ars-metrik can.*

. . . is worked this way. Release the striking arm
(marked A on diagram) by means of the
End ratchet on the cylinder marked B.
Slight humming noises should not cause alarm,
But if explosions, or loud coughing sounds,
Seem to be coming from the diaphragm,
It might be well to disengage the cam
Before examining the guards for grounds.

123

So far so good. The automatic trail
Guide bracket post should be secured against
Vibration of the flange, but do not fail
At any time to keep the wire tensed
That in the event of fire throws the switch
(marked Jettison) that breaks the circuit which . . .


AN ISSUE OF LIFE

Here: wear this spectacle bra. It is the fashion.
Soon now you may vacation on the moon.
They want young men like you, hardy, alert
And trained to scientific observation
(not blinded or befooled by any passion).
In twenty years, that is. Maybe your son
Will go instead of you. Man is like dirt
Wherever there is Martian domination.

Here: these iron things were found inside a cow.
Her churning stomach made this hairball hard.
The cow of course is dead. Cattle like this
Were frozen standing up in last week's snow.
Time now for bed. P. S. Analysis
May synthesize small men from melted lard.


DIALOGUE

O father, answer me,
Why, why must money be?
The stones along the shore,
The leaves upon the tree

Are worth as much and more.
Why must we labor for

124

Our greasy greenery
When such fine things are free?

\*   \*   \*   \*

The leaf, alas, will die,
And crumble in your hand,
And the stone's color dry
To dullness on the sand.

And only money, son,
Retains its character
When withered in the sun
Or dried in the salt air.


## THE DEPOSITION

A King
Speaks:    Of the incertain game
           I know death is the mate.
           My enemy tears down
           Ancestral tombs, and names
           Old ways with a new name.
           His horses desecrate
           The golden stair, and flames
           By his command eat at
           Our palace and the town.
           All elements are his,
           All dreadful energies
           Compound him up his right,
           And every task they bless
           That serves unruliness.
           Such elements are his
           That I, because in death
           I recognize my wish,
           Can feel the empty joy
           That shakes the brain of man
           When his strength cries, Destroy.

Did not the statues crash,
The laws become as dust
And order die, man must,
Who could not make his state
But from uncertain fate.

His
Enemy:    Order and law on power
Bear, and feed on fears.
Propriety soon falls
When the rich blood goes sour
From standing a still hour.
The state that your command
Raised for some thousand years,
One generation spanned
Before the revolted dead
Dragged up against the walls
Their rusty sieging guns
And blew up what they bred,
That like the Gorgon's head
Had turned men into stones.

The
King:    In triumph you speak this,
And love antithesis.
Here, in my place and right,
You see your waiting doom.
The warrior in his turn
Becomes the warred upon
And perishes in steel,
As in his living tomb
He cannot see forgone
His all-invested might.
Peace feeds on wars
As, turning on the night,
The planets forage on
New pasture of the stars;
And this, as the wise learn,
Moves by the holy wheel

That out of all respect
Men's fortunes and their lives
Determines in the skies
And yet is man's free choice.

His
Enemy: He does not need to choose,
For strength is choice enough
And makes its man elect
To do what must be done:
Choose ruin for a roof
And rack the rafters loose,
So somewhere there is stuff
That richer, wiser men
Have put their souls upon,
Nesting in the tree-top
Rather than the root.
I must not ever stop;
For tell me, where's the gun
That was not made to shoot?

The
King: The thing is obvious.
I make, that you destroy,
And when you have destroyed
You make it up again—
What have you left to do
But build your filthy den
That soon your little boy
Will make luxurious?
Might I not pity you?

His
Enemy: You might. You may be right.
I may live to regret
The future like a debt;
Old and benign, I might
Build roads and legislate,
And offer to the gods

My fight against the odds.
Your view of history
Goes round and round, while mine
Because of *now* is free,
And even libertine.
For now I am the state,
I beg you to relax
Lest your neck impede my axe.

Both:      This moment on the wheel
Is made of time and zeal.
Most personal is pain,
And aches to come again.
The representative
Is suffered still to live,
And the incarnate earth
Must shudder at his birth;
While the heroic I
Goes forth only to die.

The
King:      I am your freedom. Murder me.

His
Enemy:      I strike as your necessity.

# 5

## THE SNOW GLOBE

A long time ago, when I was a child,
They left my light on while I went to sleep,
As though they would have wanted me beguiled
By brightness if at all; dark was too deep.

And they left me one toy, a village white
With the fresh snow and silently in glass
Frozen forever. But if you shook it,
The snow would rise up in the rounded space

And from the limits of the universe
Snow itself down again. O world of white,
First home of dreams! Now that I have my dead,
I want so cold an emblem to rehearse
How many of them have gone from the world's light,
As I have gone, too, from my snowy bed.


## AN OLD PICTURE

Two children, dressed in court costume,
Go hand in hand through a rich room.
He bears a scepter, she a book;
Their eyes exchange a serious look.

High in a gallery above,
Grave persons frown upon their love;
Yonder behind the silken screen
Whispers the bishop with the queen.

These hold the future tightly reined,
It shall be as they have ordained:
The bridal bed already made,
The crypt also richly arrayed.


## CENTRAL PARK

The broad field darkens, but, still moving round
So that they seem to hover off the ground,
Children are following a shadowy ball;
Shrill, as of birds, their high voices sound.

The pale December sky at darkfall seems
A lake of ice, and frozen there the gleams
Of the gaunt street-lamps and the young cold cries,
The ball falling in the slow distance of dreams.

Football, long falling in the winter sky,
The cold climate of a child's eye
Had kept you at the height so long a time;
His ear had kept the waiting player's cry,

That after years, coming that way then,
He might be pity's witness among men
Who hear those cries across the darkening field,
And see the shadow children home again.


## THE QUARRY

The place is forgotten now; when I was a child
And played here, its ruins were already old
And the cracked granite face already green
To begin again; while now the wild
Overgrowth of briar and birch and pine
Keeps my hollow castle in the hill

Hidden and still.
                    Long silent years
Have split the walls that men with crowbars
And blast had split before; and all repairs
—I know it now—but ravage and ruin again
For the life's sake. The stone and vine-grown crater
I stare on, my dry wound in nature,
Is absence everywhere: what curbs or schools
Or monuments were squared by such rude rules,
Quarried and carried away and dressed in line,
Before the stone could be split by the tree,
And the tree be brought down by the vine?


TRUTH

Around, above my bed, the pitch-dark fly
Buzzed in the darkness till in my mind's eye
His blue sound made the image of my thought
An image that his resonance had brought
Out of a common midden of the sun—
A garbage pit, and pile where glittering tin
Cans turned the ragged edges of their eyes
In a mean blindness on mine, where the loud flies
Would blur the summer afternoons out back
Beyond the house. Sleepy, insomniac, black
Remainder of a dream, what house? and when?
Listening now, I knew never again
That winged image as in amber kept
Might come, summoned from darkness where it slept
The common sleep of all such sunken things
By the fly's loud buzzing and his dreaming wings.

I listened in an angry wakefulness;
The fly was bitter. Between dream and guess
About a foundered world, about a wrong
The mind refused, I waited long, long,
And then that humming of the garbage heap

131

I drew beneath the surface of my sleep
Until I saw the helmet of the king
Of Nineveh, pale gold and glittering
On the king's brow, yet sleeping knew that I
But thought the deepening blue thought of the fly.


## THE MARKET-PLACE

*Do you know me, my lord?*
*Excellent well; you are a fishmonger.*

The armored salmon jewel the ice with blood
Where cobblestones are steaming in the sun.
Witness my heart drains deep, if now, at noon,
Soft August of the salt corrupting year
Stirs a chill cloud, raises a silver flood
To savage in the marrow of my weir.


## THE BOOK OF KELLS

Out of the living word
Come flower, serpent and bird.

All things that swim or fly
Or go upon the ground,
All shapes that breath can cry
Into the sinews of sound,
That growth can make abound
In the river of the eye
Till speech is three-ply
And the truth triply wound.

Out of the living word
Come flower, serpent and bird.

# THE PRIEST'S CURSE ON DANCING

"Dance for a year and a day!" he cried
When we danced in the chantry of church
And before his altar and down the nave,
Leaping like fish in a wave,
And danced out the door and over the dead
While he stood there calling his curse—
"Dance for a year and a day!" he said,
"Dance till you die!" and some of us did.

Joan who was the priest's own daughter,
With hair unbound, with dancing eyes,
Led us through England and over the water
Until we landed at Champayne Fair,
And for a year we danced there
Happy as people in Paradise,
While rich and poor paid on the drum
To see the scandal in Christendom.

No cloak nor shoe wore thin that year,
Nor needed we eat or drink or sleep,
But with legs of iron and lungs of leather
We went in every weather
To the same tune and the single step
And the curse of the priest who kept us there,
And then those French put up a tent
Around and over us as we went.

Now Joan and some others are buried there
Thigh deep in the labyrinth of the dance,
Who trod their grave in the merry year,
Leaping like fish in a weir.
The other of us by curse or chance
Cried from the pit for cane and crutch
To steady our quivering legs to church,
For the flesh dances on out of sense.

## SLEEPING BEAUTY

They told me this story a long time ago,
When I was a child, to make me go to sleep.
I never should have been surprised,
But then, being young, I could not know they meant
My eyes to be the ones that closed
When the time came and the clock struck
And the dream was tolled by the steeple bell.

I listen to the castle sleep, the grooms
In the stables, courtiers on the marble floors,
The scratch of dust descending and the rose
Thickets breaking forth flowers and thorns;
And I ask in sleep, is this my sleep?
Am I the one the wide world cannot find
Nor even the prince in the forest foresee?

This ends only with a kiss, the story said.
Then all the snoring barons will arise
And the dogs begin to bark, the king and queen
Order their coach and four—all on a kiss
The whole world will begin to happen again,
People will yawn, stretch, begin to forget
Whatever they dreamed that was so like a dream.

And shall I also, with the kiss, forget
That I was the one who dreamed them all,
Courtier and king, scullion and cook,
Horse in the stable and fly on the wall?
Forget the petal's whisper when they drift
Down where the untold princes die in blood
Because I dreamed the thicket and the thorn?

# DEEP WOODS

Such places are too still for history,
Which slows, shudders, and shifts as the trucks do,
In hearing-distance, on the highway hill,
And staggers onward elsewhere with its load
Of statues, candelabra, buttons, gold;
But here the heart, racing strangely as though
Ready to stop, reaches a kind of rest;
The mind uneasily rests, as if a beast,
Being hunted down, made tiredness and terror
Its camouflage and fell asleep, and dreamed,
At the terrible, smooth pace of the running dogs,
A dream of being lost, covered with leaves
And hidden in a death like any sleep
So deep the bitter world must let it be
And go bay elsewhere after better game.
Even the restless eye, racing upon
Reticulated branch and vine which go
Nowhere, at last returns upon itself
And comes into a flickering kind of rest,
Being lost in the insanity of line.

Line, leaf, and light; darkness invades our day;
No meaning in it, but indifference
Which does not flatter with profundity.
Nor is it drama. Even the giant oak,
Stricken a hundred years or yesterday,
Has not found room to fall as heroes should
But crookedly leans on an awkward-squad of birch,
The tragic image and the mighty crash
Indefinitely delayed in favor of
Fresh weaving of vines, rooting of outer branches,
Beginning again, in spaces still more cramped,
A wandering calligraphy which seems
Enthralled to a magic constantly misspelled.

It is the same, they say, everywhere.
But that's not so. These here are the deep woods

Of now, New England, this October, when
Dry gold has little left to change, and half
The leaves are gone to ground, and half of those
Rained into the leaf-mold which tenses in
The fastenings of frost; where the white branches
Of birch are dry bones airborne in assaults
Which haven't worked yet. This unlegended land
Is no Black Forest where the wizard lived
Under a bent chimney and a thatch of straw;
Nor the hot swamp theatrical with snakes
And tigers; nor the Chinese forest on
The mountainside, with bridge, pagoda, fog,
Three poets in the foreground, drinking tea
(there is no tea, and not so many as three)—
But this land, this, unmitigated by myth
And whose common splendors are comparable only to
Themselves; this leaf, line, light, are scrawled alone
In solar definitions on a lump
Of hill like nothing known since Nature was
Invented by Watteau or Fragonard
In the Old Kingdom or the time of Set
Or before the Flood of Yao (or someone else
Of the same name) in the Fourth, or Disney, Dimension.

And this is yours to work; plant it to salt
Or men in armor who destroy each other,
Sprinkle with dragon's blood early in spring
And see what happens, epic or pastoral:
A sword in every stone, small minotaurs
Looking for thread, and unicorns for girls,
And Glastonbury thorns to make December
Bleed for the Saviour; the nightingale of Sarras
Enchants the traveler here three hundred years
And a day which seem but as a single day.
More probably nothing will happen. This
Place is too old for history to know
Beans about; these trees were here, are here,
Before King Hannibal had elephants
Or Frederick grew his red beard through the table

Or Mordecai hung Haman at the gate.
The other Ahasuerus has not spat
Nor walked nor cobbled any shoe, nor Joseph
So much as dreamed that he will found the Corn
Exchange Bank in the baked country of Egypt.
Not even those burnt beauties are hawked out,
By the angry Beginner, on Chaos floor
Where they build Pandemonium the Palace
Back in the high old times. Most probably
Nothing will happen. Even the Fall of Man
Is waiting, here, for someone to grow apples;
And the snake, speckled as sunlight on the rock
In the deep woods, still sleeps with a whole head
And has not begun to grow a manly smile.

# MIRRORS
AND
WINDOWS
# (1958)

*To Paul Terence Feeley*

1

## THE MIRROR

O room of silences, alien land
Where likeness lies, how should I understand
What happens here as in the other world
But silently, the branch, the same leaf curled
Against the branch, stirred in the same breeze,
And all those quivering duplicities
Rendered again under a distant light?

Now slowly the snow drifts down, and coming night
Darkens the room, while in the leaden glass
I watch with observed eyes the stranger pass.

## TREES

To be a giant and keep quiet about it,
To stay in one's own place;
To stand for the constant presence of process
And always to seem the same;
To be steady as a rock and always trembling,
Having the hard appearance of death
With the soft, fluent nature of growth,
One's Being deceptively armored,
One's Becoming deceptively vulnerable;
To be so tough, and take the light so well,
Freely providing forbidden knowledge
Of so many things about heaven and earth
For which we should otherwise have no word—
Poems or people are rarely so lovely,
And even when they have great qualities

141

They tend to tell you rather than exemplify
What they believe themselves to be about,
While from the moving silence of trees,
Whether in storm or calm, in leaf and naked,
Night or day, we draw conclusions of our own,
Sustaining and unnoticed as our breath,
And perilous also—though there has never been
A critical tree—about the nature of things.


## THE TOWN DUMP

*"The art of our necessities is strange,*
*That can make vile things precious."*

A mile out in the marshes, under a sky
Which seems to be always going away
In a hurry, on that Venetian land threaded
With hidden canals, you will find the city
Which seconds ours (so cemeteries, too,
Reflect a town from hillsides out of town),
Where Being most Becomingly ends up
Becoming some more. From cardboard tenements,
Windowed with cellophane, or simply tenting
In paper bags, the angry mackerel eyes
Glare at you out of stove-in, sunken heads
Far from the sea; the lobster, also, lifts
An empty claw in his most minatory
Of gestures; oyster, crab, and mussel shells
Lie here in heaps, savage as money hurled
Away at the gate of hell. If you want results,
These are results.
                    Objects of value or virtue,
However, are also to be picked up here,
Though rarely, lying with bones and rotten meat,
Eggshells and mouldy bread, banana peels
No one will skid on, apple cores that caused
Neither the fall of man nor a theory

Of gravitation. People do throw out
The family pearls by accident, sometimes,
Not often; I've known dealers in antiques
To prowl this place by night, with flashlights, on
The off-chance of somebody's having left
Derelict chairs which will turn out to be
By Hepplewhite, a perfect set of six
Going to show, I guess, that in any sty
Someone's heaven may open and shower down
Riches responsive to the right dream; though
It is a small chance, certainly, that sends
The ghostly dealer, heavy with fly-netting
Over his head, across these hills in darkness,
Stumbling in cut-glass goblets, lacquered cups,
And other products of his dreamy midden
Penciled with light and guarded by the flies.

For there are flies, of course. A dynamo
Composed, by thousands, of our ancient black
Retainers, hums here day and night, steady
As someone telling beads, the hum becoming
A high whine at any disturbance; then,
Settled again, they shine under the sun
Like oil-drops, or are invisible as night,
By night.
      All this continually smoulders,
Crackles, and smokes with mostly invisible fires
Which, working deep, rarely flash out and flare,
And never finish. Nothing finishes;
The flies, feeling the heat, keep on the move.

Among the flies, the purefying fires,
The hunters by night, acquainted with the art
Of our necessities, and the new deposits
That each day wastes with treasure, you may say
There should be ratios. You may sum up
The results, if you want results. But I will add
That wild birds, drawn to the carrion and flies,
Assemble in some numbers here, their wings

Shining with light, their flight enviably free,
Their music marvelous, though sad, and strange.


## THE SUNGLASSES

The terrible temper of the day gone dim
Against this lucid calm, the green lagoon
That turns my drowning eyes to precious stone,
I stare unpunished at the sun's wild limb
Of Satan wavering westward past the noon
In a mild fire, foolish gold; whose trim
Of wicked brilliance not the seraphim
Could hold a candle to, or light a moon.

Against my glass, all light is pacified
Here where I lie in green gone deeper green,
All colors colder; I, dreaming I died
Where in still waters on illusion's coast
The cold-eyed sirens sang to sailor men
Of jewels that charred the zenith, and were lost.


## STORM WINDOWS

People are putting up storm windows now,
Or were, this morning, until the heavy rain
Drove them indoors. So, coming home at noon,
I saw storm windows lying on the ground,
Frame-full of rain; through the water and glass
I saw the crushed grass, how it seemed to stream
Away in lines like seaweed on the tide
Or blades of wheat leaning under the wind.
The ripple and splash of rain on the blurred glass
Seemed that it briefly said, as I walked by,
Something I should have liked to say to you,

Something . . . the dry grass bent under the pane
Brimful of bouncing water . . . something of
A swaying clarity which blindly echoes
This lonely afternoon of memories
And missed desires, while the wintry rain
(Unspeakable, the distance in the mind!)
Runs on the standing windows and away.


SHELLS

You pick one up along the shore.
It is empty and light and dry,
And leaves a powdery chalk on your hands.

The life that made it is gone out.
That is what is meant when people say,
"A hollow shell," "a shell of his former self,"

Failing to take into account
The vital waste in composition
With the beauty of the ruined remainder

Which is no use to anyone,
Of course, unless as decoration:
A Souvenir of Sunset Beach, etc.

Its form is only cryptically
Instructive, if at all: it winds
Like generality, from nothing to nothing

By means of nothing but itself.
It is a stairway going nowhere,
Our precious emblem of the steep ascent,

Perhaps, beginning at a point
And opening to infinity,
Or the other way, if you want it the other way.

Inside it, also, there is nothing
Except the obedient sound of waters
Beat by your Mediterranean, classic heart

In bloody tides as long as breath,
Bringing by turns the ebb and flood
Upon the ruining house of histories,

Whose whitening stones, in Africa,
Bake dry and blow away, in Athens,
In Rome, abstract and instructive as chalk

When children scrawl the blackboard full
Of wild spirals every which way,
To be erased with chalk dust, then with water.


## THE STATUES IN THE PUBLIC GARDENS

Alone at the end of green *allées,* alone
Where a path turns back upon itself, or else
Where several paths converge, green bronze, grey stone,
The weatherbeaten famous figures wait
Inside their basins, on their pedestals,
Till time, as promised them, wears out of date.

Around them rise the willow, birch, and elm,
Sweet shaken pliancies in the weather now.
The granite hand is steady on the helm,
The sword, the pen, unshaken in the hand,
The bandage and the laurel on the brow:
The last obedience is the last command.

Children and nurses eddying through the day,
Old gentlemen with newspapers and canes,
And licit lovers, public as a play,
Never acknowledge the high regard of fame

Across their heads—the patriot's glare, the pains
Of prose—and scarcely stop to read a name.

Children, to be illustrious is sad.
Do not look up. Those empty eyes are stars,
Their glance the constellation of the mad
Who must be turned to stone. To save your garden,
My playful ones, these pallid voyagers
Stand in the streak of rain, imploring pardon.

At night the other lovers come to play
Endangered games, and robbers lie in wait
To knock old ladies with a rock; but they
Tremble to come upon these stony men
And suffragettes, who shine like final fate
In the electric green of every glen.

For it is then that statues suffer their
Sacrificed lives, and sigh through fruitless trees
After the flesh. Their sighs tremble the air,
They would surrender scepters, swords, and globes,
Feeling the soft flank shudder to the breeze
Under the greatcoats and the noble robes.

In darker glades, the nearly naked stone
Of athlete, goddess chaste as any snows
That stain them winters, tempts maiden and man
From their prosthetic immortality:
Pythagoras' thigh, or Tycho's golden nose,
For a figleaf fallen from the withered tree.


A DAY ON THE BIG BRANCH

Still half drunk, after a night at cards,
with the grey dawn taking us unaware
among our guilty kings and queens, we drove

147

far North in the morning, winners, losers,
to a stream in the high hills, to climb up to a place
one of us knew, with some vague view
of cutting losses or consolidating gains
by the old standard appeal to the wilderness,
the desert, the empty places of our exile,
bringing only the biblical bread and cheese
and cigarettes got from a grocer's on the way,
expecting to drink only the clear cold water
among the stones, and remember, or forget.
Though no one said anything about atonement,
there was still some purgatorial idea
in all those aching heads and ageing hearts
as we climbed the giant stair of the stream,
reaching the place around noon.

It was as promised, a wonder, with granite walls
enclosing ledges, long and flat, of limestone,
or, rolling, of lava; within the ledges
the water, fast and still, pouring its yellow light,
and green, over the tilted slabs of the floor,
blackened at shady corners, falling in a foam
of crystal to a calm where the waterlight
dappled the ledges as they leaned
against the sun; big blue dragonflies hovered
and darted and dipped a wing, hovered again
against the low wind moving over the stream,
and shook the flakes of light from their clear wings.
This surely was it, was what we had come for,
was nature, though it looked like art with its
grey fortress walls and laminated benches
as in the waiting room of some petrified station.
But we believed; and what it was we believed
made of the place a paradise
for ruined poker players, win or lose,
who stripped naked and bathed and dried out on the rocks
like gasping trout (the water they drank
making them drunk again), lit cigarettes and lay back
waiting for nature to say the last word

—as though the stones were Memnon stones,
which, caught in a certain light, would sing.

The silence (and even the noise of the waters
was silence) grew pregnant; that is the phrase,
grew pregnant; but nothing else did.
The mountain brought forth not a mouse, and the rocks,
unlike the ones you would expect to find
on the slopes of Purgatory or near Helicon,
mollified by muses and with a little give to 'em,
were modern American rocks, and hard as rocks.
Our easy bones groaned, our flesh baked
on one side and shuddered on the other; and each man
thought bitterly about primitive simplicity
and decadence, and how he had been ruined
by civilization and forced by circumstances
to drink and smoke and sit up all night
inspecting those perfectly arbitrary cards
until he was broken-winded as a trout on a rock
and had no use for the doctrines of Jean Jacques
Rousseau, and could no longer afford
a savagery whether noble or not; some
would never batter that battered copy of Walden
again.

        But all the same,
the water, the sunlight, and the wind
did something; even the dragonflies
did something to the minds full of telephone
numbers and flushes, to the flesh
sweating bourbon on one side and freezing on the other.
And the rocks, the old and tumbling boulders
which formed the giant stair of the stream,
induced (again) some purgatorial ideas
concerning humility, concerning patience
and enduring what had to be endured,
winning and losing and breaking even;
ideas of weathering in whatever weather,
being eroded, or broken, or ground down into pebbles

by the stream's necessitous and grave currents.
But to these ideas did any purgatory
respond? Only this one: that in a world
where even the Memnon stones were carved in soap
one might at any rate wash with the soap.

After a time we talked about the War,
about what we had done in the War, and how near
some of us had been to being drowned, and burned,
and shot, and how many people we knew
who had been drowned, or burned, or shot;
and would it have been better to have died
in the War, the peaceful old War, where we were young?
But the mineral peace, or paralysis, of those
great stones, the moving stillness of the waters,
entered our speech; the ribs and blood
of the earth, from which all fables grow,
established poetry and truth in us,
so that at last one said, "I shall play cards
until the day I die," and another said,
"in bourbon whisky are all the vitamins
and minerals needed to sustain man's life,"
and still another, "I shall live on smoke
until my spirit has been cured of flesh."

Climbing downstream again, on the way home
to the lives we had left empty for a day,
we noticed, as not before, how of three bridges
not one had held the stream, which in its floods
had twisted the girders, splintered the boards, hurled
boulder on boulder, and had broken into rubble,
smashed practically back to nature,
the massive masonry of span after span
with its indifferent rage; this was a sight
that sobered us considerably, and kept us quiet
both during the long drive home and after,
till it was time to deal the cards.

# AN OLD WARPLANE

Even a thing like this takes pathos
After the years; rust flaking the paint
And oil stains streaked as if by speed
Along the fairing aft of the engines.

Low down and level on the bay,
Pounding her heart out going slow,
Lost at last in the horizon cloud,
She carried pity like a gun.

For only a moment, as she passed
Close to the shore, we heard again
The empty thunder of the war
By engines drummed on the stretched sky;

Burnt patches on the cannon ports
And under the exhaust pipes flared
Like danger and experience,
And all that dirty camouflage,

Of mackerel-back and belly of
The hanging rain-cloud on the sea,
Ran past, reminding of the old
Inflexible will and devious wile.

Now not the young men lost she hurts,
Who mastered her weapons and her ways
And dove her into seven dead seas:
Their blood is thin as water. But

We live whom she endangers now.
Pity reddens beneath the paint
As all our future rusts inside
The bright invention of the war;

And memory is seen at last
As obsolete and simplified,

Inadequately armed, camouflaged
Like a backdrop in vaudeville,

And now reduced to training flights
Through skies where, envied, far ahead,
Late imitations of the will
Scream rapidly to the real war.


SANDPIPERS

In the small territory and time
Between one wave and the next, they run
Down the beach and back, eating things
Which seem, conveniently for them,
To surface only when the sand gets wet.
Small, dapper birds, they make me think
Of commuters seen, say, in an early movie
Where the rough screen wavers, where the light
Jerks and seems to rain; of clockwork dolls
Set going on the sidewalk, drawing a crowd
Beside the newsstand at five o'clock; their legs
Black toothpicks, their heads nodding at nothing.
But this comedy is based upon exact
Perceptions, and delicately balanced
Between starvation and the sea:
Though sometimes I have seen one slip and fall,
From either the undertow or greed,
And have to get up in the wave's open mouth,
Still eating, I have never seen
One caught; if necessary he spreads his wings,
With the white stripe, and flutters rather than flies
Out, to begin eating again at once.
Now they are over every outer beach,
Procrastinating steadily southwards
In endlessly local comings and goings.

Whenever a flock of them takes flight,
And flies with the beautiful unison

Of banners in the wind, they are
No longer funny. It is their courage,
Meaningless as the word is when compared
With their thoughtless precisions, which strikes
Me when I watch them hidden and revealed
Between two waves, lost in the sea's
Lost color as they distance me; flying
From winter already, while I
Am in August. When suddenly they turn
In unison, all their bellies shine
Like mirrors flashing white with signals
I cannot read, but I wish them well.


## A CLOCK WITH NO HANDS

A moon with Roman numerals, there,
Backed to the wall, in the dim air
Of the abandoned waiting-room.
The door has long since lost its lock,
The track its trains (they run elsewhere).
The empty-headed, run-down clock,
   Doom-stricken, is struck dumb.

Woe to the empty-handed vandal
(Time on his hands!) who made this scandal!
What will he do with a pair of hands
Defaced, what will the idle dial,
Short-handed, do? And will time handle
With care the lost goods at the rail-
   head where the boxcar stands?

Impossible to tell the hour
That threw the switch, cut off the power,
Rerouted or derailed the last
Express some stations down the line
Forever; the high signal tower
Stands in the yard and gives no sign
   Of passage to the past.

Idolater, this moony god,
Whose sleight-of-hand will run no road,
May blandly yet discountenance
Your travels where the still mainspring,
Behind the even and the odd,
Hides in its coiled continuing
    A venomous tense past tense.

2

LIGHTNING STORM ON FUJI

(*Hokusai*)

1

The storm, darkness, a cracked hurdle of lightning,
Take place in the foreground and down below.
And out of all that, above the green forest,
Above the blue of the sea, the curly clouds,
Into the white of the sky and almost beyond
Into the charred blue-black wherein the zenith
Reflects the sea, the serene mountain rises
And falls in a clear cadence. The snowy peak,
Where the brown foliage falls away, is white
As the sky behind it, so that line alone
Seems to be left, and the hard rock become
Limpid as water, the form engraved on glass.
There at the left, hanging in empty heaven,
A cartouche with written characters proclaims
Even to such as do not know the script
That this is art, not nature. The gold lightning
Proclaims it too, for all that jagged speed
And linked immensity follow at a distance
The mountain's high serenity of thought,
Giving it depth and huge solidity.

A picture, then, touching eternity
From time, the way Fuji touches the sky,
Transparently, so that the summit might
Be substance thin enough to pierce with light.
The subject, you may say, is violence,
Or storm, and calm rising above the storm
To the region of serenity and splendor

Where earthly things are seen as a clear light.
This subject is imitated in the form.

2

Across an ocean and a continent,
A difference of a hundred and fifty years
And much in the way of manners, seeing mountains
And making images, I've watched this thing
Under the changes of the local light
All afternoon, turning from time to time
To see Mount Anthony framed in my window:
Named for Mad Anthony Wayne, a man of war
Who died a few years before Hokusai
Painted the Views of Fuji, this is a hill
Symmetrical, not stormy now, and small,
But deepening as that does, and ageing as
That does, while the day sinks in indistinction.
Between eternity and time there is
Space for the terrible thought that all things fail.
I try to think it through the evening, while
Shadows emerge and merge upon the mountain
And night grows up the slow flank heaved like a wave
Out of the first fault of the ancient earth,
To hold in silence till another morning
The folded history which will dream away,
Defined or not in nature, action, art,
Mad Anthony and Hokusai and me.


HOME FOR THE HOLIDAYS

While the train waited for an hour in Troy
And its engines were changed, the neon crosses,
Ladders, flowers, blinked rapidly on and off,
Eyes trying not to cry. The snowy stone,
Square darkness of this station, back of which
A dreamy town flowed away, somewhat depressed me

Going home for Christmas. When I was a boy
The mystery of railroads was more enthralling
As witnessed from outside. Across the water,
On the embankment, the iron wheels used to roll
All day and roar, the long trains disappear
Into the tunnel under Mundy's Hill.
For hours in the winter dusk I watched
The lighted sleeping cars go up the grade
To vanish in the dark of dark (I hoped
To see a naked woman, but never did).
Or else, going the other way, the high
Black engine spurting smoke burst from
The smoky hole, the released smoke burst high
In the still air and hung there white and solid
As galloping marble, while the whistle screamed
Telling the agony of distances
I could not go.
    Back there, all towns were Troy,
The iron horse breaching the wall would carry away
Priam's treasure and Helen's too. Oh, Greeks,
The sack of Santa Claus was deep and black
Inside, sleeveless and smoky as the spiral
Coalsack behind Orion, out where time
And distance cross. The neon city burns
And Christ is born time and again, stars fallen
From railing wheels by the iron axle thrown.
Those wheels a man beneath my window now
Taps with a hammer. The smoke of his breath
Drifts up along the pane, clouding with frost
My view of Troy, one station on the way
Which has become all towns, all neon signs,
Stars, planets, meteors, and signal lights.
Slowly the train begins to move again,
Across a street, between high walls, and through
Backyards of tenements where children watch
Me riding high to spend Christmas at home.

Tomorrow night we decorate the tree
With globes of light, with stars, with candied snow

And chains of ice; and we shall sing old songs,
While underneath the tree, as in childhood,
Our parents will have placed every good thing,
Treasure of Priam, treasure of Helen too,
So much of which no one is able to use:
Those neckties, watch chains, nightgowns, fountain pens,
Accustomed signs of His nativity
Who in the darkest hour of the year
Relights the planets of the evergreen
Axle of heaven, whereon presently
He is to hang.
    But oh, Greek bearing gifts,
As the train gathers speed and Troy dissolves
In dreamy slums, developments unbuilt
And hills of snowy coal, I see your smile,
Reflected on the violent windowpane,
As permanent against the moving scene.


## THE LOON'S CRY

On a cold evening, summer almost gone,
I walked alone down where the railroad bridge
Divides the river from the estuary.
There was a silence over both the waters,
The river's concentrated reach, the wide
Diffusion of the delta, marsh and sea,
Which in the distance misted out of sight.

As on the seaward side the sun went down,
The river answered with the rising moon,
Full moon, its craters, mountains and still seas
Shining like snow and shadows on the snow.
The balanced silence centered where I stood,
The fulcrum of two poised immensities,
Which offered to be weighed at either hand.

But I could think only, Red sun, white moon,
This is a natural beauty, it is not

Theology. For I had fallen from
The symboled world, where I in earlier days
Found mysteries of meaning, form, and fate
Signed on the sky, and now stood but between
A swamp of fire and a reflecting rock.

I envied those past ages of the world
When, as I thought, the energy in things
Shone through their shapes, when sun and moon no less
Than tree or stone or star or human face
Were seen but as fantastic Japanese
Lanterns are seen, sullen or gay colors
And lines revealing the light that they conceal.

The world a stage, its people maskers all
In actions largely framed to imitate
God and His Lucifer's long debate, a trunk
From which, complex and clear, the episodes
Spread out their branches. Each life played a part,
And every part consumed a life, nor dreams
After remained to mock accomplishment.

Under the austere power of the scene,
The moon standing balanced against the sun,
I simplified still more, and thought that now
We'd traded all those mysteries in for things,
For essences in things, not understood—
Reality in things! and now we saw
Reality exhausted all their truth.

As answering my thought a loon cried out
Laughter of desolation on the river,
A savage cry, now that the moon went up
And the sun down—yet when I heard him cry
Again, his voice seemed emptied of that sense
Or any other, and Adam I became,
Hearing the first loon cry in paradise.

For sometimes, when the world is not our home
Nor have we any home elsewhere, but all

Things look to leave us naked, hungry, cold,
We suddenly may seem in paradise
Again, in ignorance and emptiness
Blessed beyond all that we thought to know:
Then on sweet waters echoes the loon's cry.

I thought I understood what that cry meant,
That its contempt was for the forms of things,
Their doctrines, which decayed—the nouns of stone
And adjectives of glass—not for the verb
Which surged in power properly eternal
Against the seawall of the solid world,
Battering and undermining what it built,

And whose respeaking was the poet's act,
Only and always, in whatever time
Stripped by uncertainty, despair, and ruin,
Time readying to die, unable to die
But damned to life again, and the loon's cry.
And now the sun was sunken in the sea,
The full moon high, and stars began to shine.

The moon, I thought, might have been such a world
As this one is, till it went cold inside,
Nor any strength of sun could keep its people
Warm in their palaces of glass and stone.
Now all its craters, mountains and still seas,
Shining like snow and shadows on the snow,
Orbit this world in envy and late love.

And the stars too? Worlds, as the scholars taught
So long ago? Chaos of beauty, void,
O burning cold, against which we define
Both wretchedness and love. For signatures
In all things are, which leave us not alone
Even in the thought of death, and may by arts
Contemplative be found and named again.

The loon again? Or else a whistling train,
Whose far thunders began to shake the bridge.

And it came on, a loud bulk under smoke,
Changing the signals on the bridge, the bright
Rubies and emeralds, rubies and emeralds
Signing the cold night as I turned for home,
Hearing the train cry once more, like a loon.


## SUNDERLAND

*an eclogue*

HE

It was on a winter's day, as cold, as clear
As water running underneath the ice,
Green starwort bending in the water-bed,
Swayed by invisible power.

SHE

                              Cold and clear,
So that when their mouths met in a first kiss
The meaning of it made them spirit-cold,
Or so they thought, while the two woolen bundles
Of body stood helplessly apart and watched,
While from within the warm and sighing breaths
Mingled together and went up in smoke,
Cold smoke.

HE

                  That was the moment that they would
Have wished to keep, if anyone had asked,
Years afterward, when soot and kitchen fat
Resulted from their fires, when a damp wool
Of children steamed around their winter's hearth,
When time came for the burial of friends.

SHE

                  If anyone had asked them, What do you
Remember best? they would have said, The day
In winter with the current clear and cold
Under the ice, the wild beast of the future

161

Baffled in leather and cloth, so that our kiss,
The first kiss, when it came, was spirit-cold,
Forbidding what it fed.

HE

                              Time, O dear time
Not only takes us but we ask for it,
Current we cannot bear the nearness of
Without we touch it.

SHE

                        But the world goes on,
Of course, and time goes on from bearing
To burying and back without *our* love.
And though we say, That was the way it was
One winter afternoon in Sunderland,
Some might reply, The lovers would have died
As certainly had they refused their love;
Or had they tried to nourish it on smoke
And make a progeny of vapors, no
Miraculous result would have resulted
When they had wasted all their breath in frost—
They would have died.

HE

                        This world is such you must
Sell it like hot cakes or sell it not at all.

SHE

                    What lesson then from this?

HE

                          None. There is none,
I guess, but that the lovers felt that way
Years afterward.

SHE

                        Or else, again, suppose
That they, arrested on the single kiss

Between all past time and the future which
Could happen only as they let it happen,
Refused to let it happen.

HE

That's been done,

I know, many a time, among lovers
Whose families or whose countries were at odds,
Forbidding them the future.

SHE

They died too.

HE

But dying they became, in marble lines,

Like gods, or, more than gods, like boys and girls
Immortal of limb and youth, such bodies as
Titian and Tintoretto drew, blood-warm,
Blood-live, but with a cast of coldness there
In that deep blue of distance and the stars,
Which signed them to eternity, not time.

SHE

You mean that they became like works of art?

Like, say, that Montague and Capulet
Whose high example from the marble tomb
Beckons all boys and girls to emulate
Their fever, not their fate?

HE

The circle closed,

We end as we began.

SHE

A winter's day

In Sunderland, a kiss which though it could
Not be all spirit, would not yet be flesh.
Is this our moment of nobility,
Where every move's a sacrifice?

163

HE

O world,

What wickedness is yours.

SHE

Is ours.

HE

Is yours.

Those men and women walking in the street
Were boys and girls who on a single kiss,
A breath, weighed one against the other kingdom—

SHE

And ignominiously fell?

HE

It was no fall.

These bodies crouching in the woolen jungle
Already bear the weapons and the scars
Of that old war where veteran Lucifer
Was beaten from the field, and it was here
He made his winter quarters—and it is
And was and will be one long winter yet.

SHE

I think we stand so near Jerusalem
The Golden, only the thickness of a hair,
Or not so much, no greater distance than
A kiss consumes, holds guard at the bright gate.

HE

You mean that we too must—?

SHE

Now our time's come,

What can we do but fail?

HE

I mean that too.

164

# MOSES

THE FINDING OF THE ARK

Down by the Nile water,
Below the palace, where the steps left off
In the mild, shallow water stiff with reeds,
Came Pharaoh's daughter to bathe
With her maidens beside her, the mild
Girls of the morning, in the pale gold sun-
Light, bent over the ark, the sleeping child.

Lone as the ship of Noah
Sealed and surrendered to the high flood
Which was over every land,
The cradle of rushes caulked with pitch and mud
Rocked at the river's hand.
Neither the circle of the fish's splash
Nor the crane's rusty cry
Troubled the sleeping reaches of the stream
Which brought the child where Pharaoh's daughter stood,
Who smiled to watch him while he slept.

Now as the sun grew red,
The pale Nile thickened up to blood.
And when the child awaked, he wept.

A SONG OF PHARAOH'S DAUGHTER

I, daughter of Osiris, and sister,
Sister and bride to Horus, hawk
Of the spring, who will become Osiris
Over the river, in the West;
I, mother of Osiris, and
His widow in all the coasts of Egypt,
Have mothered, not from my womb,
And given to nurse among another people,
A child, a stranger, whose name is from the river.

The sun stands, and the shadows stand
On the burnt sand and the baked stone,

High on the face of a painted wall
And in the angles of the tomb.
Pharaoh raises his face to the sun
And the golden snake stares from his brow.
Pithom and Raamses harden in
The cruel, steady blaze of the years,
And Egypt waits, and the end waits
Like a lion asleep among tombs
Under the sun standing at noon.

My son, stranger, not of my name
But of the river which covers Osiris,
In the day when the dynasties are broken
Stones in a field which the shifting sand
Discovers and conceals, and when
This Egypt is the nome of dead
Men and dead gods, remember Isis
Who brought you up out of the river
When you were small and helpless,
Against the commandment of Osiris.

PHARAOH'S MEDITATION ON THE EXODUS

The thing is finished now, there is no more
Administration worth attending to,
And I have withdrawn to this inner room
To think, or dream. From the ridiculous
To death itself we have traveled in the space
Of ten days more or less (and my child dead),
But the damp stone may weep, the wall sweat blood
(And he may take his god and go elsewhere),
Since I no longer care? Why did I care?

To come from Midian, and need his brother's help
To turn a rod into a snake—there's no
Magician here who wouldn't be ashamed
To deal in parlor magic; yet his snake
Certainly swallowed theirs, and they were out
That many rods, and had their tempers up

Besides, that they could do what he could do.
So when he turned the water all to blood,
My idiots had to have fresh wells dug out
And turn them bloody too, assisting him
While seeming to compete; if he brought frogs,
And thousands of 'em, each wizard of mine
Must proudly add some six or seven frogs
To the total disaster and say it wasn't hard—
But luckily they stuck at the lice and flies
(Though by then we were past what luck could do).

The thing is finished, and I've had enough.
If the nation break, and the rude tribes
Flood in over the marches of the South;
If the commanders elaborate confusion
Because they have heard nothing; if one whole
Division has been drowned with its equipment—
It is nothing to me, it means nothing,
I will refuse to hear. All the last week
Things were bled white of meaning, and I say,
Enough! and have imposed my solitude
On kingdom and court, so that I may have time,
In this inner room, where I need not endure
Daylight or darkness but am soothed by lamps,
To think, should there be anything left to think.
Alone, in the cool silence of the stone,
Where only my heartbeats happen, and my thoughts
Follow the small flame's wavering against the wall
Until that meaningless motion is my thought,
It may be that the world outside has stopped,
The fountains dried up, and the brickwork broken
Under the insane silence of the sun
Centuries ago, and the whole course of the world
Shifted like sand; and I alone, the brain
In this room the skull of Egypt, am alive.

My first-born son is dead, the first-born sons
Of all Egypt are dead, but that's no matter.
I am astounded, but I do not weep.

How did that power come? Out of the desert?
Out of the empty land of Midian?
May he take his god and go back there
Again, and die there.
                              But he will not die.
I'll be the one to die, and when I do,
When they replace my gut with spices, wrap
My body in the rich cloth, and write me
Immortal on the soul's stone hull I sail
Beneath the world, into some inner room
Like this, where blue Polaris, through a shaft,
Shines coldly on my smile, Egypt and I
Shall triumph. And have I hardened my heart?
I harden it again, for the greatest virtues
Are cut from stone. And on the day I rise
Once more, driving my horses up the East,
Let him and all his people fear the whip
And run to their confusion through the world.


AHASUERUS

*homage to George Herbert*

Christ passed before my shop, and as I spat
The crowd applauded; only He looked at
Me angrily; and that, I thought, was that.
                    Was ever grief like mine?


He was three days beyond the tomb, they tell
How He went in this time harrowing Hell.
During these days, thy servant lived well.
                    Was ever grief like mine?


When he came forth to wear the crown of glory
My walk in the world began. He young, I hoary,
No end to either His or to my story.
                    Was ever grief like mine?

I aged, He eternal at the prime;
He, instantly forever, I, all time
For my atonement to confirm my crime.
                    Was ever grief like mine?

He, nailed upon the Cross, became the theme
Which might all suffering but mine redeem:
The world my night, history my long dream.
                    Was ever grief like mine?

I have witnessed the battles and the blood,
The armor and the bedclothes soaked with blood,
And seen man answer Him with blood for Blood.
                    Was ever grief like mine?

I have seen the world in vomit, tears and turd,
Stained, muddied and bepissed; for debt incurred
Returning endless words to His one Word.
                    Was ever grief like mine?

Their pleasures I have seen also; when they,
The drunk and sober, with one single cry
Would hang Him on the Tree again to die.
                    Was ever grief like mine?

Not pains and pleasures only—duties too;
His order maintained by the austere few
Whose millions punish Child and murder Jew.
                    Was ever grief like mine?

And I have seen them, rulers in His Name,
Extend dominion, and His golden fame,
Over the Orient whence the three kings came.
                    Was ever grief like mine?

Priests go among the peoples brown and black,
Gospel in hand and merchant on the back,
Preaching the fellowship of stick and sack.
                    Was ever grief like mine?

They batter with the weapon of the Rood
The savages who worship gods of wood—
Here is distinction, nicely understood.
                    Was ever grief like mine?

I see the good grow ugly day by day,
Who know what is not black or white as grey;
Anemia, wasting soul with body away.
                    Was ever grief like mine?

And see that all encourage guiltiness
And ineradicable sinfulness;
The apple stuck in the craw none can confess.
                    Was ever grief like mine?

The toadstool-shapen cloud is seen on high;
By night, the pillar of fire lights the sky.
—Leading, through desert, to the new Sinai?
                    Was ever grief like mine?

Many cry Armageddon and the end,
But I, walking the world and time, contend
It is no end, though nothing of it mend.
                    Was ever grief like mine?

And if it be, I will not have it end.
Let Gog, Magog and Prester John offend
From Asia's plains, and Anti-Christ ascend.
                    Was ever grief like mine?

And in the Valley of Jehoshaphat
The dry bones rise and wrap themselves in fat
And living spirit enter into that—
                    Was ever grief like mine?

And God, the Father, Son & Holy Ghost,
Summon the quick and dead to the last post,
Parade there, and dismiss the angelic host—
                    Was ever grief like mine?

And explode judgment through the universe,
The good made better and the bad made worse,
And Hell closed like a coffin in a hearse—
    Was ever grief like mine?

To go careening through the Orient void
Like Phaethon's chariot burning from inside—
Let star and planet darken far and wide—
    Was ever grief like mine?

No end can altogether be the End
If His Ahasuerus still offend
And will not bend—
    Was ever grief like mine?

I know not what will happen on that Day.
But if the floor of the world be taken away,
On foot I will cross Nothing, till He say—
    Was ever grief like mine?

Ahasuerus? and I say, Yes, Lord?
And look askance. Then He: What of My Word?
And I will say: Thou saidst a mighty Word.
    Was ever grief like mine?

But yet I come no closer. He will ask:
Do your feet bleed after the weary task?
Come, now I give you leave to drop the mask.
    Was ever grief like mine?

The mask, my Lord, has hardened to my face,
I say, and formed the features of a race
Uncertain if it cares to bear Thy grace.
    Was ever grief like mine?

Now He will glance at me with His shrewd eye,
As long ago He did. Child, with a sigh
He says, Come home to life eternal. Die.
    Was ever grief like mine?

171

And we two stand upon the empty height,
I in my darkness, He alone in light,
Nought else left in the world but spit, my spite—
                    Was ever grief like mine?

Which still is wet, and glitters on His cheek,
My portion of eternity, antique
And ever new, import of time, a freak.
                    Was ever grief like mine?

And He: Come home to life, my dear Jew. Die.
And there I stick in my own throat, and I
Know not, things being thus, what to reply.
                    Was ever grief like mine?

What is it happens then? Will I give in,
Sit on a darkened planet, hand on chin,
And cast away the great weight of my sin?
                    Was ever grief like mine?

Or would we laugh together in the void,
Talking of battles we had both enjoyed,
Of saints, and massacres, and girls destroyed?
                    Was ever grief like mine?

Seeing, agreeing, that the world did seem
A something, nothing, which He might redeem
One day—or had He? It faded like a dream.
                    Was ever grief like mine?

Since we were brothers then, so might it be.
I suffered Time as He Eternity.
And my shoes were nailed with nails from His Tree.
                    Was ever grief like mine?

But, God of my fathers whom I have forgot,
Old exiled Anger, Moralist, Marplot,
So be it, Father, that I do it not.
                    Was ever grief like mine?

We two must walk the vast void separate,
His business to forgive, but mine to hate
Even till Nothing too be out of date.
                              Was ever grief like mine?

Shall I have spirit, when He tells me then,
Give over, Child, and be as other men,
To spit at Him? Eternally? Again?
                              Was ever grief like mine?


ORPHIC SCENARIO

*for a movie of* Hamlet

Bear Hamlet, like a soldier, to the stage
(The world a stage). And bid the soldiers shoot.
Loud music, drums and guns, the lights go up.
Cheap? Yes, of course it's cheap. Reality
Comes dearer, but reality's much the same
As this dark malodorous box of taken tricks,
Reality's where the hurled light beams and breaks,
Against the solemn wall, a spattered egg,
The seed and food of being. If the seed
And food, split open thus, splayed as a blaze
On the blank of limit, focused on the yolk
Or might-be-meat of things, should still entrance
The vacant stare, fix it with visions of,
However dripping and impure, an order,
That is enough, or the abstract of enough.
And should the seed and food of order also
Resemble the things we think we see and know,
Lips, noses, eyes, the grimaces thereof
Compounded, playing on the fetal night,
That too is enough, if not too much. Order
Is fused of such refuse, eternity
Lusts after the productions of time.

173

Fastidious prince, consider. It is a play
Within a play, a mystery of infinite
Reflexions, nor since Phineas Pluto's Cave
No catch-all for the conscience has been found
Meatier, nor more meet. Let each man pay
His own admission: his prismatic self
Will break the godhead into comedy.
He will be purged, order will be restored,
And he may hear something to his advantage,
Viewing, at little cost, his Karma pass
And the wheel spin to honey and to blood.

It is the egg of the great bird of light,
Phoenix of Araby, splayed on the dark,
Its planes of cleavage, rhythms of its growth
Rudely abrupted for the sakes of us
The understanders. Its violated yolk
Will shadow forth the form and pressure of
The body of the age, its shadows move
Us, shadow-man come forth of shadow-woman,
Shedding their light without our heat, their sweetness
Cast accidentally from corrupted substance.
This moment of the close-up and the clinch
Desire sighs, prudence makes up its mind,
While terror moistens on the shining lips
And the dry tips of the hair gigantically
Shake and are swayed: Our stars have fire hearts.

So the great bull staggers, and his blood spouts
At the throat and drips between the cracked floorboards
Over the blackened pit, raining on bowed
And naked heads. The bull's fall shakes the floor
To thunder, splinters, dung, dust, as his knees
Break under him.
                              Priestess and priest display
The new Veronica, the stiffened face,
Light of the world, cast on a hanging cloth,
The egghead's Rorschach in the Holy Wood.

Minos is dead and Pharaoh buried.
All gone where the green grass goes winters.

This way to the Egress.

                And see, sweet prince,
How all the buildings rise in a colder sky,
Cheaper, and yet more golden, than before,
More high and solemn, borne on a great stage
In a failing light.
          Goodnight.
                 The soldiers shoot.

That's what life is, you may be moved to say,
Reality. And sometimes, in reality,
You may remember how the honey and blood
Fell from the huge lips of those murdered gods.

# 3

## THE WHEEL KING

Men, ropes, horses, strain
To breaking, but the great siege gun
On the mountain road
Stands axle-deep in mud
Till the light is gone.

The rowers sweat all afternoon
At the sweeps, yet the huge sea-wain
Behind them slacks her helm
Hulled down in the calm
Till the light is gone.

O coming night will make all one,
The Wheel King cried, all might and main,
All muscle and brain,
The ship and the rusted gun,
When the light is gone.


## DISTRACTION

The God of being demoralized
Has, roughly speaking, a human form
And two hands only, which are shown
Sometimes in icons as seven because
They tremble incessantly; the fingers
Are burning cigarettes. His feet
Really are four, though, and they walk
Both widdershins and otherwise
Around him while he is standing still.

176

One head he has, with but one face
Which spins until it blurs, for like
A compass in an iron mine, he
Is always arriving where he is.

No one has seen or dared to draw
The genitals, if any, of this
Divinity. In self-embrace,
However, he is said to engender
The species of bug that never bites
Nor alights, but buzzes around
The God's adorers' darkened rooms
Infecting their dreams with wakefulness;
Until they rise up hollow-eyed
To go about their daily business
Of praising, pursuing, dreaming Him.

## FALSE SOLOMON'S SEAL

I wanted wisdom, yet the indifferent glance
Of one young probable virgin sets my knees
To splashing like two waves. Sister and spouse,
Garden with walls and towering city, *fons*
*Signatus*, let us die in abstinence
Of one another, sigh gales, yet refuse
To speak the solving word which opens chaos
And fuses Shebas with their Solomons.

We sublimate—sublime!—all tidal waves,
Tornadoes, temblors of the earth, for good
And all, finding the separateness that saves
Garden and city from the wilderness
Where lust and wisdom tremble to undress:—
So may we die before both Fall and Flood.

# THE MURDER OF WILLIAM REMINGTON

It is true, that even in the best-run state
Such things will happen; it is true,
What's done is done. The law, whereby we hate
Our hatred, sees no fire in the flue
But by the smoke, and not for thought alone
It punishes, but for the thing that's done.

And yet there is the horror of the fact,
Though we knew not the man. To die in jail,
To be beaten to death, to know the act
Of personal fury before the eyes can fail
And the man die against the cold last wall
Of the lonely world—and neither is that all:

There is the terror too of each man's thought,
That knows not, but must quietly suspect
His neighbor, friend, or self of being taught
To take an attitude merely correct;
Being frightened of his own cold image in
The glass of government, and his own sin,

Frightened lest senate house and prison wall
Be quarried of one stone, lest righteous and high
Look faintly smiling down and seem to call
A crime the welcome chance of liberty,
And any man an outlaw who aggrieves
The patriotism of a pair of thieves.


# THE OLD SOLDIERS' HOME

Trumpet and drum, the old soldier said,
What has become of the regiment,
What of the company and the squad?
Some must be living, though cracked or bent,
But I can't get it out of my head

How trumpet and drum paraded before
The marching young men, how they led
Us, green and dumb, where the war
    Opened his mouth to be fed.

There was a hill, the old soldier said.
The military and manly thing
Was to take the hill, and we near did.
We got our fill and had our fling
And sowed our wild oats and our blood
All up and down the slope, before
We turned back, broken, and fled,
Bleeding and chill, where the war
    Opened his mouth to be fed.

God bless the State! the old soldier said,
Which lets me wait in a fine house
With a bronze gate and an iron bed,
Reciting the roll call, win or lose,
The order of battle, the old parade
Climbing the hill. How long before
Trumpet and drum prate over my head?
I, chill and dumb, where the war
    Opens his mouth to be fed.


SUBURBAN PROPHECY

On Saturday, the power-mowers' whine
Begins the morning. Over this neighborhood
Rises the keening, petulant voice, begin
Green oily teeth to chatter and munch the cud.

Monsters, crawling the carpets of the world,
Still send from underground against your blades
The roots of things battalions green and curled
And tender, that will match your blades with blades
Till the revolted throats shall strangle on

The tickle of their dead, till straws shall break
Crankshafts like camels, and the sun go down
On dinosaurs in swamps. A night attack
Follows, and by the time the Sabbath dawns
All armored beasts are eaten by their lawns.


## A PRIMER OF THE DAILY ROUND

A peels an apple, while B kneels to God,
C telephones to D, who has a hand
On E's knee, F coughs, G turns up the sod
For H's grave, I do not understand
But J is bringing one clay pigeon down
While K brings down a nightstick on L's head,
And M takes mustard, N drives into town,
O goes to bed with P, and Q drops dead,
R lies to S, but happens to be heard
By T, who tells U not to fire V
For having to give W the word
That X is now deceiving Y with Z,
    Who happens just now to remember A
    Peeling an apple somewhere far away.


## EPIGRAMS

### I   Invocation

Wasp, climbing the window pane
And falling back on the sill—
What buzz in the brain
And tremor of the will,
What climbing anger you excite
Where my images brim and spill
In failures of the full light.

180

## II   Lucilius

Lucilius the poet has informed me,
Defending his somewhat pedantic songs,
That "Memory is the Mother of the Muses."
May he continue making love to the mother.

## III   An Old Story

They gathered shouting crowds along the road
To praise His Majesty's satin and cloth-of-gold,
   But "Naked! Naked!" the children cried.

Now when the gaudy clothes ride down the street
No child is found sufficiently indiscreet
   To whisper "No Majesty's inside."

## IV   Mythological Beast

Four-footed, silent, resilient, feathered,
It waits by daylight, standing alert and tethered.
Come night, it bears me through the jungle of
The images, where are victims enough.

But this fat beast, responsive to my weight,
I know for a wild hunter grown to hate
Patiently the rider in his high seat,
Blind rider whom it will pluck down and eat.

## V   The Hunt Goes By

The dogs ran in the woods today,
Their note sounded from far away.
Tonight the shallow snowfall clears
The dogs' track and the deer's.

## VI   Political Reflexion

*loquitur the sparrow in the zoo.*

No bars are set too close, no mesh too fine
To keep me from the eagle and the lion,

Whom keepers feed that I may freely dine.
This goes to show that if you have the wit
To be small, common, cute, and live on shit,
Though the cage fret kings, you may make free with it.

## VII    A Spiral Shell

A twist along the spine begins the form
And hides itself inside a twisted house
Which turns once wide and slow, then speeds to close
Whirled on a point. Divine and crippled norm,
O Vulcan of the secret forging flame!
A hollow life is beautiful with shame.

## VIII    April

Today was a day of cold spring showers
Between bouts of sun; the fine, literary weather
We used to have so often, some Boris or other bidding farewell
To Nastasya; Lisbeth, Priscilla,
     Jane hastening back to the vicarage
Lest their taffeta crumple; a young man and a bicycle
Posed on the puddled lane. These days are rare lately,
And I remember college girls who declared
They loved to walk bare-headed in the rain.

## IX    Absent-Minded Professor

This lonely figure of not much fun
Strayed out of folklore fifteen years ago
Forever. Now on an autumn afternoon,
While the leaves drift past the office window,
His bright replacement, present-minded, stays
At the desk correcting papers, nor ever grieves
For the silly scholar of the bad old days,
Who'd burn the papers and correct the leaves.

## THE FOURTH OF JULY

Because I am drunk, this Independence Night,
I watch the fireworks from far away,
From a high hill, across the moony green
Of lakes and other hills to the town harbor,
Where stately illuminations are flung aloft,
One light shattering in a hundred lights
Minute by minute. The reason I am crying,
Aside from only being country drunk,
That is, may be that I have just remembered
The sparklers, rockets, roman candles, and
So on, we used to be allowed to buy
When I was a boy, and set off by ourselves
At some peril to life and property.
Our freedom to abuse our freedom thus
Has since, I understand, been remedied
By legislation. Now the authorities
Arrange a perfectly safe public display
To be watched at a distance; and now also
The contribution of all the taxpayers
Together makes a more spectacular
Result than any could achieve alone
(A few pale pinwheels, or a firecracker
Fused at the dog's tail). It is, indeed, splendid:
Showers of roses in the sky, fountains
Of emeralds, and those profusely scattered zircons
Falling and falling, flowering as they fall
And followed distantly by a noise of thunder.
My eyes are half-afloat in happy tears.
God bless our Nation on a night like this,
And bless the careful and secure officials
Who celebrate our independence now.

## REFLEXIONS ON THE SEIZURE OF THE SUEZ, AND ON A PROPOSAL TO LINE THE BANKS OF THAT CANAL WITH BILLBOARD ADVERTISEMENTS

From Molepolole and Morogoro,
Dongola, Dungun, Dush,
From Kongor and Gojjam and Juba,
Gagag and Segag and Geba Geba,
The bracelets of brass and the calico hankies
Come back a thousandfold.

   *Smoke Pyramids for Appearances' Sake*

From Kanker and Kurnool and Bhor,
Bellary, Trivandrum, Nellore,
From Gooty and Owsa, Hubh and Alur,
Adoni and Chik- and Dod-Ballapur,
The glass beads and obsolete Lee Enfields
Return upon the makers.

   *Drink Pyramids the World's Premier Aperient*

In Hebron, Jabal, Zebara,
In Jebel Tathlith and Wafi Harid,
Asterabad, Washraf, Miskin, Sham,
In Jask and Ras Nus, Beni Auf, Jauf,
It is the same. Everywhere the givers
Are in the hands of the receivers.

   *For That Serious Fear, Take a Pyramid*

So also in Bumpass and Mauch Chunk,
Tallulah, Wabuska, Markle and Lair,
The burden of Tupelo, Tunica, Nampa, Dufur,
Of Grundy and Presho and Stackhouse and Bland.
Though oil cast upon the troubled waters
May be returned as capital gains.

   *Pyramids Are Silent, Speedy, Safe.*
       *—Next Time, Go by Pyramid.*

## SEVEN MACABRE SONGS

*dedicated to Louis Calabro*

### 1   *a dream*

The ground swayed like a sea,
Uneasily, where the dead fought free
Of my preserved desires. In one bed
Godhead and maidenhead
Wrestled out of necessity.
I slept, but restlessly,
Lusting for what I dreamt I saw
Under the deserts of the law.

### 2

The officer wore a thin smile
Over his dental plate.

The nurse had carrot hair,
But I saw black at the roots.

The doctor's eye frightened me,
And it was made of glass.

The priest had fair hair as he knelt.
I saw the seam and smelt the glue.

My death bugged from my eyes
At recognizing theirs.

### 3   *from the last dream of a dying woman*
*aged eighty (see Ella Freeman Sharpe,* Dream Analysis)

I did not want to suffer again
    Or ever feel pain.
Last night I dreamed that I could see
    My sicknesses in me
Gathered together, each a rose.
    And I saw that all those

185

Roses were planted and grew again
    Out of my pain.


4

Under the pie crust,
Behind the attic door,
Inside the camera or
The cathode tube, I must—
(Inside the frigidaire,
Under the manhole cover
Where rumpsteak and lover
Run out of air)—It is there
I must—(under the rug,
Behind the arras, dug
Into the basement floor)—
Though there may be no more
Than dust,
        I must.


5   *Bluebeard's wife*

My husband Bluebeard has a blue beard.
I have heard this story before. It is night
In the palace, and the Minotaur,
Our janitor, is smoking in the cellar,
Sitting alone among turds and bones and dottle.
To him, enter the naked Athenian youths and maidens.

Now moms and dads are shrunken into sleep,
And Bluebeard's beard curtains the tiny room
Where I have always been forbidden to go
(Husband, I come!), why, it is now and never
That I may beard him and unlock the door
Where the Athenian adolescents fell,
And find his soul, maybe, and crack it like an egg.


6

It is forbidden to go further.

Darkness stands in the wall
Spattered with blood.

These are the Gates of Hercules.
You shall not pass again
Those giant knees,

Not to the open Atlantic water,
Not to the blessed Mount.
No son or daughter dares

Stand with unbandaged eyes
Before the bloodied black seawall,
Before the opening seas.

7

My death with a nail in his foot
Came dragging at the ground.
He carried a long tooth for a cane,
He carried his eye cast down.

The sunlight pierced his body through
With shafts of shadow; hung
Under the shadows of his breast
A perching sparrow sang.

My crippled death for my sake bears
(While life is, life is long)
Both tooth and nail, and for my heart
The sweetly beating song.


A SINGULAR METAMORPHOSIS

We all were watching the quiz on television
Last night, combining leisure with pleasure,
When Uncle Henry's antique *escritoire*,

Where he used to sit making up his accounts,
Began to shudder and rock like a crying woman,
Then burst into flower from every cubbyhole
(For all the world like a seventy-four of the line
Riding the swell and firing off Finisterre.)
Extraordinary sight! Its delicate legs
Thickened and gnarled, writhing, they started to root
The feet deep in a carpet of briony
Star-pointed with primula. Small animals
Began to mooch around and climb up this
Reversionary desk and dustable heirloom
Left in the gloomiest corner of the room
Far from the television.
                                    I alone,
To my belief, remarked the remarkable
Transaction above remarked. The flowers were blue,
The fiery blue of iris, and there was
A smell of warm, wet grass and new horse-dung.

The screen, meanwhile, communicated to us
With some fidelity the image and voice
Of Narcisse, the cultivated policewoman
From San Francisco, who had already
Taken the sponsors for ten thousand greens
By knowing her Montalets from Capegues,
Cordilleras from Gonorrheas, in
The Plays of Shapesmoke Swoon of Avalon,
A tygers hart in a players painted hide
If ever you saw one.
                              When all this was over,
And everyone went home to bed, not one
Mentioned the *escritoire*, which was by now
Bowed over with a weight of fruit and nuts
And birds and squirrels in its upper limbs.
Stars tangled with its mistletoe and ivy.

# LORE

Man walks, I learn, in fear of woman,
Possession of the constant moon;
Because the moon has strength to summon
Her blood to the full and ebb again,
And gives her strength beyond her own.

A girl then, Graves writes in his book,          *The White Goddess*
Can fade the purple out of cloth
And tarnish mirrors with her look,
And by the power of her thought
Make one branch grow and another rot.

And if she should, at such a time,
Go further, lifting up her dress
She can find out the hidden crime,
Flatten a storm on the high seas,
Cure either boils or barrenness.

So great the power of her moon
That, as the Talmud said,
If she should walk between two men
And no appropriate prayer is read,
The one of them will drop down dead.


# DRAMA

　　　　—Ah, green Elysia,
Scuttled at last into the western sea,
Thou crownéd, fragile sea-nymph, slender bodied,
Thy lobes and processes have trancéd me,
My lust begins to rule.

　　　　　　—False Wentletrap!
Avaunt. My maiden mantle may not blush
For thee or thine, all towering as thou art

189

And turreted. For thee do I disdain
As doth the warty Venus of the shore
The prickly cockle's Tarquin-like approach.
Sea-lemon, with thy tricksy tentacles
And feather-gills, thou granulated thing,
I deprecate on thee.

                              —Alas! I pale,
And all my whorls 'gin waver. Wrinkle me,
Or else I perish.

                              —Horny, let thy drawn
Operculum defend thee now. .

                                        —Elysia,
Upon thy cruel tentacles I die.

—And now I am alone.


TALE

*"Goethe said of the tails of vertebrates
that they allude as it were to the potential
infinity of organic existence."*
*Symmetry,* by Herman Weyl

Well then, a man has got to stop somewhere,
I can't go along with that. They say the brain
Is nothing but a flower on the spine,
But at the other end . . . ? Too true, it's gone.
(If we *had* roots, they'd only lash the air).
But it's the greatness of the loss I doubt
Will be the last thing that we think about.

Dear chicken, one more kiss. I don't feel
Any different, do you? I mean, now that we know?
So near divine, my animal, but who

190

Gives much of a damn for that? Potential, was all.
It kind of takes the almighty virtue, though,
From uprightness, if we have gained a soul
—Ah, *if* we have!—only to lose a tail.


## ENDEGEESTE

*anecdote after Ortega y Gasset*

Through my window and across the lawn
I look to Endegeeste, now an insane
Asylum, whence the elms lengthen their huge
Shadows, all afternoon, over my page.

In that same house, three hundred years gone out,
Lazy Descartes described the modern thought.
Now on his lawn the mindless come and go
In the State's hand, and the stately elms grow.

I live in a great and terrifying time,
As Descartes did. For both of us the dream
Has turned like milk, and the straight, slender tree
Twisted at root and branch hysterically.

I keep my reasonable doubt as gay
As any—though on the lawn they seem to say,
Those patient, nodding heads, "sum, ergo sum."
The elms' long shadows fall cold in my room.


## MOONSHINE

The old men, son, drink whisky, for they know
How time goes to the head, grey head, bald head
Where histories lie. They stagger from the fumes
That make the dreams that make the dead seed grow

High in the sun, the rain, the wind—those dreams
Can shake the living, they can wake the dead.

The sour mash distilled is history.
Old men have known it, they bear it in mind;
Those minds, coiling in cloud over the vat
Of the strong belly, or like flowers spined
On the stalk of seventy years of flesh and fat,
Breathe out their ruined perfumes till they die.

It dies when those minds die, the hundred proof
Aged in the cask, that time's remembered by.
Historians may bottle theirs in bond,
Nations take it in taxes or go dry,
But when the old men pass their whisky round
There is the ferment, son, will raise the roof.


CANOSSA

The image, now proverbial, stands alone:
    A shoeless king and a grey wall.
    He "comes to his Canossa," small
As in a Book of Hours, under the stone
    Rampart where the cold wizard lies
    Silent and pitiless, who has said:
    "Drink of the wine, eat of the bread—
        "Which of us falsifies,
        "May God strike him dead."

Proverbial it is, and meaningless:
    Emperor and priest go on,
    And nothing that is done is done.
The sport of it is, to curse until they bless,
    Kiss and make up, and curse again.
    So let the lion and unicorn
    Ramp, till they wear, for change of scorn,
        The unicorn a mane,
        The lion a single horn.

192

## STUDENT DIES IN 100 YARD DASH

This way or that way, student, in the sprint
Or the intestine marathon of age,
The body of this death is adamant
And stumbles toward the finish after heart
Has broken, earth opened under the feet.
Horizon lines are fine, but no mirage,
Student, though breathless now on the cinder path
Where planets run against time in a dead heat.

# 4

MAIA

Reality! said the stone-minded man
With his eye on a sky-scraper,
    This world is hard lines.

Suffer! said the thorny-minded man
Who sat at the cross-roads,
    The world is a tangled vine.

The sun on the streaming water
Imagines rock and branch, the moon
    Imagines the sun,

I die into these images while
The black water and the white
    Water race and remain.


CLOUD SEEDING

The tragic man stares at the sun
Until the sun blacks both his eyes.
The comic man lies on his back
And with his tent-pole bears the skies.
The virgin nymphomaniac
Is swollen with her father's son,

    *That it rain again in the spring.*

Poets, in their majestic wigs,
Pen canzonetti on these themes,
And by the fruits ye know the trees:

194

By sour grapes, by withered figs.
Those Minotaurs and Semeles
Are raddled through all modern dreams,

*That it rain again in the spring.*

It is my black desire to see
The brutal and divine synod
Gather again in thunder, ride on
In lightning splitting the seed-pod,
Till thought be driven as Poseidon,
The salt-bearded teamster, drives the sea,

*That it rain again in the spring.*


## THE MAP-MAKER ON HIS ART

After the bronzed, heroic traveler
Returns to the television interview
And cocktails at the Ritz, I in my turn
Set forth across the clean, uncharted paper.
Smiling a little at his encounters with
Savages, bugs, and snakes, for the most part
Skipping his night thoughts, philosophic notes,
Rainy reflexions, I translate his trip
Into my native tongue of bearings, shapes,
Directions, distances. My fluent pen
Wanders and cranks as his great river does,
Over the page, making the lonely voyage
Common and human.
                This my modest art
Brings wilderness well down into the range
Of any budget; under the haunted mountain
Where he lay in delirium, deserted
By his safari, they will build hotels
In a year or two. I make no claim that this
Much matters (they will name a hotel for him
And none for me), but lest the comparison

Make me appear a trifle colorless,
I write the running river a rich blue
And—let imagination rage!—wild green
The jungles with their tawny meadows and swamps
Where, till the day I die, I will not go.


BRAINSTORM

The house was shaken by a rising wind
That rattled window and door. He sat alone
In an upstairs room and heard these things: a blind
Ran up with a bang, a door slammed, a groan
Came from some hidden joist, and a leaky tap,
At any silence of the wind, walked like
A blind man through the house. Timber and sap
Revolt, he thought, from washer, baulk and spike.
Bent to his book, continued unafraid
Until the crows came down from their loud flight
To walk along the rooftree overhead.
Their horny feet, so near but out of sight,
Scratched on the slate; when they were blown away
He heard their wings beat till they came again,
While the wind rose, and the house seemed to sway,
And window panes began to blind with rain.
The house was talking, not to him, he thought,
But to the crows; the crows were talking back
In their black voices. The secret might be out:
Houses are only trees stretched on the rack.
And once the crows knew, all nature would know.
Fur, leaf and feather would invade the form,
Nail rust with rain and shingle warp with snow,
Vine tear the wall, till any straw-borne storm
Could rip both roof and rooftree off and show
Naked to nature what they had kept warm.

He came to feel the crows walk on his head
As if he were the house, their crooked feet

Scratched, through the hair, his scalp. He might be dead
It seemed, and all the noises underneath
Be but the cooling of the sinews, veins,
Juices, and sodden sacks suddenly let go;
While in his ruins of wiring, his burst mains,
The rainy wind had been set free to blow
Until the green uprising and mob rule
That ran the world had taken over him,
Split him like seed, and set him in the school
Where any crutch can learn to be a limb.

Inside his head he heard the stormy crows.


## LIMITS

*"Florida Frogmen Find New World"*
The *New York Times*

Within the limestone mantle of the shelf
   Beneath the swamp, the cypress root,
     The great resort hotels
     Of Florida, other hells
   Are trespassed by the webbéd foot
Beating to print the water's self with self.

     Leaching the whole of truth,
     Ruined heroes of the daily mind,
Those undergoing scholars climb upstream
Into a darkness prior to their dream,
     Where the dividing eye is blind.
     Therein they spend their youth.

Inside the pouched, hard hide of the riddled earth
   They flutter, determined frogmen, ready
     To carry air and light
     Into the condemned, tight

Tenements of the old landlady
Till she have rent them more than bed and birth.

Under the rib, inside,
Air gone, and battery burned out,
Is there a second, till the lungs have burst,
Of a second freedom, greater than the first,
When the young frog prince, born of doubt,
Swims down upon his bride?

She drags him to her as a mirror would.
Now shrieking Oedipus is blind
And fair Narcissus cold,
The dragon-guarded gold,
All that was lost, they fall to find,
Losing their science, which is understood.


## TO LU CHI

*(author of the* Wen Fu, *or Prose Poem*
*on the Art of Letters, A.D. 302)*

Old sir, I think of you in this tardy spring,
Think of you for, maybe, no better reason
Than that the apple branches in the orchard
Bear snow, not blossoms, and that this somehow
Seems oddly Chinese. I too, when I walk
Around the orchard, pretending to be a poet
Walking around the orchard, feel Chinese,
A silken figure on a silken screen
Who tries out with his eye the apple branches,
The last year's shriveled apples capped with snow,
The hungry birds. And then I think of you.

Through many centuries of dust, to which
We both belong, your quiet voice is clear
About the difficulties and delights

Of writing well, which are, it seems, always
The same and generally unfashionable.
In all the many times I have read your poem,
Or treatise, where the art of letters turns
To the inspection of itself—the theme
(I take your phrase) of how to hold the axe
To make its handle,—your words have not failed
To move me with their justice and their strength,
Their manner gentle as their substance is
Fastidious and severe. You frighten me
When you describe the dangers of our course,
And then you bring, by precept and example,
Assurance that a reach of mastery,
Some still, reed-hidden and reflective stream
Where the heron fishes in his own image,
Always exists. I have a sight of you,
Your robes tucked in your belt, standing
Fishing that stream, where it is always dawn
With a mist beginning to be burned away
By the lonely sun. And soon you will turn back
To breakfast and the waking of the world
Where the contending war lords and the lords
Of money pay to form the public taste
For their derivative sonorities;
But yet that pure and hidden reach remains.

Lu Chi, it's said the world has changed, and that
Is doubtless something which is always said
(Though now to justify, and not in scorn)—
Yet I should think that on our common theme
That sort of change has never mattered much.
In letters as in many other trades
The active man and the contemplative
May both engage, and both in different ways
Succeed. The alphabet, the gift of god
Or of the gods (and modern as we are,
We have no better theory yet), was not
Devised to one use only, but to all
The work that human wit could find for it;

Is honorably employed in government
And all techniques; without it, nothing. Yet
The active man, because he is active,
Expropriates as if by natural right
The common ground to his singular use,
And spits on everything he cannot use;
Not knowing, or not caring, that to use
Means also to use up. So I have read,
In works by sages of the active side,
And heard them say, that poetry is dead.
This ancient paragon and type of arts,
They say, was magic when the world began,
And when the old magicians died in scorn
Among the ruins of unsuccessful spells,
Their childish children, living in the dawn
Of intellect and conscience, said those spells
(Which could not move a mountain or a mouse
In a real world) for courage and consolation,
Making those holy places in their hearts
Not masonry nor magic made elsewhere.
But now, in the objective, brazen light
Shed by the sciences, they say, the arts,
And poetry first, considered as their trunk,
The nearest to the root, and bearing branches
Aloft with flower and fruit, and spreading seed
To all societies, must wither away
By supersession in nature and all hearts.
So in our day wisdom cries out in the streets
And some men regard her. And in your day,
Lu Chi? We know these theories, which are not new,
And know the sort of man these theories
Produce, intelligent and serviceable
So long as he can see his language as
Coin of the realm, backed up by church and state,
Each word referring to a thing, each thing
Nicely denominated by a word—
A good mind at its best, a trifle dry. . . .
But in bad times, when the word of command
Fails to command, and when the word for bread

Dries and grows mouldy, he is, of all men,
The likeliest to panic as he sits
In his bomb shelter and commissions war songs
From active poets with aggressive views.
Nor on the day when all civilisation
Quite visibly and audibly collapses,
When Paris burns as merrily as Sodom,
When London looks like Hell, or Hiroshima,
Not even then will this man of his own
Free choice consult those who consult the source—
Who by then, in any case, can do nothing.
Meanwhile, in riches, insolence and honor
Pride is twisting his tongue. What an old joke!
These things, Lu Chi, cannot have changed so much.

What then? Nothing but this, old sir: *continue*.
And to the active man, if he should ask
(If he should bother asking) Why? say nothing.
And to the thinker, if he should ask us once
Instead of telling us, again say nothing,
But look into the clear and mirroring stream
Where images remain although the water
Passes away. Neither action nor thought,
Only the concentration of our speech
In fineness and in strength (your axe again),
Till it can carry, in those other minds,
A nobler action and a purer thought.

So much I gather from your poem: *continue*.
And now the sun shines on the apple trees,
The melting snow glitters with a great wealth,
The waxwings, drunk on last year's rotten apples,
Move through the branches, uttering pretty cries,
While portly grosbeaks, because they do not drink
That applejack, chatter with indignation.
How fine the Chinese day! delicate, jeweled,
Exactly spaced, peaceably tense with life.
I shall pretend to be a poet all
This afternoon, a Chinese poet, and

My marvelous words must bring the springtime in
And the great tree of speech to flower
Between the two realms of heaven and earth. So now
Goodbye, Lu Chi, and thank you for your poem.

Note: For Lu Chi & the Wen Fu, see *The Art of Letters*,
a translation and comparative study by E. R. Hughes, N.Y.,
Bollingen series XXIX, 1951.


ART SONG

Down where the dog-toothed tide
   Crawled at the bay,
I held in my fingers the feather of a gull,
   Black, white and gray,
   Lighter than the wind
Which twisted and tried to tear it away.

That single feather danced
   In a welter where
Twelve winds contended with my hand.
   Shattered in focus there,
   The once-gulled feather seemed
A divining rod of ocean and the wild air.

Now the plume dowsing the poem
   Under my hand
Angles in waves after the lost
   Life of the gull from land
   Gone on horizon wings
Where neither feather can follow nor any poet stand.


WRITING

The cursive crawl, the squared-off characters
these by themselves delight, even without
a meaning, in a foreign language, in

Chinese, for instance, or when skaters curve
all day across the lake, scoring their white
records in ice. Being intelligible,
these winding ways with their audacities
and delicate hesitations, they become
miraculous, so intimately, out there
at the pen's point or brush's tip, do world
and spirit wed. The small bones of the wrist
balance against great skeletons of stars
exactly; the blind bat surveys his way
by echo alone. Still, the point of style
is character. The universe induces
a different tremor in every hand, from the
check-forger's to that of the Emperor
Hui Tsung, who called his own calligraphy
the 'Slender Gold.' A nervous man
writes nervously of a nervous world, and so on.

Miraculous. It is as though the world
were a great writing. Having said so much,
let us allow there is more to the world
than writing: continental faults are not
bare convoluted fissures in the brain.
Not only must the skaters soon go home;
also the hard inscription of their skates
is scored across the open water, which long
remembers nothing, neither wind nor wake.


PAINTING A MOUNTAIN STREAM

Running and standing still at once
is the whole truth. Raveled or combed,
wrinkled or clear, it gets its force
from losing force. Going it stays.

Pulse beats, and planets echo this,
the running down, the standing still,

all thunder of the one thought.
The mind that thinks it is unfounded.

I speak of what is running down.
Of sun, of thunder bearing the rain
I do not speak, of the rising flame
or the slow towering of the elm.

A comb was found in a girl's grave
(ah heartsblood raveled like a rope).
The visible way is always down
but there is no floor to the world.

Study this rhythm, not this thing.
The brush's tip streams from the wrist
of a living man, a dying man.
The running water is the wrist.

In the confluence of the wrist
things and ideas ripple together,
as in the clear lake of the eye,
unfathomably, running remains.

The eye travels on running water,
out to the sky, if you let it go.
However often you call it back
it travels again, out to the sky.

The water that seemed to stand is gone.
The water that seemed to run is here.
Steady the wrist, steady the eye;
paint this rhythm, not this thing.


SARABANDE

*Honoring the Musicians*

Whatever may be going through our heads
in time to your noted bowing and scraping,

our faces all express the naked, rapt
stupidity which more than other arts
yours can evoke, wearing our masks away
till pride relaxes and hypocrisy
forgets his knowing smile—we might be cows
rather than cousins of Mme. Verdurin.

The vacuous expressions of lovers, mourners,
children and pregnant women, people asleep,
racial and strange and sullenly at ease
as African faces or roughly featured stones
with looks eroded in the rain of time,
those were the faces waiting in our faces
For your divisions to divide us from
ourselves till we lost the burden in the ground.

Lascivious dances, melancholy songs,
whose right articulation strikes us dumb,
these shake us in a core that wit forgets
and self wants to deny, in tomb-town where
the dancing-steps are beating in the streets,
where maskers carry away both flower crown
and flowerless torch; from such unsounded chambers,
heartbeaten, how have the dead comforted us!


STEPS FOR A DANCER

Not with an iron will, no. More like a whip,
whose flexible command is always pain,
you buy geometry from poor dogsbody
who is led on a leash, and who will die.

Difficult saint, what do you mortify,
yourself or the brutal other? Can you buy
redemption of a bond whose interest
alone makes a revenge of discipline?

Salmon can manage, and the comedian crow
can do his turn, even the cat can rise,

a natural, into grace; but as for us,
not fish, not flesh, not fowl, our ecstasies

are never groundless, and even in those rare
and really airborne times, old Shylock there
in the wings, still unredeemed, is showing off
to his audience the raw pound of your flesh.

What then? I think yours is the hardest art,
least heretic, of all. You would ascend
not as the pure fantastic fire alone
but bringing this analphabetic ape

to leave those mortally awkward parodies
and fly of his own refined will to number
among the elect; which till he do I see,
young lady, nothing for it but the whip.


## THE DANCER'S REPLY

Your body may be a sack
For the soul to carry on its back,
Whining and groaning with its heavy thought,

But my body is not.
My body is more sweetly wrought,
Nor dances to the whip but at its will,

And says in its own style
What's left when your words fail,
Stumble from rhythm and cannot find a rime.

For isn't it your shame,
Old gentleman, to live in time
Our terrible dream, and lose the beat of it?

But if you have such wit,

Then go, become a timeless thought.
But when our bodies and souls, on the last day,

Couple and dance away,
Your soul will be made to stay
And learn its dancing-lesson after school,

And beg your body's full
Pardon for being such a fool,
And wear it like a dunce-cap for a while.


## HOLDING THE MIRROR UP TO NATURE

Some shapes cannot be seen in a glass,
those are the ones the heart breaks at.
They will never become valentines
or crucifixes, never. Night clouds
go on insanely as themselves
though metaphors would be prettier;
and when I see them massed at the edge
of the globe, neither weasel nor whale,
as though this world were, after all,
non-representational, I know
a truth that cannot be told, although
I try to tell you, "We are alone,
we know nothing, nothing, we shall die
frightened in our freedom, the one
who survives will change his name
to evade the vengeance for love. . . ."
Meanwhile the clouds go on clowning
over our heads in the floodlight of
a moon who is known to be Artemis
and Cynthia but sails away anyhow
beyond the serious poets with their
crazy ladies and cloudy histories,
their heroes in whose idiot dreams
the buzzard circles like a clock.

# NEW
# POEMS
# (1960)

## MOMENT

Now, starflake frozen on the windowpane
All of a winter night, the open hearth
Blazing beyond Andromeda, the sea-
Anemone and the downwind seed, O moment
Hastening, halting in a clockwise dust,
The time in all the hospitals is now,
Under the arc-lights where the sentry walks
His lonely wall it never moves from now,
The crying in the cell is also now,
And now is quiet in the tomb as now
Explodes inside the sun, and it is now
In the saddle of space, where argosies of dust
Sail outward blazing, and the mind of God,
The flash across the gap of being, thinks
In the instant absence of forever: now.

## RUNES

"... insaniebam salubriter et moriebar vitaliter."
St. Augustine

### I

This is about the stillness in moving things,
In running water, also in the sleep
Of winter seeds, where time to come has tensed
Itself, enciphering a script so fine
Only the hourglass can magnify it, only
The years unfold its sentence from the root.

211

I have considered such things often, but
I cannot say I have thought deeply of them:
That is my theme, of thought and the defeat
Of thought before its object, where it turns
As from a mirror, and returns to be
The thought of something and the thought of thought,
A trader doubly burdened, commercing
Out of one stillness and into another.

II

About Ulysses, the learned have reached two
Distinct conclusions. In one, he secretly
Returns to Ithaca, is recognized
By Euryclea, destroys the insolent suitors,
And makes himself known to Penelope,
Describing the bed he built; then, at the last
Dissolve, we see him with Telemachus
Leaving the palace, planning to steal sheep:
The country squire resumes a normal life.
But in the other, out beyond the gates
Of Hercules, gabbling persuasively
About virtue and knowledge, he sails south
To disappear from sight behind the sun;
Drowning near blessed shores he flames in hell.
I do not know which ending is the right one.

III

Sunflowers, traders rounding the horn of time
Into deep afternoons, sleepy with gain,
The fall of silence has begun to storm
Around you where you nod your heavy heads
Whose bare poles, raking out of true, will crack,
Driving your wreckage on the world's lee shore.
Your faces no more will follow the sun,
But bow down to the ground with a heavy truth
That dereliction learns, how charity
Is strangled out of selfishness at last;
When, golden misers in the courts of summer,

You are stripped of gain for coining images
And broken on this quarter of the wheel,
It is on savage ground you spill yourselves,
And spend the tarnished silver of your change.

## IV

The seed sleeps in the furnaces of death,
A cock's egg slept till hatching by a serpent
Wound in his wintry coil, a spring so tight
In his radical presence that every tense
Is now. Out of this head the terms of kind,
Distributed in syntax, come to judgment,
Are basilisks who write our sentences
Deep at the scripture's pith, in rooted tongues,
How one shall marry while another dies.
Give us our ignorance, the family tree
Grows upside down and shakes its heavy fruit,
Whose buried stones philosophers have sought.
For each stone bears the living word, each word
Will be made flesh, and all flesh fall to seed:
Such stones from the tree; and from the stones, such blood.

## V

The fat time of the year is also time
Of the Atonement; birds to the berry bushes,
Men to the harvest; a time to answer for
Both present plenty and emptiness to come.
When the slain legal deer is salted down,
When apples smell like goodness, cold in the cellar,
You hear the ram's horn sounded in the high
Mount of the Lord, and you lift up your eyes
As though by this observance you might hide
The dry husk of an eaten heart which brings
Nothing to offer up, no sacrifice
Acceptable but the canceled-out desires
And satisfactions of another year's
Abscess, whose zero in His winter's mercy
Still hides the undecipherable seed.

## VI

White water now in the snowflake's prison,
A mad king in a skullcap thinks these thoughts
In regular hexagons, each one unlike
Each of the others. The atoms of memory,
Like those that Democritus knew, have hooks
At either end, but these? Insane tycoon,
These are the riches of order snowed without end
In this distracted globe, where is no state
To fingerprint the flakes or number these
Moments melting in flight, seeds mirroring
Substance without position or a speed
And course unsubstanced. What may the spring be,
Deep in the atom, among galactic snows,
But the substance of things hoped for, argument
Of things unseen? White water, fall and fall.

## VII

*Unstable as water, thou shalt not excel*
—Said to the firstborn, the dignity and strength,
And the defiler of his father's bed.
Fit motto for a dehydrated age
Nervously watering whisky and stock,
Quick-freezing dreams into realities.
Brain-surgeons have produced the proustian syndrome,
But patients dunk their tasteless madeleines
In vain, those papers that the Japanese
Amused themselves by watering until
They flowered and became Combray, flower
No more. The plastic and cosmetic arts
Unbreakably record the last word and
The least word, till sometimes even the Muse,
In her transparent raincoat, resembles a condom.

## VIII

To go low, to be as nothing, to die,
To sleep in the dark water threading through
The fields of ice, the soapy, frothing water

214

That slithers under the culvert below the road,
Water of dirt, water of death, dark water,
And through the tangle of the sleeping roots
Under the coppery cold beech woods, the green
Pinewoods, and past the buried hulls of things
To come, and humbly through the breathing dreams
Of all small creatures sleeping in the earth;
To fall with the weight of things down on the one
Still ebbing stream, to go on to the end
With the convict hunted through the swamp all night.
The dog's corpse in the ditch, to come at last
Into the pit where zero's eye is closed.

## IX

In this dehydrated time of digests, pills
And condensations, the most expensive presents
Are thought to come in the smallest packages:
In atoms, for example. There are still
To be found, at carnivals, men who engrave
The Lord's Prayer on a grain of wheat for pennies,
But they are a dying race, unlike the men
Now fortunate, who bottle holy water
In plastic tears, and bury mustard seeds
In lucite lockets, and for safety sell
To be planted on the dashboard of your car
The statues, in durable celluloid,
Of Mary and St. Christopher, who both
With humble power in the world's floodwaters
Carried their heavy Savior and their Lord.

## X

White water, white water, feather of a form
Between the stones, is the race run to stay
Or pass away? Your utterance is riddled,
Rainbowed and clear and cold, tasting of stone,
Its brilliance blinds me. But still I have seen,
White water, at the breaking of the ice,
When the high places render up the new

Children of water and their tumbling light
Laughter runs down the hills, and the small fist
Of the seed unclenches in the day's dazzle,
How happiness is helpless before your fall,
White water, and history is no more than
The shadows thrown by clouds on mountainsides,
A distant chill, when all is brought to pass
By rain and birth and rising of the dead.

XI

A holy man said to me, "Split the stick
And there is Jesus." When I split the stick
To the dark marrow and the splintery grain
I saw nothing that was not wood, nothing
That was not God, and I began to dream
How from the tree that stood between the rivers
Came Aaron's rod that crawled in front of Pharaoh,
And came the rod of Jesse flowering
In all the generations of the Kings,
And came the timbers of the second tree,
The sticks and yardarms of the holy three-
masted vessel whereon the Son of Man
Hung between thieves, and came the crown of thorns,
The lance and ladder, when was shed that blood
Streamed in the grain of Adam's tainted seed.

XII

Consider how the seed lost by a bird
Will harbor in its branches most remote
Descendants of the bird; while everywhere
And unobserved, the soft green stalks and tubes
Of water are hardening into wood, whose hide,
Gnarled, knotted, flowing, and its hidden grain,
Remember how the water is streaming still.
Now does the seed asleep, as in a dream
Where time is compacted under pressures of
Another order, crack open like stone
From whose division pours a stream, between

The raindrop and the sea, running in one
Direction, down, and gathering in its course
That bitter salt which spices us the food
We sweat for, and the blood and tears we shed.

## XIII

There sailed out on the river, Conrad saw,
The dreams of men, the seeds of commonwealths,
The germs of Empire. To the ends of the earth
One many-veined bloodstream swayed the hulls
Of darkness gone, of darkness still to come,
And sent its tendrils steeping through the roots
Of wasted continents. That echoing pulse
Carried the ground swell of all sea-returns
Muttering under history, and its taste,
Saline and cold, was as a mirror of
The taste of human blood. The sailor leaned
To lick the mirror clean, the somber and
Immense mirror that Conrad saw, and saw
The other self, the sacred Cain of blood
Who would seed a commonwealth in the Land of Nod.

## XIV

There is a threshold, that meniscus where
The strider walks on drowning waters, or
That tense, curved membrane of the camera's lens
Which darkness holds against the battering light
And the distracted drumming of the world's
Importunate plenty.—Now that threshold,
The water of the eye where the world walks
Delicately, is as a needle threaded
From the reel of a raveling stream, to stitch
Dissolving figures in a watered cloth,
A damask either-sided as the shroud
Of the lord of Ithaca, labored at in light,
Destroyed in darkness, while the spidery oars
Carry his keel across deep mysteries
To harbor in unfathomable mercies.

## XV

To watch water, to watch running water
Is to know a secret, seeing the twisted rope
Of runnels on the hillside, the small freshets
Leaping and limping down the tilted field
In April's light, the green, grave and opaque
Swirl in the millpond where the current slides
To be combed and carded silver at the fall;
It is a secret. Or it is not to know
The secret, but to have it in your keeping,
A locked box, Bluebeard's room, the deathless thing
Which it is death to open. Knowing the secret,
Keeping the secret—herringbones of light
Ebbing on beaches, the huge artillery
Of tides—it is not knowing, it is not keeping,
But being the secret hidden from yourself.


## ON CERTAIN WITS

*who amused themselves over the simplicity of*
*Barnett Newman's paintings shown at Bennington*
*College in May of 1958*

When Moses in Horeb struck the rock,
And water came forth out of the rock,
Some of the people were annoyed with Moses
And said he should have used a fancier stick.

And when Elijah on Mount Carmel brought the rain,
Where the prophets of Baal could not bring rain,
Some of the people said that the rituals of the prophets of Baal
Were aesthetically significant, while Elijah's were very plain.

## TO H. M.

*On Reading His Poems*

As when the gannet goes deep down
And splashes like a stone,
The splash may be windblown
Until a rainbow in the spray
Scatters and falls away
Whether or no the gannet gets his fish:—
So with the poet and the secret wish.


## MAESTRIA

Is where you find it,
And you need not agree with its views
About money or the meaning of numbers,
About the immaculate conception or the divine
Ancestry of Augustus. After a few years,
The smoke having blown off those battlefields
And the dead having buried their dead,
Only the scholar will revisit that silence
To inspect the rusting, controversial wheels
Of the abandoned machinery.
                              There remains
A singular lucidity and sweetness, a way
Of relating the light and the shade,
The light spilling from fountains, the shade
Shaken among the leaves.
                              Doubtless
It would be better to be always right, refraining
From those millennial expectations, but strangely,
Rising sometimes from hatred and wrong,
The song sings itself out to the end,
And like a running stream which purifies itself
It leaves behind the mortality of its maker,
Who has the skill of his art, and a trembling hand.

# GOING AWAY

Now as the year turns toward its darkness
the car is packed, and time come to start
driving west. We have lived here
for many years and been more or less content;
now we are going away. That is how
things happen, and how into new places,
among other people, we shall carry
our lives with their peculiar memories
both happy and unhappy but either way
touched with the strange tonality
of what is gone but inalienable, the clear
and level light of a late afternoon
out on the terrace, looking to the mountains,
drinking with friends. Voices and laughter
lifted in still air, in a light
that seemed to paralyze time.
We have had kindness here, and some
unkindness; now we are going on.
Though we are young enough still
and militant enough to be resolved,
keeping our faces to the front, there is
a moment, after saying all farewells,
when we taste the dry and bitter dust
of everything that we have said and done
for many years, and our mouths are dumb,
and the easy tears will not do. Soon
the north wind will shake the leaves,
the leaves will fall. It may be
never again that we shall see them,
the strangers who stand on the steps,
smiling and waving, before the screen doors
of their suddenly forbidden houses.

# LIFE CYCLE OF COMMON MAN

Roughly figured, this man of moderate habits,
This average consumer of the middle class,
Consumed in the course of his average life span
Just under half a million cigarettes,
Four thousand fifths of gin and about
A quarter as much vermouth; he drank
Maybe a hundred thousand cups of coffee,
And counting his parents' share it cost
Something like half a million dollars
To put him through life. How many beasts
Died to provide him with meat, belt and shoes
Cannot be certainly said.
                              But anyhow,
It is in this way that a man travels through time,
Leaving behind him a lengthening trail
Of empty bottles and bones, of broken shoes,
Frayed collars and worn out or outgrown
Diapers and dinnerjackets, silk ties and slickers.

Given the energy and security thus achieved,
He did . . . ? What? The usual things, of course,
The eating, dreaming, drinking and begetting,
And he worked for the money which was to pay
For the eating, et cetera, which were necessary
If he were to go on working for the money, et cetera,
But chiefly he talked. As the bottles and bones
Accumulated behind him, the words proceeded
Steadily from the front of his face as he
Advanced into the silence and made it verbal.
Who can tally the tale of his words? A lifetime
Would barely suffice for their repetition;
If you merely printed all his commas the result
Would be a very large volume, and the number of times
He said "thank you" or "very little sugar, please,"
Would stagger the imagination. There were also
Witticisms, platitudes, and statements beginning
"It seems to me" or "As I always say."

221

Consider the courage in all that, and behold the man
Walking into deep silence, with the ectoplastic
Cartoon's balloon of speech proceeding
Steadily out of the front of his face, the words
Borne along on the breath which is his spirit
Telling the numberless tale of his untold Word
Which makes the world his apple, and forces him to eat.


## BOOM!

### SEES BOOM IN RELIGION, TOO

*Atlantic City, June 23, 1957* (AP).—*President Eisenhower's pastor said tonight that Americans are living in a period of "unprecedented religious activity" caused partially by paid vacations, the eight-hour day and modern conveniences.*

*"These fruits of material progress," said the Rev. Edward L. R. Elson of the National Presbyterian Church, Washington, "have provided the leisure, the energy, and the means for a level of human and spiritual values never before reached."*

Here at the Vespasian-Carlton, it's just one
religious activity after another; the sky
is constantly being crossed by cruciform
airplanes, in which nobody disbelieves
for a second, and the tide, the tide
of spiritual progress and prosperity
miraculously keeps rising, to a level
never before attained. The churches are full,
the beaches are full, and the filling-stations
are full, God's great ocean is full
of paid vacationers praying an eight-hour day
to the human and spiritual values, the fruits,
the leisure, the energy, and the means, Lord,
the means for the level, the unprecedented level,
and the modern conveniences, which also are full.
Never before, O Lord, have the prayers and praises

from belfry and phonebooth, from ballpark and barbecue
the sacrifices, so endlessly ascended.

It was not thus when Job in Palestine
sat in the dust and cried, cried bitterly;
when Damien kissed the lepers on their wounds
it was not thus; it was not thus
when Francis worked a fourteen-hour day
strictly for the birds; when Dante took
a week's vacation without pay and it rained
part of the time, O Lord, it was not thus.

But now the gears mesh and the tires burn
and the ice chatters in the shaker and the priest
in the pulpit, and Thy Name, O Lord,
is kept before the public, while the fruits
ripen and religion booms and the level rises
and every modern convenience runneth over,
that it may never be with us as it hath been
with Athens and Karnak and Nagasaki,
nor Thy sun for one instant refrain from shining
on the rainbow Buick by the breezeway
or the Chris Craft with the uplift life raft;
that we may continue to be the just folks we are,
plain people with ordinary superliners and
disposable diaperliners, people of the stop'n'shop
'n'pray as you go, of hotel, motel, boatel,
the humble pilgrims of no deposit no return
and please adjust thy clothing, who will give to Thee,
if Thee will keep us going, our annual
Miss Universe, for Thy Name's Sake, Amen.


MRS. MANDRILL

On the night that Mrs. Mandrill entered Nature,
squirrels and mice and crickets everywhere

were squeaking, while the dark spilled up the sky
and the marble moon rolled out over the hills.

"I had not thought of this," that lady said.
"Involved with crowsfeet, husbands, lawsuits, I
paid it no heed. But now it is plain as day
that subways and wires run among the roots
to stations with outlandish names, if not
no names at all. I can see now," she said,
"how I should have thought of this before I came
out in the noisy night, before I heard
the rumor of betrayal in me, or learned
corruption meant to criticize my heart.
One might have known, though it wasn't said at school,
that there was more to this than met the eye.
Now, I suppose, it is too late." So mooning,
went Mrs. Mandrill over the wild meadows,
through marshes, in the unofficial land
of squirrels and bats and tiny creatures whining
like her refrigerator, where two cold
bottles of milk whitely awaited her
desire, and slowly soured where they stood.

"God?" Mrs. Mandrill said, "I have no God,
and not afraid or ashamed to tell Him so
either, if it should come to that. I am
fatigued, and would find no fault with these arrangements,
did they not cause me pain."
                          But while she said,
her skinny feet troubled the waters, rattled
the leaves, and picked at the nervous vines where crossed
every last telephone in the weird world,
with all the crickety conversations of them
describing how the moon rolled out like a marble,
and how the dark spilled up instead of down.

It was the pain that lady felt, went chirping
through wires and waters of her grasping heart's
exchange, converting stones to vegetables

224

and blood to stars for sweet speculation's sake.
—"Such unintelligible things." She sighed.
"But they mean me now, and meant me even when
I was a little thing, before my face
broke like a cheese, before my vanity
caught me in netted veins and I went in
for litigation more than lechery.
It hasn't been easy," Mrs. Mandrill cried
to the crickets and other creatures who now silenced
their conversations at her heart, "for though
I knew the lead behind my looking-glass
better than some, I was the more deceived
by the way things looked. But for the love of God
all's one, I see that now, since I shall be
converted even against my will, and my will
converted with me, hearing this creature cry
before her wet heart spills and goes to seed."


## THE VIEW FROM AN ATTIC WINDOW

*for Francis and Barbara*

1

Among the high-branching, leafless boughs
Above the roof-peaks of the town,
Snowflakes unnumberably come down.

I watched out of the attic window
The laced sway of family trees,
Intricate genealogies

Whose strict, reserved gentility,
Trembling, impossible to bow,
Received the appalling fall of snow.

All during Sunday afternoon,
Not storming, but befittingly,
Out of a still, grey, devout sky,

The snowflakes fell, until all shapes
Went under, and thickening, drunken lines
Cobwebbed the sleep of solemn pines.

Up in the attic, among many things
Inherited and out of style,
I cried, then fell asleep awhile,

Waking at night now, as the snow-
flakes from darkness to darkness go
Past yellow lights in the street below.


2

I cried because life is hopeless and beautiful.
And like a child I cried myself to sleep
High in the head of the house, feeling the hull
Beneath me pitch and roll among the steep
Mountains and valleys of the many years
    That brought me to tears.

Down in the cellar, furnace and washing machine,
Pump, fuse-box, water heater, work their hearts
Out at my life, which narrowly runs between
Them and this cemetery of spare parts
For discontinued men, whose hats and canes
    Are my rich remains.

And women, their portraits and wedding gowns
Stacked in the corners, brooding in wooden trunks;
And children's rattles, books about lions and clowns;
And headless, hanging dresses swayed like drunks
Whenever a living footstep shakes the floor;
    I mention no more;

But what I thought today, that made me cry,
Is this, that we live in two kinds of thing:
The powerful trees, thrusting into the sky
Their black patience, are one, and that branching

Relation teaches how we endure and grow;
   The other is the snow,

Falling in a white chaos from the sky,
As many as the sands of all the seas,
As all the men who died or who will die,
As stars in heaven, as leaves of all the trees;
As Abraham was promised of his seed;
   Generations bleed,

Till I, high in the tower of my time
Among familiar ruins, began to cry
For accident, sickness, justice, war and crime,
Because all died, because I had to die.
The snow fell, the trees stood, the promise kept,
   And a child I slept.


## DEATH AND THE MAIDEN

Once I saw a grown man fall from a tree
and die. That's years ago, I was a girl.
My father's house is sold into a home
for the feeble-minded gentlefolk who can't
any longer stand the world, but in those days
there was money to maintain the mile or so
of discipline that kept the hungry grass
parading to the lake, and once a year
bring men to prune the files of giant trees
whose order satisfied and stood for some
euclidean ancestor's dream about the truth:
elms, most of them, already dying of
their yellow blight, and blackened with witches' broom
in the highest branches—but they could die for years,
decades, so tall their silence, and tell you nothing.
Those men came in October every year,
and among the last leaves, the driven leaves,
would set their ladders for assault and swarm

like pirates into the shrouds, thrusting with hook
and long-handled bill against the withered members
of those great corporations, amputating
death away from the center. They were called
tree surgeons, on the ground they were surly-
polite and touched their caps, but in the air
they dared. I would watch one straddle a branch
on a day of rainy wind, his red shirt patched
on the elm's great fan of sky, his pruning-claw
breaking the finger-bones from the high hand
which held him, and I'd dream of voyages.
My father said: "It looks more dangerous
than really it is." But if your hand offend,
I thought, cut off the hand, and if your eye
offend, pluck out the eye. I looked at him
out of my window all one afternoon,
and I think he looked back once, a young man
proud and probably lecherous, while I—
was a maiden at a window. Only he died
that day. "Unlucky boy," my father said,
who then was dying himself without a word
to anyone, the crab's claw tightening
inside the bowel that year to the next
in a dead silence. I do not know if things
that happen can be said to come to pass,
or only happen, but when I remember
my father's house, I imagine sometimes
a dry, ruined spinster at my rainy window
trying to tally on dumb fingers a world's
incredible damage—nothing can stand it!—and
watching the red shirt patched against the sky,
so far and small in the webbed hand of the elm.


ANGEL AND STONE

In the world are millions and millions of men, and each man,
With a few exceptions, believes himself to be at the center,
A small number of his more or less necessary planets careering

Around him in an orderly manner, some morning stars singing
    together,
More distant galaxies shining like dust in any stray sunbeam
Of his attention. Since this is true not of one man or of two,
But of ever so many, it is hard to imagine what life must be like.
But if you drop a stone into a pool, and observe the ripples
Moving in circles successively out to the edges of the pool and
    then
Reflecting back and passing through the ones which continue
    to come
Out of the center over the sunken stone, you observe it is
    pleasing.
And if you drop two stones it will still be pleasing, because now
The angular intersections of the two sets form a more
    complicated
Pattern, a kind of reticulation regular and of simple origins.
But if you throw a handful of sand into the water, it is
    confusion,
Not because the same laws have ceased to obtain, but only
    because
The limits of your vision in time and number forbid you to
    discriminate
Such fine, quick, myriad events as the angels and archangels,
    thrones
And dominations, principalities and powers, are delegated to
    witness
And declare the glory of before the Lord of everything that is.

Of these great beings and mirrors of being, little at present is
    known,
And of the manner of their perceiving not much more. We
    imagine them
As benign, as pensively smiling and somewhat coldly smiling,
    but
They may not be as we imagine them. Among them there are
    some who count
The grassblades and the grains of sand by one and one and one
And number the raindrops and memorize the eccentricities of
    snowflakes.

229

One of the greater ones reckons and records the tides of time,
Distinguishing the dynasties of mountains, races, cities,
As they rise, flower and fall, to whom an age is as a wave,
A nation the spray thrown from its crest; and one, being charged
With all the crossing moments, the comings-together and
    drivings-apart,
Reads in the chromatin its cryptic scripture as the cell divides;
And one is the watcher over chance events and the guardian of
    disorder
According to the law of the square root of n, so that a certain
    number
Of angels or molecules shall fall in irrelevance and be retrograde.

So do they go, those shining creatures, counting without
    confusion
And holding in their slow immeasurable gaze all the transactions
Of all the particles, item by atom, while the pyramids stand still
In the desert and the deermouse huddles in his hole and the
    rain falls
Piercing the skin of the pool with water in water and making a
    million
And a million designs to be pleasingly latticed and laced and
    interfused
And mirrored to the Lord of everything that is by one and one
    and one.


THE REMORSE FOR TIME

When I was a boy, I used to go to bed
By daylight, in the summer, and lie awake
Between the cool, white, reconciling sheets,
Hearing the talk of birds, watching the light
Diminish through the shimmering planes of leaf
Outside the window, until sleep came down
When darkness did, eyes closing as the light
Faded out of them, silencing the birds.

230

Sometimes still, in the sleepless dark hours
Tormented most by the remorse for time,
Only for time, the mind speaks of that boy
(he did no wrong, then why had he to die?)
Falling asleep on the current of the stars
Which even then washed him away past pardon.


MOUSEMEAL

My son invites me to witness with him
a children's program, a series of cartoons,
on television. Addressing myself to share
his harmless pleasures, I am horrified
by the unbridled violence and hostility
of the imagined world he takes in stride,
where human beings dressed in the skins of mice
are eaten by portcullises and cowcatchers,
digested through the winding corridors
of organs, overshoes, boa constrictors
and locomotive boilers, to be excreted
in waters where shark and squid and abalone
wait to employ their tentacles and jaws.
It seems there is no object in this world
unable to become a gullet with great lonely teeth,
sometimes a set of teeth all by itself
comes clacking over an endless plain
after the moving mouse; and though the mouse
wins in the end, the tail of one cartoon
is spliced into the mouth of the next, where his
rapid and trivial agony repeats itself
in another form. My son has seen these things
a number of times, and knows what to expect;
he does not seem disturbed or anything more
than mildly amused. Maybe these old cartoons
refer to my childhood and not to his
(The ogres in them wear Mussolini's face),
so that when mice are swallowed by skeletons

or empty suits of armor, when a tribe
of savage Negro mice is put through a wringer
and stacked flat in the cellar, he can take
the objective and critical view, while I
am shaken to see the giant picassoid
parents eating and voiding their little mice
time and again. And when the cheery announcer
cries, "Well, kids, that's the end," my son gets up
obediently and runs outside to play.
I hope he will ride over this world as well,
and that his crudest and most terrifying dreams
will not return with such wide publicity.


## THE ICEHOUSE IN SUMMER

*see* Amos, 3:15

A door sunk in a hillside, with a bolt
thick as the boy's arm, and behind that door
the walls of ice, melting a blue, faint light,
an air of cedar branches, sawdust, fern:
decaying seasons keeping from decay.

A summer guest, the boy had never seen
(a servant told him of it) how the lake
froze three foot thick, how farmers came with teams,
with axe and saw, to cut great blocks of ice,
translucid, marbled, glittering in the sun,
load them on sleds and drag them up the hill
to be manhandled down the narrow path
and set in courses for the summer's keeping,
the kitchen uses and luxuriousness
of the great houses. And he heard how once
a team and driver drowned in the break of spring:
the man's cry melting from the ice that summer
frightened the sherbet-eaters off the terrace.

Dust of the cedar, lost and evergreen
among the slowly blunting water walls
where the blade edge melted and the steel saw's bite
was rounded out, and the horse and rider drowned
in the red sea's blood, I was the silly child
who dreamed that riderless cry, and saw the guests
run from a ghostly wall, so long before
the winter house fell with the summer house,
and the houses, Egypt, the great houses, had an end.

# THE NEXT ROOM OF THE DREAM (1962)

*As with a dream interpreted by one still sleeping,*
*The interpretation is only the next room of the dream.*
  "To Clio, Muse of History"

*To Kay Boyle*

# 1 Effigies

## TO CLIO, MUSE OF HISTORY

*On learning that The Etruscan Warrior*
*in the Metropolitan Museum of Art*
*is proved a modern forgery*

One more casualty,
One more screen memory penetrated at last
To be destroyed in the endless anamnesis
Always progressing, never arriving at a cure.
My childhood in the glare of that giant form
Corrupts with history, for I too fought in the War.

He, great male beauty
That stood for the sexual thrust of power,
His target eyes inviting the universal victim
To fatal seduction, the crested and greaved
Survivor long after shield and sword are dust,
Has now become another lie about our life.

Smash the idol, of course.
Bury the pieces deep as the interest of truth
Requires. And you may in time compose the future
Smoothly without him, though it is too late
To disinfect the past of his huge effigy
By any further imposition of your hands.

But tell us no more
Enchantments, Clio. History has given
And taken away; murders become memories,
And memories become the beautiful obligations:
As with a dream interpreted by one still sleeping,
The interpretation is only the next room of the dream.

For I remember how
We children stared, learning from him
Unspeakable things about war that weren't in the books;
And how the Museum store offered for sale
His photographic reproductions in full color
With the ancient genitals blacked out.


## SANTA CLAUS

Somewhere on his travels the strange Child
Picked up with this overstuffed confidence man,
Affection's inverted thief, who climbs at night
Down chimneys, into dreams, with this world's goods.
Bringing all the benevolence of money,
He teaches the innocent to want, thus keeps
Our fat world rolling. His prescribed costume,
White flannel beard, red belly of cotton waste,
Conceals the thinness of essential hunger,
An appetite that feeds on satisfaction;
Or, pregnant with possessions, he brings forth
Vanity and the void. His name itself
Is corrupted, and even Saint Nicholas, in his turn,
Gives off a faint and reminiscent stench,
The merest soupçon, of brimstone and the pit.

Now, at the season when the Child is born
To suffer for the world, suffer the world,
His bloated Other, jovial satellite
And sycophant, makes his appearance also
In a glitter of goodies, in a rock candy glare.
Played at the better stores by bums, for money,
This annual savior of the economy
Speaks in the parables of the dollar sign:
Suffer the little children to come to Him.

At Easter, he's anonymous again,
Just one of the crowd lunching on Calvary.

# TO THE MANNEQUINS

Adorable images,
Plaster of Paris
Lilies of the field,
You are not alive, therefore
Pathos will be out of place.

But I have learned
A fact about your fate,
And it is this:

After you go out of fashion
Beneath your many fashions,
Or when your elbows and knees
Have been bruised powdery white,
So that you are no good to anybody—

They will take away your gowns,
Your sables and bathing suits,
Leaving exposed before all men
Your inaccessible bellies
And pointless nubilities.

Movers will come by night
And load you into trucks
And take you away to the Camps,
Where soldiers, or the State Police,
Will use you as targets
For small-arms practice,

Leading me to inquire,
Since pathos is out of place,
What it is that they are practicing.

# FONTENELLE

At night, passing the open door
Of the power station, you look inside
At an immense, immaculate, lofty space
Of marble floors and green iron grille work
Climbing on windows cathedrally tall.

The shields of their backs showing as giant humps,
The dynamos gleam deep in their own light.
They have been sunk partly into the floor
And set apart behind railings, as man sets apart
Whatever he would find famous and disturbing:
The way the great globe is in the Daily News
Building, or Grant is in Grant's Tomb.

An old man in a grey sweater sits by the door,
The night watchman, reading a comic book.
Sometimes he stops to spit on the floor,
And after the comic book he has an obscene
Magazine. It is a long night
In the power plant.

Fontenelle wrote these books among others:
The *Apologie des Tourbillons*, the *Dialogues des Morts*,
The *Entretiens sur la Pluralité des Mondes*.
He lived to be one hundred years old.

The dynamos, deep sunken in their own light,
Hum to themselves. Not of the dragon's wake,
The moonlit rinsings of the China Sea,
Not of the wind in the furnace of the North.
They are of the type called "self-exciting."

Someone asked Fontenelle, Did he never laugh?
*Non non, monsieur, je ne fais jamais ah-ah-ah.*
And when he got to be a hundred years old,
Somebody asked him what he felt about being
    a hundred years old.
*Rien, seulement une certaine difficulté d'être.*

# THE IRON CHARACTERS

The iron characters, keepers of the public confidence,
The sponsors, fund raisers, and members of the board,
Who naturally assume their seats among the governors,
Who place their names behind the issue of bonds
And are consulted in the formation of cabinets,
The catastrophes of war, depression, and natural disaster:
They represent us in responsibilities many and great.
It is no wonder, then, if in a moment of crisis,
Before the microphones, under the lights, on a great occasion,
One of them will break down in hysterical weeping
Or fall in an epileptic seizure, or if one day
We read in the papers of one's having been found
Naked and drunk in a basement with three high school boys,
Of one who jumped from the window of his hospital room.
For are they not as ourselves in these things also?
Let the orphan, the pauper, the thief, the derelict drunk
And all those of no fixed address, shed tears of rejoicing
For the broken minds of the strong, the torn flesh of the just.


# DON JUAN TO THE STATUE

Dominant marble, neither will I yield!
The soul endures at one with its election,
Lover to bed or soldier to the field,
Your daughter's the cause of this & that erection.


# JOURNEY OF THE SNOWMEN

Gradually in gardens
The cold men melted,
Becoming featureless
As powerful Pharaohs
Slumped in the long sleep.
That's how things were
In the Old Kingdom.

241

Now, by a miracle
Reborn, they assemble
Under the influence
Of light, they crowd
At the highest corners
To testify in a babble
Of tongues that they are going
To glitter in the gutters
And snakedance down all hills
And hollows, on the long fall
That makes the sewers sing.


## THE DAILY GLOBE

Each day another installment of the old
Romance of Order brings to the breakfast table
The paper flowers of catastrophe.
One has this recurrent dream about the world.

Headlines declare the ambiguous oracles,
The comfortable old prophets mutter doom.
Man's greatest intellectual pleasure is
To repeat himself, yet somehow the daily globe

Rolls on, while the characters in comic strips
Prolong their slow, interminable lives
Beyond the segregated photographs
Of the girls that marry and the men that die.


## A PICTURE

Of people running down the street
Among the cars, a good many people.
You could see that something was up,
Because people in American towns

Don't ordinarily run, they walk,
And not in the street. The camera caught
A pretty girl tilted off-balance
And with her mouth in O amazed;
A man in a fat white shirt, his tie
Streaming behind him, as one flat foot
Went slap on the asphalt—you could see
He was out of breath, but dutifully
Running along with all the others,
Maybe at midday, on Main Street somewhere.

The running faces did not record
Hatred or anger or great enthusiasm
For what they were doing (hunting down
A Negro, according to the caption),
But seemed rather solemn, intent,
With the serious patience of animals
Driven through a gate by some
Urgency out of the camera's range,
On an occasion too serious
For private feeling. The breathless faces
Expressed a religion of running,
A form of ritual exaltation
Devoted to obedience, and
Obedient, it might be, to the Negro,
Who was not caught by the camera
When it took the people in the street
Among the cars, toward some object,
Seriously running.


NOTHING WILL YIELD

Nothing will yield. The pretty poems are dead,
And the mad poets in their periwigs,
Bemused upon a frontispiece before
The ruined Temple of Art, and supervised
By the Goddess of Reason leaning from a cloud,

In reality died insane. Alas, for the grave
And gaudy forms! Lord Hi and Lady Ho,
Those brazen effigies upon a plinth
Of pink granite, seem immutable,
But seem. In time, they have many tongues,
But in eternity Latin is spoken.

Or else, perhaps, it is all a matter of hats,
The helmet, the biretta, the iron crown,
The crown of thorns. Lachrymae Christi is
A beautiful sound, a Neapolitan wine,
The Tears of Christ. And yet nothing will yield.
How many are the uniforms of time
That men and women wear, how grave the glitter
Of epaulets and emblems as the grand
Procession passes, how nobly they speak
The language of the court, the holy language
That scorns the isolation of the heart.
It takes great courage to go on the stage.


ONE FOREVER ALIEN

When I become the land, when they will build
Blast furnaces over me, and lay black asphalt
For hundreds of miles across my ribs, and wheels
Begin to bounce interminably on the bone;
When I enter, at last, America, when I am
Part of her progress and a true patriot,
And the schoolchildren sing of my sacrifice,
Remembering the burial day of my birth—
Then even the efficient will have to forgive me,
The investigators approve my security,
And those that harden their hearts welcome me home.

Then, in that day, my countrymen,
When I shall come among you fleeced as the lamb
And in the diaper of the grave newly arrayed,
The Adam Qadmon, the greenhorn immigrant,

244

Shall pass the customs at the port of entry
Where the Guardian Lady lifts her flaming sword.
Forgiven the original sin of his origin,
He comes as a bond redeemed, as newly negotiable,
  To be as a soybean before you.


## A PREDECESSOR OF PERSEUS

Since he is older than Hamlet or Stavrogin,
Older than Leopold Bloom; since he has been
Stravaging through the Dark Wood several years
Beyond the appointed time, meeting no wolf,
Leopard, or lion, not to mention Virgil;
And long since seen the span of Keats conclude,
And the span of Alexander,—he begins
At last to wonder.

              Had his sacred books
Misled him? Or had he deceived himself?
Like some he knew, who'd foolishly confused
The being called and being chosen; they
Ran down the crazy pavement of their path
On primrose all the way.

              An old friend said,
"The first thing to learn about wisdom is
This, that you can't do anything with it."
Wisdom. If that was what he had, he might,
Like a retired witch, keep it locked up
In the broom closet. But he rides his road,
Passing the skinless elder skeletons
Who smile, and maybe he will keep on going
Until the grey unbearable she of the world
Shall raise her eyes, and recognize, and grin
At her eternal amateur's approach,
All guts no glass, to meet her gaze head on
And be stricken in the likeness of himself
At least, if not of Keats or Alexander.

245

# 2 Emblems

## A SPELL BEFORE WINTER

After the red leaf and the gold have gone,
Brought down by the wind, then by hammering rain
Bruised and discolored, when October's flame
Goes blue to guttering in the cusp, this land
Sinks deeper into silence, darker into shade.
There is a knowledge in the look of things,
The old hills hunch before the north wind blows.

Now I can see certain simplicities
In the darkening rust and tarnish of the time,
And say over the certain simplicities,
The running water and the standing stone,
The yellow haze of the willow and the black
Smoke of the elm, the silver, silent light
Where suddenly, readying toward nightfall,
The sumac's candelabrum darkly flames.
And I speak to you now with the land's voice,
It is the cold, wild land that says to you
A knowledge glimmers in the sleep of things:
The old hills hunch before the north wind blows.

## HUMAN THINGS

When the sun gets low, in winter,
The lapstreaked side of a red barn
Can put so flat a stop to its light
You'd think everything was finished.

Each dent, fray, scratch, or splinter,
Any gray weathering where the paint

246

Has scaled off, is a healed scar
Grown harder with the wounds of light.

Only a tree's trembling shadow
Crosses that ruined composure; even
Nail holes look deep enough to swallow
Whatever light has left to give.

And after sundown, when the wall
Slowly surrenders its color, the rest
Remains, its high, obstinate
Hulk more shadowy than the night.


WINTER EXERCISE

A man out walking alone in the snow,
Painfully cold, blinded by wind and snow,
And with nowhere in particular to go
But round in a circle, over the wooded hill
And down, back round by the road and past the mill
And up street again to his own doorsill—
Now what may such a man be but a lost
Man, aimlessly battling the snowy host
To get nowhere but home, where his own ghost
Will meet him, bowing, on the parlor floor,
Join him again when he's scarce through the door,
Enjoin him against wandering any more?

Suppose, instead, he really did get lost
There on the hill, beyond surveyor's post
And sidewalk, and Bohemia grew a coast
Which loomed before him, white as the white storm
Blowing into his eyes? With what good form
Would things be kept up by his ghost at the warm
Hearthside at home: His slippers and his drink,
No dust on the floor, or dishes in the sink;
It might be days till anyone would think
There was a kind of stillness to all this

Which made the house, though cheerful, an abyss,
And unidentifiably remiss.

Meanwhile his seven-league, left-handed heart
Had kept him circling up there, far apart
From what his ghost, out of domestic art,
Could manage in the way of keeping life
Respectable and decent (keep his wife
From noticing, for instance). His hard strife
Against the storm had long begun to seem
Unduly long, a walk around a dream
Whose nonsense only waking could redeem;
Till, seeing everywhere nothing but deep
Snow and dark woods, he knew he was asleep,
And, to wake up, lay down and went to sleep.

He dreamed a warm, familiar dream of home,
Went, like an auctioneer, from room to room.
Table and chair, razor and brush and comb
He catalogued, and the lady too whose lord
He was, who shared his castle, bed and board,
And realized in his dream that he was bored.
"There's nothing in this for me," he said aloud;
"Better the snow should be my lonely shroud."
The ghost at home heard, looked around, allowed
The force of this, and followed: Up the hill
He went, through snow, across the same doorsill
Stepped into dream; and soon the lady will.


IDEA

Idea blazes in darkness, a lonely star.
The witching hour is not twelve, but one.
Pure thought, in principle, some say, is near
Madness, but the independent mind thinks on,
Breathing and burning, abstract as the air.

248

Supposing all this were a game of chess.
One learned to do without the pieces first,
And then the board; and finally, I guess,
Without the game. The lightship gone adrift,
Endangering others with its own distress.

O holy light! All other stars are gone,
The shapeless constellations sag and fall
Till navigation fails, though ships go on
This merry, mad adventure as before
Their single-minded masters meant to drown.


## SOMEWHERE

A girl this evening regrets her surrender with tears,
A schoolboy knows he will be unprepared tomorrow.
A father, aware of having behaved viciously,
Is unable to speak; his child weeps obstinately.
Somewhere a glutton waits for himself to vomit,
An unfaithful wife resists the temptation to die.

The stones of the city have been here for centuries,
The tides have been washing backwards and forwards
In sunlight, in starlight, since before the beginning.
Down in the swamp a red fox runs quietly, quietly
Under the owl's observation, those yellow eyes
That eat through the darkness. Hear the shrew cry!

Somewhere a story is told, someone is singing
Of careless love in the hands of its creditors.
It is of Yseult, Antigone, Tarquin with Lucrece,
The Brides in the Bath. . . . Those who listen
Lean forward bemused, rapt with the sweet seductions
Punishable by death, with the song's word: long ago.

# DE ANIMA

Now it is night, now in the brilliant room
A girl stands at the window looking out,
But sees, in the darkness of the frame,
Only her own image.

And there is a young man across the street
Who looks at the girl and into the brilliant room.
They might be in love, might be about to meet,
If this were a romance.

In looking at herself, she tries to look
Beyond herself, and half become another,
Admiring and resenting, maybe dreaming
Her lover might see her so.

The other, the stranger standing in cold and dark,
Looks at the young girl in her crystalline room.
He sees clearly, and hopelessly desires,
A life that is not his.

Given the blindness of her self-possession,
The luminous vision revealed to his despair,
We look to both sides of the glass at once
And see no future in it.

These pure divisions hurt us in some realm
Of parable beyond belief, beyond
The temporal mind. Why is it sorrowful?
Why do we want them together?

Is it the spirit, ransacking through the earth
After its image, its being, its begetting?
The spirit sorrows, for what lovers bring
Into the world is death,

The most exclusive romance, after all,
The sort that lords and ladies listen to

With selfish tears, when she draws down the shade,
When he has turned away,

When the blind embryo with his bow of bees,
His candied arrows tipped with flower heads,
Turns from them too, for mercy or for grief
Refusing to be, refusing to die.


## THE DIAL TONE

A moment of silence, first, then there it is.
But not as though it only now began
Because of my attention; rather, this,
That I begin at one point on its span
Brief kinship with its endless going on.

Between society and self it poses
Neutrality perceptible to sense,
Being a no man's land the lawyer uses
Much as the lover does: charged innocence,
It sits on its own electrified fence,

Is neither pleased nor hurt by race results
Or by the nasty thing John said to Jane;
Is merely interrupted by insults,
Devotions, lecheries; after the sane
And mad hang up at once, it will remain.

Suppose that in God a black bumblebee
Or colorless hummingbird buzzed all night,
Dividing the abyss up equally;
And carried its neither sweetness nor its light
Across impossible eternity.

Now take this hummingbird, this bee, away;
And like the Cheshire smile without its cat
The remnant hum continues on its way,

Unwinged, able at once to move and wait,
An endless freight train on an endless flat.

Something like that, some loneliest of powers
That never has confessed its secret name.
I do not doubt that if you gave it hours
And then lost patience, it would be the same
After you left that it was before you came.


## GOLDFISH

The bearded goldfish move about the bowl
Waving disheveled rags of elegant fin
Languidly in the light; their mandarin
Manner of life, weary and cynical,

Rebukes the round world that has kept them in
Glass bubbles with a mythological
Decor of Rhineland castles on a shoal
Of pebbles pink and green. Like light in gin,

Viscous as ice first forming on a stream,
Their refined feathers fan them on to no
Remarkable purpose; they close their eyes
As, mouths reopening in new surprise
About their long imprisonment in O,
They cruise the ocean of an alien dream.


## POLONIUS PASSING THROUGH A STAGE

Try to be yourself, they told the child.
I tried. Accumulating all those years
The blue annuities of silence some called
Wisdom, I heard sunstorms and exploding stars,

The legions screaming in the German wood—
Old violence petrifying where it stood.

The company in my Globe Theater rants
Its Famous Histories, the heroes fall
In ketchup and couplets. Ten heavenly don'ts
Botch up a selfhood, but where there's a Will
He's away. Rotting at ease, a ghostly doll—
What is that scratching on my heart's wall?

I tried to be myself. The silence grew
Till I could hear the tiniest Mongol horde
Scuffle the Gobi, a pony's felted shoe. . . .
Then from the fiery pit that self-born bird
Arose. A rat! The unseen good old man—
That sort of thing always brings the house down.


THE VIEW FROM PISGAH

Our God was to be a breath, and not a postcard
Of the sun setting over Niagara Falls:
"Wish you were here." Our God was first the breath
That raised a whirlwind in the desert dust,
The Wilderness of Sin. And then a word
Unspeakable, a stillness, and a standing stone
Set in the road; you would not raise a chisel
Upon that stone. Nothing but sky and sand
To purify a forbidden generation
Of Egypt's kitchens. In that wilderness
I've wandered for my forty years also,
Lifting mirages to break horizons, dreaming
Idolatries to alphabet the void,
Sending these postcards to the self at home:
Sunlight on pouring water; wish I were here.

## MAIDEN WITH ORB AND PLANETS

She stands now, shy among the destinies,
Daughter and mother of the silent crossings.
That is what beauty is, the petaled time
In a child's tomb, the basalt time that waits
In the Valley of the Kings, the swaying time
That smoothes the rivers through the summer nights
And polishes the stone and dulls the eye.
A china dynasty, the May fly's day,
Tremble to balance at her either hand,
And her blood moves as the dark rivers move,
While all the sailing stars pass and return.
Her stillness makes the moment of the world
Strike once, and that is what beauty is,
To stand as Agamemnon's daughter stood
Amid great armies waiting on the wind.


## THE FIRST POINT OF ARIES

After the morning of amazing rain
(How fiercely it fell, in slanting lines of light!)
A new breeze blew the clouds back to the hills,
And the huge day gloried in its gold and blue.

The road they walked was shoe-top deep in mud,
But the air was mild. And water of the spring,
The new, cold water, spread across the fields,
The running, the wind-rippled, the still-reflecting.

Life with remorseless joy possessed them then,
Compelling happiness beyond the power
Of prudence to refuse; perforce they gave
To splendor their impersonal consent.

What god could save them from this holy time?
The water, blinking in the sun's blue eye,

254

Watches them loiter on the road to death,
But stricken helpless at the heart with love.


THE DRAGONFLY

Under the pond, among rocks
Or in the bramble of the water wood,
He is at home, and feeds the small
Remorseless craving of his dream,

His cruel delight; until in May
The dream transforms him with itself
And from his depths he rises out,
An exile from the brutal night.

He rises out, the aged one
Imprisoned in the dying child,
And spreads his wings to the new sun:
Climbing, he withers into light.


THE JUNCTION, ON A WARM AFTERNOON

Out of the small domestic jungle,
The roadside scribble of wire and stick
Left over from last fall as we come
Into spring again, a slow freight
Incongruously rises into view.
The tall boxcars, rounding the bend,
Rattle their chains, and from the high
Cab of the engine, from the caboose,
The old men in caps and spectacles,
Gentle old men, some smoking pipes,
Nod with a distant courtesy,
Kindly and yet remote, their minds
On other things.

Sunlight is warm
And grateful. The old railroad men
Are growing obsolete with the great
Engines whose demands they meet,
And yet they do not fail in their
Courtly consideration of the stranger
Standing in sunlight while the freight
Passes slowly along the line
To disappear among small trees,
Leaving empty the long, shining rails
That curve, divide, vanish, and remain.


## BLUE SUBURBAN

Out in the elegy country, summer evenings,
It used to be always six o'clock, or seven,
Where the fountain of the willow always wept
Over the lawn, where the shadows crept longer
But came no closer, where the talk was brilliant,
The laughter friendly, where they all were young
And taken by the darkness in surprise
That night should come and the small lights go on
In the lonely house down in the elegy country,
Where the bitter things were said and the drunken friends
Steadied themselves away in their courses
For industrious ruin or casual disaster
Under a handful of pale, permanent stars.


## THESE WORDS ALSO

There is her mother's letter on the table
Where it was opened and read and put down
In a morning remaining what it never was,
Remaining what it will not be again.

These words also, earth, the sun brings forth
In the moment of his unbearable brilliancy:
"After a night of drink and too much talk,
After the casual companions had gone home,
She did this. . . ." How the silence must have grown
Austere, as the unanswerable phone
Rang in a room that wanted to be empty.

The garden holds its sunlight heavy and still
As if in a gold frame around the flowers
That nod and never change, the picture-book
Flowers of somebody's forbidden childhood,
Pale lemony lilies, pansies with brilliant scowls
Pretending to be children. Only they live,
And it is beautiful enough, to live,
Having to do with hunger and reflection,
A matter of thresholds, of thoughtless balancings.

The black and gold morning goes on, and
What is a girl's life? There on the path
Red ants are pulling a shiny beetle along
Through the toy kingdom where nobody thinks.


VERMEER

Taking what is, and seeing it as it is,
Pretending to no heroic stances or gestures,
Keeping it simple; being in love with light
And the marvelous things that light is able to do,
How beautiful! a modesty which is
Seductive extremely, the care for daily things.

At one for once with sunlight falling through
A leaded window, the holy mathematic
Plays out the cat's cradle of relation
Endlessly; even the inexorable
Domesticates itself and becomes charm.

257

If I could say to you, and make it stick,
A girl in a red hat, a woman in blue
Reading a letter, a lady weighing gold . . .
If I could say this to you so you saw,
And knew, and agreed that this was how it was
In a lost city across the sea of years,
I think we should be for one moment happy
In the great reckoning of those little rooms
Where the weight of life has been lifted and made light,
Or standing invisible on the shore opposed,
Watching the water in the foreground dream
Reflectively, taking a view of Delft
As it was, under a wide and darkening sky.

## AT A COUNTRY HOTEL

(*a young widow with two pretty children*)

"I watched the seeds come down this afternoon
Over the lawn, the garden and the gravel drive.
Even on the pool, where the children sailed
The paper boats you made them—paper boats
Among the lilies, frightening the frogs—
Seeds fell and were sailing.

"I never get tired of watching how the seeds
Break from that high sea of silver and green
Branches to tumble and drift, to glide and spin
Down. It makes me think of falling asleep,
The way people say, I mean, 'falling' asleep,
As if it were really a falling.

"Summer is gone, and the fire is almost out. . . .
How tired they were with playing! Will they dream
About their boats? Autumn is here, the night
Is rainy, with a cold wind; and still the seeds

Are falling, falling in darkness. Or else it is
The rain, that taps at the window."

It is late. He does not speak, will never speak.
She goes to the children sleeping, and he dreams
A kindly harbor, delicate with waves,
Where the tethered dories, rocking, rise and fall,
Until the high sail heightens, coming home
To landfalls of the lily and the ash.


THE END OF SUMMER SCHOOL

At dawn today the spider's web was cold
With dew heavy as silver to the sight,
Where, kicked and spun, with clear wings befouled,
Lay in the shrouds some victims of the night.

This morning, too, as if they had decided,
A few first leaves came loose and drifted down
Still slopes of air; in silence they paraded
Their ominous detachment to the lawn.

How strange and slow the many apples ripened
And suddenly were red beneath the bough.
A master of our school has said this happened
"Quiet as grass can ruminate a cow."

And now the seeds go on their voyages,
Drifting, gliding, spinning in quiet storms
Obedient to the air's lightest laws;
And where they fall, a few will find their forms.

And baby spiders, on their shining threads,
The middle air make glisten gold all day;
Sailing, as if the sun had blessed their roads,
Hundreds of miles, and sometimes out to sea.

This is the end of summer school, the change
Behind the green wall and the steady weather:
Something that turns upon a hidden hinge
Brings down the dead leaf and live seed together,

And of the strength that slowly warps the stars
To strange harbors, the learned pupil knows
How adamant the anvil, fierce the hearth
Where imperceptible summer turns the rose.


BURNING THE LEAVES

This was the first day that the leaves
Came down in hordes, in hosts, a great wealth
Gambled away over the green lawn
Belonging to the house, old fry and spawn
Of the rich year converted into filth
In the beds by the walls, the gutters under the eaves.
We thought of all the generations gone
Like that, flyers, migrants, fugitives.

We come like croupiers with rakes,
To a bamboo clatter drag these winnings in,
Our windfall, firstfruits, tithes and early dead
Fallen on our holdings from overhead,
And taxable to trees against our sin.
Money to burn! We play for higher stakes
Than the mere leaves, and, burdened with treasure, tread
The orbit of the tree that heaven shakes.

The wrath of God we gather up today,
But not for long. In the beginning night
We light our hoarded leaves, the flames arise,
The smell of smoke takes memory by surprise,
And we become as children in our sight.
That is, I think, the object of this play,
Though our children dance about the sacrifice
Unthinking, their shadows lengthened and cast away.

## ELEGY FOR A NATURE POET

It was in October, a favorite season,
He went for his last walk. The covered bridge,
Most natural of all the works of reason,
Received him, let him go. Along the hedge

He rattled his stick; observed the blackening bushes
In his familiar field; thought he espied
Late meadow larks; considered picking rushes
For a dry arrangement; returned home, and died

Of a catarrh caught in the autumn rains
And let go on uncared for. He was too rapt
In contemplation to recall that brains
Like his should not be kept too long uncapped

In the wet and cold weather. While we mourned,
We thought of his imprudence, and how Nature,
Whom he'd done so much for, had finally turned
Against her creature.

His gift was daily his delight, he peeled
The landscape back to show it was a story;
Any old bird or burning bush revealed
At his hands just another allegory.

Nothing too great, nothing too trivial
For him; from mountain range or humble vermin
He could extract the hidden parable—
If need be, crack the stone to get the sermon.

And now, poor man, he's gone. Without his name
The field reverts to wilderness again,
The rocks are silent, woods don't seem the same;
Demoralized small birds will fly insane.

Rude Nature, whom he loved to idealize
And would have wed, pretends she never heard
His voice at all, as, taken by surprise
At last, he goes to her without a word.

## THE FALL AGAIN

It is the Old Man through the sleeping town
Comes oil dark to a certain lip, and breaks
By the white rain's beard the word he speaks,
A drunken Babel that spills upon a stone
And leaps in shatterings of light against
Its pouring fall, and falls again to spill
Asleep its dreaming strength along the kill
On those great sinews' curves twisted and tensed.

Between the vineyard and the drunken dark,
O sorrow, there the rainbow shines no more.
There promises are broken in the roar
Of that Old Man, the staggered Patriarch
And white beard falling naked to the floor
Ashamed, who was himself both Flood and Ark.

# 3 Vaudeville & Critique

LOT LATER

*Vaudeville for George Finckel*

I

It seems now far off and foolish, a memory
Torn at the hem from the fabric of a dream
In drunken sleep, but why was I the one?
God knows, there were no fifty righteous, nor
Ten righteous, in town just at that very moment;
Gone south for the winter, maybe. And moreover,
I wouldn't have been one of the ten or fifty
Or whatever, if there had been. Abraham
Stood up to Him, but not for me—more likely
For the principle of the thing. I've always been
Honest enough for this world, and respected
In this town—but to be taken by the hair
Like that, and lifted into that insane story,
Then to be dropped when it was done with me . . .
I tell you, I felt *used*.
                          In the first place,
I never knew the two of them were angels:
No wings, no radiance. I thought they might be students
Going from town to town, seeing the country.
I said "Come in the house, we'll have a drink,
Some supper, why not stay the night?" They did.
The only oddity was they didn't bother
With evening prayers, and that made me suspect
They might be Somebody. But in my home town
It doesn't take much; before I thought it out
People were coming round beating the door:
"Who you got in the house, let's have a party."
It was a pretty nice town in those days,

263

With always something going on, a dance
Or a big drunk with free women, or boys
For those who wanted boys, in the good weather
We used to play strip poker in the yard.
But just then, when I looked at those young gents,
I had a notion it was not the time,
And shouted through the door, "Go home, we're tired."
Nobody went. But all these drunks began
To pound the door and throw rocks at the windows
And make suggestions as to what they might do
When they got hold of the two pretty young men.
Matters were getting fairly desperate
By this time, and I said to those outside,
"Look, I got here my two daughters, virgins
Who never been there yet. I send them out,
Only my guests should have a peaceful night."
That's how serious the situation was.
Of course it wasn't the truth about the kids,
Who were both married, and, as a matter of fact,
Not much better than whores, and both the husbands
Knocking their horns against the chandeliers
Of my own house—but still, it's what I said.
It got a big laugh out there, and remarks,
Till the two young men gave me a nice smile
And stretched out one hand each, and suddenly
It got pitch dark outside, people began
Bumping into each other and swearing; then
They cleared away and everything was quiet.
So one young man opens his mouth, he says,
"You've got till sunrise, take the wife and kids
And the kids' husbands, and go. Go up to the hills."
The other says, "The Lord hath sent us to
Destroy this place" and so forth and so forth.
You can imagine how I felt. I said,
"Now look, now after all . . ." and my wife said,
"Give me a few days till I pack our things,"
And one of them looked at his watch and said,
"It's orders, lady, sorry, you've got till dawn."
I said, "Respectfully, gentlemen, but who

Lives in the hills? I've got to go, so why
Shouldn't I go to Zoar, which is a nice
Town with a country club which doesn't exclude
Jews?" "So go to Zoar if you want," they said.
"Whatever you do, you shouldn't look back here."
We argued all night long. First this, then that.
My son-in-laws got into the act: "You're kidding,
Things of this nature simply do not happen
To people like us." I said, "These here are angels,
But suit yourselves." The pair of them said, "We'll stay,
Only deed us the house and furniture."
"I wouldn't deed you a dead fish," I said,
"Besides, I'm going to take the girls along."
"So take," they said, "they weren't such a bargain."
The two visitors all this time said nothing,
They might as well not have been there. But I
Believed what I was told, and this, I think,
Makes all the difference—between life and death,
I mean—to feel sincerely that there's truth
In something, even if it's God knows what.
My poor old woman felt it too, that night,
She only couldn't hold it to the end.
The girls just packed their biggest pocketbooks
With candy and perfume; they'd be at home
Most anywhere, even in a hill.
                              At last
I knelt down and I spoke to my God as follows:
"Dear Sir," I said, "I do not understand
Why you are doing this to my community,
And I do not understand why, doing it,
You let me out. There's only this one thing,
So help me, that with all my faults I do
Believe you are able to do whatever you say
You plan to do. Myself, I don't belong
In any operation on this scale.
I've always been known here as a nice fellow,
Which is low enough to be or want to be:
Respectfully I ask to be let go
To live out my declining years at peace

In Zoar with my wife and the two kids
Such as they are. A small house will do.
Only I shouldn't be part of history."
Of course no one answered. One of them said:
"If you're about through, please get on your feet,
It's time to go." My daughters' gorgeous husbands
Were drinking on the porch before we left.


## II

My relative Abraham saw it happen: the whole
Outfit went up in smoke, he said. One minute
There was the town, with banks and bars and grills
And the new sewage disposal plant, all looking
(he said) terribly innocent in the first light; ·
Then it ignited. It went. All those old pals
Gone up, or maybe down. I am his nephew,
Maybe you know, he had troubles himself,
With the maid, and his own son. That's neither here
Nor there. We'd been forbidden to look, of course,
But equally of course my old girl had to look.
She turned around, and in one minute there
She was, a road sign or a mileage marker.
By this time, though, I knew that what we were in
Was very big, and I told the kids Come on.
We didn't stop to cry, even. Also
We never went to Zoar. I began to think
How real estate was high, how I'd been told
To go up in the hills, and how I'd always
Wanted to live in the country, a gentleman
Like Abraham, maybe, and have my flocks
Or whatever you call them—herds. Well, I found out.
A cave, we lived in, a real cave, out of rock.
I envied those bums my son-in-laws, until
I remembered they were dead. And the two girls,
My nutsy kids, getting the odd idea
That the whole human race had been destroyed
Except for us, conceived—this word I love,
Conceived—the notion that they should be known
In carnal union by their poppa. Me.

Poor dear old Dad. Most any man might dream
About his daughters; darling and stupid chicks
As these ones were, I'd dreamed, even in daytime,
Such brilliant dreams. But they? They bought some booze,
Having remembered to bring money along,
Something I never thought of, considering
I was in the hand of God, and got me boiled.
And then—I'm told—on two successive nights
Arrived on my plain stone couch and—what shall I say?
Had me? I was completely gone at the time,
And have no recollection. But there they were,
The pair of them, at the next moon, knocked up,
And properly, and by their Dad. The kids
Turned out to be boys, Moab and Ben-Ammi
By name. I have been given to understand
On competent authority that they will father
A couple of peoples known as Moabites
And Ammonites, distinguished chiefly by
Heathenish ways and ignorance of the Law.
And I did this? Or this was done to me,
A foolish man who lived in the grand dream
One instant, at the fuse of miracle and
The flare of light, a man no better than most,
Who loves the Lord and does not know His ways,
Neither permitted the pleasure of his sins
Nor punished for them, and whose aging daughters
Bring him his supper nights, and clean the cave.


THE PRIVATE EYE

To see clearly, not to be deceived
By the pretended burial of the dead,
    The tears of the bereaved,
    The stopped clock
    Or impenetrable lock,
Or anything that possibly was said
Simply to see who might have been misled;

To dig down deep enough to find the truth,
To penetrate and check, balance and sift,
   Pretending to be uncouth
   And a little dumb
   Till the truth come,
Till the proud and wicked give away their drift
Out of security—that is my gift,

To seem omnivorous in my belief,
Ready to swallow anything at first,
   (Knowing the corrupt chief
   Had rigged the raid
   So no arrest was made)
And, acting guileless as an infant nursed,
Believe in nothing till I get the worst.

I know what cannot possibly be known,
And never know I know it till the end.
   When justice must be done
   I give the word
   To the honestly bored
Survivors of my lust to apprehend,
And then, with the bourbon and the blonde, unbend.


TO DAVID, ABOUT HIS EDUCATION

The world is full of mostly invisible things,
And there is no way but putting the mind's eye,
Or its nose, in a book, to find them out,
Things like the square root of Everest
Or how many times Byron goes into Texas,
Or whether the law of the excluded middle
Applies west of the Rockies. For these
And the like reasons, you have to go to school
And study books and listen to what you are told,
And sometimes try to remember. Though I don't know
What you will do with the mean annual rainfall

On Plato's Republic, or the calorie content
Of the Diet of Worms, such things are said to be
Good for you, and you will have to learn them
In order to become one of the grown-ups
Who sees invisible things neither steadily nor whole,
But keeps gravely the grand confusion of the world
Under his hat, which is where it belongs,
And teaches small children to do this in their turn.


AN INTERVIEW

Young man, the world's outside that door.
A theater full of risky charms,
With real and paranoid alarms:
Great heights for throwing oneself down
And shallows of a depth to drown—
Sawdust enough to save a clown.
Let others stay and mind the store:
What are you saving yourself for?

Young man, don't wait till you know more.
Too much the combat course around,
You'll never find the battleground.
The graves of some that played it cool,
And took no chance, nor looked the fool,
Are hid beneath the graduate school.
This music is to face before
You find out even what's the score.

So to the youth spoke old wisdom,
With leathery face and polished knob,
With golden smile and gold watch fob,
Arthritic knuckles, creaking knees,
And yet in this world well at ease
On sixty years of dignities.
The young man wondered, going home,
What was he saving himself from?

# GNOMES

### A SACRIFICED AUTHOR

Father, he cried, after the critics' chewing,
Forgive them, for they know not what I'm doing.

### LOVE

A sandwich and a beer might cure these ills
If only Boys and Girls were Bars and Grills.

### MINIM

The red butterflies are so beautiful!
But they will not stand still to be looked at.


# REALITIES

She told him, "You were in my dream last night."
She was a bold one, anyhow, and he
Had never cared much for that kind; but now
She'd started something, he wondered.

The dream itself didn't amount to much.
The two of them had been in swimming, she said.
So that weekend they went out to the beach
To see what the dream had to say about that.

You metaphysicians, consider their four kids.
You couldn't hope for a nicer lot of kids
Or for a prettier split-level ranch-type home
To come from a dry swim in a dream.


# DEBATE WITH THE RABBI

You've lost your religion, the Rabbi said.
    It wasn't much to keep, said I.

You should affirm the spirit, said he,
And the communal solidarity.
　　I don't feel so solid, I said.

We are the people of the Book, the Rabbi said.
　　Not of the phone book, said I.
Ours is a great tradition, said he,
And a wonderful history.
　　But history's over, I said.

We Jews are creative people, the Rabbi said.
　　Make something, then, said I.
In science and in art, said he,
Violinists and physicists have we.
　　Fiddle and physic indeed, I said.

Stubborn and stiff-necked man! the Rabbi cried.
　　The pain you give me, said I.
Instead of bowing down, said he,
You go on in your obstinacy.
　　We Jews are that way, I replied.


## TO THE BLEEDING HEARTS ASSOCIATION
## OF AMERICAN NOVELISTS

My grown-ups told me when I started out,
"You have to suffer in order to create."
It took me twenty years of stubborn doubt
Before I found the half-truth in all that.

We have so many fancy fellows now
That cannot leave their sufferings alone.
They spend their precious talents learning how
To paint a sigh, and decorate a groan.

Realistic till it hurts while it astounds
(And to conceal some small defects of art),

They slop their ketchup in the statue's wounds
And advertise that blood as from the heart.

I like those masters better who expound
More inwardly the nature of our loss,
And only offhand let us know they've found
No better composition than a cross.


## THE POET AT FORTY

A light, a winged, & a holy thing,
Who if his God's not in him cannot sing.
Ah, Socrates, behold him here at last
Wingless and heavy, still enthusiast.


## FROM THE DESK OF THE LAUREATE:
## FOR IMMEDIATE RELEASE

Because Great Pan is dead, Astraea gone,
Because the singing has ceased upon Sion,
The Well at Helicon choked up with mud,
The Master of Songs tenders his resignation.

He cannot even do the Birthday Ode
For the Queen Mother, much less manage the
Elaborated forms of Elegy
And Epithalamion, when these fall due.

The Court will simply have to get along
As best it can on Chronicles in prose.
The Master regrets, but from this day the news
Must go uncelebrated in his song.

Although the pay was low, the hours long,
He wrote his wretched little works with love;

And if he will not have his lute restrung,
His reasons are the ones set forth above.

He has retired to the ancient horrible hotel
Where he can still afford to be a swell,
His nightly pony, a scotch whisky neat,
Brought by the servingman on squeaking feet.


MAKE BIG MONEY AT HOME!
WRITE POEMS IN SPARE TIME!

Oliver wanted to write about reality.
He sat before a wooden table,
He poised his wooden pencil
Above his pad of wooden paper,
And attempted to think about agony
And history, and the meaning of history,
And all stuff like that there.

Suddenly this wooden thought got in his head:
A Tree. That's all, no more than that,
Just one tree, not even a note
As to whether it was deciduous
Or evergreen, or even where it stood.
Still, because it came unbidden,
It was inspiration, and had to be dealt with.

Oliver hoped that this particular tree
Would turn out to be fashionable,
The axle of the universe, maybe,
Or some other mythologically
Respectable tree-contraption
With dryads, or having to do
With the knowledge of Good and Evil, and the Fall.

"A Tree," he wrote down with his wooden pencil
Upon his pad of wooden paper
Supported by the wooden table.

And while he sat there waiting
For what would come next to come next,
The whole wooden house began to become
Silent, particularly silent, sinisterly so.


## ON THE THRESHOLD OF HIS GREATNESS, THE POET COMES DOWN WITH A SORE THROAT

*Enthusiasm is not the state of a writer's soul.*—Valéry.[1]

For years I explored the pharmacopoeia
After a new vision. I lay upon nails
While memorizing the Seven Least Nostalgias.[2]
And I lived naked in a filthy cave,
Sneering at skiers, all one awful winter;
Then condescended, and appeared in tails
At the Waldorf-Astoria,[3] where I excelled
In the dancing of the Dialecticians' Waltz
Before admiring matrons and their patrons.

Those days, I burned with a hard, gemlike phlegm,
And went up like Excelsior[4] in a huff
Of seven-veiled symbols and colored vowels.
Flying from the alone to the Alone,[5]
My name appeared on every manifest
O.
    *Everything, Bhikkhus, was on fire.*[6]
Things are so different now. My reformation,
Glittering o'er my fault.[7] . . . Anyhow,

1. "Variety," tr. by Malcolm Cowley, in "An Introduction to the Method of Leonardo da Vinci."
2. Ancient druidical chants of immense length. Also referred to, in some early writers, as "The Small End of the Egg of Wisdom."
3. An hotel in New York City.
4. A poem by Henry Wadsworth Longfellow.
5. Plotinus, in Stephen Mackenna's translation.
6. In the present tense in Buddha's Fire Sermon addressed to a thousand monks at Gaya Head in Magadha. See Henry Clarke Warren, "Buddhism in Translations" (Harvard, 1922), Ch. IV, Sec. 73. See also William Empson, "Poems" (London, 1935), and T. S. Eliot, "The Waste Land" (1922), Part III, "The Fire Sermon," ad fin. Bhikkhus = monks, or priests.
7. Shakespeare, "Henry IV Part One," 1.2.236.

It's very quiet here at Monsalvat.[8]
The kids are singing in the cupola,[9]
But quietly. The good old psychopomp
Who comes to give my shots is terribly kind:
Procurasin at night in massive doses,
Repentisol next morning when I wake.
An unpretentious life, with late quartets
Among the early frescoes, a few friars
Asleep in their coffins[10] off to one side,
Angels adoring[11] where the jet planes wailed.
Evenings, we all eat from the same Grail.

*Gin a body meet a body*[12]
*Under the boo*[13]
　　*Under the bo*
　　　　*Under the bodhi tree*
—All is illusion,[14] all is vanity[15]—
*Nobodhi there but me and me*[16]

Metaphysics at mealtime gets in my hair.[17]

8. The Grail Castle. Richard Wagner, "Parsifal," "Lohengrin." See also Nemerov, "The Melodramatists" (1949), pp. 155 & ff.

9. T. S. Eliot, "The Waste Land," line 202: "Et O ces voix d'enfants, chantant dans la coupole!" Mr. Eliot's note attributes the line to Verlaine, "Parsifal," but probably the sentiment, in one form or another, goes back to antiquity. Cf. Kafka, "The Castle," where K., telephoning for permission to enter the Castle, hears in the receiver "the hum of countless children's voices—but yet not a hum, the echo rather of voices singing at an infinite distance."

10. See James Joyce's celebrated story "The Dead," in "Dubliners."

11. Painting by Fra Angelico in the National Gallery, London.

12. Note the increased profundity of the Burns song in the new context.

13. Cf. T. S. Eliot, "Fragment of an Agon": "Under the bam / Under the boo / Under the bamboo tree."

14. The Buddha.

15. Ecclesiastes. The collocation of these two representatives of Eastern and Western tradition, here at the collapse of the poem, may not be an accident.

16. The Buddha achieved illumination and Buddhahood under the bo tree from the perception that all the forces of evil threatening him arose from within himself.

17. Wallace Stevens, "Les Plus Belles Pages": "Theology after breakfast sticks to the eye."

NOTES BY CYRIL LIMPKIN, M.A. (OXON.), FELLOW IN AMERICAN LITERATURE AT THE UNIVERSITY OF LAND'S END, ENGLAND.

Note on Notes. These notes have not the intention of offering a complete elucidation of the poem. Naturally, interpretations will differ from one reader to another, and even, perhaps, from one minute to the next. But because Modern Poetry is generally agreed to be a matter of the Intellect, and not the Feelings; because it is meant to be studied, and not merely read; and because it is valued, in the classroom, to the precise degree of its difficulty, poet and critic have agreed that these Notes will not merely adorn the Poem, but possibly supersede it altogether.

# METAMORPHOSES

*according to Steinberg*

These people, with their illegible diplomas,
Their passports to a landscape full of languages,
Carry their images on banners, or become
Porters of pedestals bearing their own
Statues, or hold up, with and against gravity,
The unbalanced scrollwork of their signatures.
Thumbprints somehow get to be sanderlings,
And the cats keep on appearing, with an air
Of looking at kings even as they claw
Their way up the latticed cage of a graph,
Balance with fish, confront photographers
In family groups, or prowl music paper
Behind the staves.
                              These in themselves, Master,
Are a great teaching. But more than for these
I am grateful for the lesson of the line,
That wandering divider of the world,
So casually able to do anything:
The extended clothesline that will carry trains,
For instance, or the lines of letters whose
Interstices vary the planes between
The far horizon and a very near nose.

The enchanted line, defying gravity and death,
Brings into being and destroys its world
Of marvelous exceptions that prove rules,
Where a hand is taken drawing its own hand,
A man with a pen laboriously sketches
Himself into existence; world of the lost
Characters amazed in their own images:
The woman elided with her rocking chair,
The person trapped behind his signature,
The man who has just crossed himself out.

# LION & HONEYCOMB

He didn't want to do it with skill,
He'd had enough of skill. If he never saw
Another villanelle, it would be too soon;
And the same went for sonnets. If it had been
Hard work learning to rime, it would be much
Harder learning not to. The time came
He had to ask himself, what did he want?
What did he want when he began
That idiot fiddling with the sounds of things?

He asked himself, poor moron, because he had
Nobody else to ask. The others went right on
Talking about form, talking about myth
And the (so help us) need for a modern idiom;
The verseballs among them kept counting syllables.

So there he was, this forty-year-old teen-ager
Dreaming preposterous mergers and divisions
Of vowels like water, consonants like rock
(While everybody kept discussing values
And the need for values), for words that would
Enter the silence and be there as a light.
So much coffee and so many cigarettes
Gone down the drain, gone up in smoke,
Just for the sake of getting something right
Once in a while, something that could stand
On its own flat feet to keep out windy time
And the worm, something that might simply be,
Not as the monument in the smoky rain
Grimly endures, but that would be
Only a moment's inviolable presence,
The moment before disaster, before the storm,
In its peculiar silence, an integer
Fixed in the middle of the fall of things,
Perfected and casual as to a child's eye
Soap bubbles are, and skipping stones.

# 4 Endor

Drama in One Act

*The action takes place during one night, at first before, and then within, the dwelling of the Witch of Endor. One imagines this to be as much cave as house, with a further recess, behind and above the fireplace, where the apparitions are seen.*

*Outside the house. Saul, alone.*

SAUL

How long it takes to learn a simple thing,
That when a man says absolutely, This
Thou shalt not, either to himself or others,
That is the thing he means to do, and will do
One day, as if to spite himself.

                        That has been true
Of my whole life.

                After the old man died,
Samuel, my father in the spirit, and was buried
In Ramah, and all Israel wept for him
Except myself, I knew and I refused to know
That the spirit was gone from my kingship,
And my ordination taken away, the mantle torn.
I knew, and I refused to know, and I forbade
Witchcraft and divination in the kingdom,
Decreeing death on any who would scry
The future, or go questioning among the dead
By means of their familiar spirits. This I did,
Not wanting to know, and hoping not to know,
What he would speak with that rusty tongue of his
That could make even my God bitter to me.
I thought to be secure of the rebuke
Of dream or prophecy, letting the future fall

278

Day upon day until I died, after a life
Which would not be a destiny.

       But now
God moves in darkness over against me, I feel it,
And like a man walking a strange road at night,
Sensing a fence before him, or a ditch,
I put my hand before my face, and grope and stumble
Where no obstacle is, but march in confidence
Over the river's edge. So to my shame
And in despair I have come secretly,
Not as a king, directed by ministers
Who snicker behind their sleeves because the king
Needs what the king forbids.

        This is the place,
And they are in there now, bargaining with the woman
To gain my peace, my terrible peace.

   (*He kneels, and beats with his fist on the ground.*)

Samuel, Samuel, cruel father, if you are
Under the world, hear me, speak, forgive
Saul who will be your obedient son, your king
In Israel.

             (*He rises.*)


   No, no, nothing. But yet
I know he listens there, and his skull wears still
The strict and secret smile of power which
Never forgives. Saul, Saul, you are a madman,
And sometimes in your heart you think that all,
Philistines, Israelites, and God himself,
Are gone, fled back and hidden away, so that you stand
On the world alone, stabbing at shadows.
Know, must you? What would you know? That you will die?
All men will die. That you will die tomorrow?
No, that's not it. You want to be at peace,
And get the old man's blessing from the deep
Sea of the grave. And as you have resolved,
Madman or not and King or not, so shall you do.

        (*He knocks at the door.*)

You in there! Have you the woman of Endor?

> (*The Witch of Endor comes forth, flanked*
> *rather menacingly by the Minister and the*
> *Commander.*)

THE WITCH

I've done nothing. I am an innocent woman,
I have no money. What do you mean to do to me?

SAUL

No harm. It is your help we are asking.
That discipline of yours among the dead,
Who tell you secrets, and with empty eyes
Peer into things to come. That is my need.

THE WITCH

I do not understand what you or these men mean.
I think you have mistaken me for someone else,
Or you have heard a scandal spread about me
(As happens to a woman all alone),
To make you think I have the second sight
Or power with the dead.

COMMANDER

                     Now that's enough.
We know about you, and there's no mistake.

MINISTER (*aside, to Saul*)

The woman is shy, my Lord, thinks we are the law,
And will admit to nothing. You shall do best,
I think, by kindness, not command; and remember,
If she should recognize you for the king,
We shall get nothing from her.

SAUL

                    Madam,
It's not for you to be afraid of us.
The powers you possess, which are well known,
Command more than respect. I am quick to say

I fear them. But I also need them, and
I am ready to pay you well for what you do.

THE WITCH

Supposing you are, that's still not good enough,
For if I had those "powers," as you call them,
I'd be a fool to show them off to strangers
Who may for all I know be spies. King Saul
Forbids this business to be practiced, and many
Who traded in the future and with spirits
Have died of his forbidding. Would you trap me?
But even so, I'm not the woman you believe me,
And have no talents that way. I am a widow,
I live quietly, there is no mystery about me.

SAUL

We have come here by night. My need is great.
What must I do to make you trust me?

COMMANDER

Since kindness will not do it,
Look, woman, at this sword, look hard at it.
Here is the immediate threat. Do you wish to die?

MINISTER

Now what will that accomplish? This is not
The situation for your soldierly bluster.

THE WITCH

It is a foolish threat. Suppose I were
The woman that you think me, would my death
Be any use to you? It's not that way
I fear you, any of you, for it comes to me
When I look hard at you three strong men
That I shall outlive some of you at least.

SAUL

What do you mean? You speak
As though of something certain. Tell me, then.

You cannot mean to say what you have said
And leave it at hints and guesses? What you tell
I will bear quietly, I swear it. And I swear
No hurt shall come to you, neither by law
Nor from the bitterness of all our hearts
If what you tell is doom.

> (*He kneels to her; the two courtiers turn away, half-*
> *smiling, in respect and scorn and shame.*)

THE WITCH

What word of power will you swear it by?

SAUL (*kneeling*)

By the Lord God of Israel, I swear there shall
No punishment happen to thee for this thing.

THE WITCH

A mighty word to take upon the tongue.
You are a strange man, possibly a foolish one.
I like your foolishness, and only for that
I will believe your word. Come in with me,
These others may remain behind.

> (*Saul and the Witch enter the house.*)

MINISTER

I am the king's first minister.
The position of personal servant to the great
Is a delicate one, requiring of a man
A keen sense not merely of where the bread is buttered,
The pot sweetened, or the fat in the fire,
But of the balance to be kept
Between his person and his office.
To serve the lusts of majesty, or its rage,
Or childish fear; to superintend
The concubine or the assassin
With equal secrecy and poise,
Is not a weakling's job. You need
To be a hypocrite, a sycophant, a pimp,

282

And, at the same time, absolutely loyal,
Utterly sincere. To be a king's servant
Is to have immense power, and know enough to know
That one will never use it where it matters.

COMMANDER

I am the commander of the king's guard,
And my profession is fidelity
Ending in death. My only power
Is the power of blind obedience.
I and my forces do not matter until disaster,
And then we do not matter. That is the meaning
Of spit and polish and golden breastplate,
The pomp and honor of parade, the armed
Solemnity at the king's riding out or at
His keeping court—that we shall be there at the end,
To demonstrate how men must meet the end.

MINISTER

So when King Saul drew me aside and said
"Find me a witch, a wizard, anyone
Who hears God, reads the future, traffics with the dead,"
I did as I was told. I did not remind him of his law
Forbidding people of that sort to practice
Their mortal arts in Israel, I simply said
"My Lord, there is such a one, a woman,
Living at Endor." Neither did he ask
Me how I knew. It is assumed between us
That I know what I must.

COMMANDER

I have been with King Saul for many years,
Since the establishing of the Kingdom,
Have been a faithful servant, have kept
(As we say in the forces) my mouth closed
And my bowels open—which is to say, I have endured
His sulks and rages, periods of baseless suspicion
And insane favoritism, and even—what was harder—
The concerts of effeminate music on the harp

To which in certain moods he is so partial.
Yet I have seen in him a good commander and my king.

MINISTER

You have been honored for it. So have I.
And in the fat times, it went easy. One might overlook
His temper, uncertainly swaying back and forth
Between an arrogance which made all things
Look possible, and melancholy so deep
He would not eat. One paid that price,
But in return one had a place, and not the lowest,
In something alive and likely to go on.
Tonight it is different.

COMMANDER

Tonight we may be near the end.
The armies of the Philistine, increased
With allies, and among them the young man David
(Who serves the King of Gath, for his own ends),
Lie in the camp at Shunem, while our force
Has occupied Gilboa. All the space between
Lies in the balance of tomorrow's battle.
I do not fear a fight, or the chance of death,
But this new desperation of the king's
Makes me uneasy. Why are we here
On this lonely hillside, consulting with a woman,
Ourselves and the king disguised?

MINISTER

It is as though the end already exists
Out there, blindly, in darkness, while we,
Like blind men, stumble toward it.
Trust me, I know the king, I know
His power has gone out of him, poor man.
Samuel destroyed him over Amalek,
When Saul refused to slaughter the survivors.
And since that time, before the old man died,
He secretly anointed the boy David,
Gave him the kingship under God, so that

Saul holds this realm only by personal force,
The blessing on him gone.

COMMANDER

                    I too have felt,
Having a professional sense for such things,
That I am on the wrong side. Nevertheless,
Morale must be kept up, and the king is wrong
To let even his trusted servants see
The fall of things hanging upon a woman's word.

MINISTER

I wonder what she can be telling him?
The future . . . does it already exist,
Waiting for us to come marching along
And fill its outlines with our flesh and blood?

COMMANDER

The soldier is not paid to think that way.

MINISTER

I know, the soldier is not paid to think.
And maybe no one knows how God
Creates tomorrow. What could He create it from?
Unless it's there already? Now, supposing
Tomorrow to be there, and knowledge possible,
Should a man want it? Have you asked yourself
Whether you would rather, all things considered,
Foreknow the future or go at it blind?

COMMANDER

Brother, that is a question
Only civilians ask. Blind, blind is better.
Where would obedience be, and discipline,
When once the end was guaranteed? If a good end,
No one would bother fighting, and that would turn it bad.
If bad to begin with, no one would bother fighting,
Since he might better die drunk and in bed on the same day.
No, let me be blind, if I'm to have a choice.

MINISTER

The question is, though, whether you and I
Will have a choice? Sometimes
A close association with the mighty
Requires that one suffer the inordinate pressures
That march with power; and then, although a man
Is but a man, with a life and a death, no more,
One must endure as though one had a destiny
In the direct glare of God's eye. How shall I,
Civilian as you say, face up to that?

COMMANDER

We in the service are not commanded to believe
That anyone foretells the future. It is
A superstition, and, besides, would be
Intolerable if it were not.

(*A cry of rage from Saul within.*)

The king calls out!
There is some danger!

MINISTER

From the woman? More likely
She has crossed him somehow, and got his temper up.
Still, let us look helpful.

COMMANDER

Come, quickly!

(*As the two courtiers enter, the curtains of the
forestage part disclosing the interior of the
Witch's dwelling: a small, shadowy room waveringly
illuminated by a fire at the back, yet giving a
dark impression of great depth; another room off
to one side.*)

SAUL (*to the Witch*)

God's thunder smite you for a liar and fraud,
And let me be the instrument! Have I none about me
But flatterers, deceivers by sweet words?

286

COMMANDER
My Lord!

MINISTER
Patience, Saul.

THE WITCH
Protect me, he is the king! I knew at once.
Remind him, gentlemen, that he swore an oath
No harm would come to me.

SAUL
Must I be taken in by fortune tellers' tricks?

MINISTER
My Lord, what has the woman done?

SAUL
She has mistaken me what I am.
For when I said to her the name of Samuel
She cries at once: The King! It is the King!

(*He imitates the woman's voice.*)

O sir, she says, no need to bring him up,
I see in the stars, I scry in the dark water,
I dreamed last night, I read in the cracked shell
Of a tortoise and from the guts of a frog. . . .
And whatnot else she babbled on, from fear,
All tending to establish endless life
And all good fortune to her kind King Saul,
Her merciful King Saul, whose mercy would
Surely protect her from a witch's death.
I say, she has misjudged me what I am!

MINISTER (*aside*)
We know that tone too well. And a king's rage
Must run its course. The end of it, for him,
Is black despair, he punishes himself.

287

SAUL

Ha ha! She feared to die for being a witch,
And the joke of it is that she shall die
For failing to be witch enough.

THE WITCH

                                        Your oath!
You swore upon the name of the living God.

MINISTER and COMMANDER

My Lord. My Lord.

SAUL

Beware. My business now is with the woman.
My dear, now that you know I am the king,
You must do what I ask, your mystery,
For nothing less will do. Deal honestly,
My oath protects you. Once more put me off
With prophecies of long life and success,
As flatterers do, as you have tried to do,
Your life pays for it.
                        It is the truth I want.

THE WITCH

And must the truth be always bitter, Saul?

SAUL

Already I suspect, and come to you
For visible certainties. It is not death
We fear, but going to
Forsaken actions, while God laughs in hiding.
Ends can be faced, but not the emptiness
Of ignorance, where folly tries conclusions
With what is already done. I say again,
Bring me up out of the grave the old wizard,
Samuel, I mean, the last judge in Israel.
Say that his king would question him. Say that.

COMMANDER

My Lord?

SAUL

Yes?

COMMANDER

If my Lord please, I have been a faithful servant,
And never one to put himself forward, either.
But now there is something I should like to say.

MINISTER

The military mind, faced with the dead,
Is getting embarrassed.

COMMANDER

That's not what I mean.

SAUL

You may speak.

COMMANDER

Consider a moment, my Lord, if it is good
To know what happens next. For once the dead
Shall rise and speak, are not our wills enthralled
Under the lips of dust? Better to doubt.
What can the dead say other than despair,
Since they know nothing else? No, better doubt,
And let tomorrow, like any other day,
Come as it will and go as it will. What are
The few more hours till our battle is drawn?
We should be resting, and readying ourselves,
Not seeking the speculations of a ghost.
Above all else, let us not start to fight
In the conviction of defeat.

SAUL

I see
You too believe we are to be defeated.

MINISTER

I'm sure my colleague does not entertain
That treasonable thought. He merely means,

289

My Lord, and he has reason on his side,
That the will to fight is delicate as a girl,
Who, once her first resistance weakens, comes near
Corrupting altogether. If the end
Inevitably must be thus and such, it might
Be well to live an hour or two more
Without the knowledge. Someone like myself,
Civilian to the core, may hear the truth
Or not, it hardly matters; but the soldier,
While this is going on, might best
Stand in the corner and stuff his fingers in his ears.

SAUL

You are eloquent. But I have lived that way
Too long. When Samuel turned away from me,
That bitter, unforgiving man of God,
I in my rage drove David from my side,
And wanted to destroy him. After that,
When Samuel died, the voice of God fell silent
Within me and around me, and my realm,
Wanting in metaphysical love and truth,
Shriveled inside, a kingdom dry as sand
Whose king was but a stone in the spirit's path
From the true father to the anointed son.
Thenceforth, not wanting to hear the Word of God,
I stoppered up the ways of access, dreams
And prophecies, and banned the necromancers.
And then, when I began to want again
The painful consolation of the truth,
My dreams were dumb, and divination failed.
So now I come, since the great gate is shut,
Round to the kitchen door, that the black art
And traffic in the filthy beds of death
May bring me to my difficult peace.
                                      Woman,
Begin your spells.

THE WITCH

Patience, my Lord. For all my preparations,

290

It's hard. They don't always want to come up,
And those that do come may not want to speak.
They're sullen, the old ones in the earth, sullen.
But I have the mastery of them in the end.

> (*She crouches before the fire. Her procedures
> consist in mutterings and croonings not intel-
> ligible to us, and in throwing powders and
> liquids from various bottles on the fire.
> This should not look awesome, or even very
> impressive; after all, it is only a sort
> of cookery.*)

MINISTER

It lowers one's opinion of the dead
To think they rise to a rigmarole like this.

SAUL

Be quiet.

> (*He is watching intently over the woman's shoulder;
> the others are somewhat withdrawn.*)

COMMANDER (*whispering*)

What can this bring us but regret?

MINISTER (*whispering*)

It's rather interesting, though, isn't it?

COMMANDER

It is horrible, it is revolting.

MINISTER

Come now, surely the soldier cannot shirk
Inspecting his professional results?

> (*The Witch gives a long, low cry.*)

SAUL

What have you seen?

THE WITCH

I see gods ascending out of the earth.
They go, they go, like bats behind the flame.
And now, look, it is an old man, his head
Is shrouded in a mantle.

(*Samuel appears.*)

SAUL (*thrusting her aside*)
It is Samuel.

(*He kneels at the fire.*)

Father and Judge, forgive. Have pity.

SAMUEL

Why have you disquieted me, to bring me up?

SAUL

The Philistines have come against me, and the Lord
Forsaken me, he answers me not by prophets
Nor comes to me in dreams. Father, I call to you
That you will tell me what thing I must do
To make whole the mantle of this land
You tore from me at Gilgal, when you killed
The King of Amalek. Father, I bow my head.
Yours is the power.

SAMUEL
The power is the Lord's.
I sleep in the dirt of the earth, you ask in vain,
Seeing that God has turned his face from you
And torn the kingdom from your hand, and given
The mantle of it to the shepherd David.
Out of your disobedience, Saul, it came,
Because you turned in the hand of power, because
You did not His vengeance and execution on Amalek,
Therefore the Lord has splintered you against a stone
And taken another instrument.

292

SAUL

What must I do?


SAMUEL

The time to do is gone; what you must suffer
Is what is already done. The Philistine
Already hangs your armor in the house
Of Ashtaroth, your body from the wall at Beth-shan.
Tomorrow you will be with me.

(*As the apparition fades on these words, Saul utters*
*a cry and falls fainting.*)


COMMANDER (*kneeling beside him*)
My Lord! Comfort, my Lord. Don't give way.
It was a trick of the fire that we saw,
The woman's voice we heard, seeming to come
From the angle of the wall, and our brains,
Troubled between fear and desire,
Perfected the illusion. Now, my Lord,
You can't believe in that, you can't believe
Tomorrow has already come and gone
In a kitchen fireplace.


SAUL

What does it matter
What I believe, what you believe? Tomorrow
Is like a town at the end of a long road
Across a desert country. First in mirages
Its towers and its walls appear, as if
In a dream, and tremble high above the ground
In a shaken air, but then, as we go on,
The real town too appears, and no less real
Although we think it another trick of the light.


COMMANDER
But he is gone, my Lord. Open your eyes.
The fire sputters there, nothing but fire.
It was illusion, or it was a dream.

MINISTER

And dreamed by all of us at once, and waking.

SAUL

I feel that I have slept. My legs are weak,
My head is heavy. Did you hear him speak?
You heard him speak. My body on the wall,
He said, down at Beth-shan. I should like to sleep
A little more. It is a weakness in me,
And I would sleep until it passes.

THE WITCH

If the king wishes to rest, there is a couch
In the further room.

COMMANDER

Come then, my Lord, get up.

　　　　　　　　　　Give me a hand (*to the Minister*),
Don't stand there dreaming. And you, my good woman,
Prepare what you have in the way of food and drink.
I'll stay with the king a while.

　　　　　　　　(*The Commander and the Minister help
　　　　　　　　　the king into the other room.*)

THE WITCH (*singing*)

Between the living and the dead,
Between the living and the dead
　　My traffic and my art.
　　The womb in the head,
　　The grave in the heart.
How time is born of time, the seed
Born of the tree, the tree of the seed.
They dream each other, the living and the dead,
In the grave of my heart, the womb of my head.

　　　　　　　　　　　　(*The Minister returns.*)

THE MINISTER

My colleague is staying there to guard the king.

294

This is the kind of emergency he finds
Acceptable, for he can deal with it,
Bring blankets and get food. It's curious
How much even of warfare is housekeeping.
Of course he has to stay and guard the king,
That is his job. And yet I should have thought
That if the king is destined to die tomorrow
He would be perfectly safe tonight. My dear,
You are a clever woman, or maybe a deep one,
I don't know which. How do you do these things?

>                  (*During the following conversation the Witch*
>                            *is preparing food and drink.*)

THE WITCH

I do nothing. And yet there is nothing
Which is not done.

MINISTER

                     Mystical talk.
I've never understood that kind of thing,
Nor greatly cared to. And I'm not pressing you for
Professional secrets. But isn't it rather odd?
The king will die tomorrow. Now we know
The king will die tomorrow, which means, I guess,
Defeat, confusion, all the baggage lost,
Some towns burnt down, the flocks and herds let stray
All over the place . . . and at the very least
The end of an order of existence which
I shall be sorry to see go. It is
An inconvenience, to put it no more strongly.
You think me, perhaps, unfeeling, but that's not so.
What is it possible to feel? We've had
The experience, but not the weight of it.
For here I am, and here you are, it is
As though nothing whatever had happened. That
May be the most uncanny thing of all,
That nothing, really, has happened.
Tell me the future. I suppose
That David will be King of Israel?

THE WITCH

    I do not know the future. Only, when I stare
Into the fire, I see strange images rising.
They mean nothing to me. My power is,
Such as it is, that others, who look with me
Into the flames, beyond the flames, can see
As I can see. But it's for them to say
If what they see is future or is past;
And what it means, if it means anything,
It means to them, never to me.

MINISTER

    Then stare with me into the fire, for I
Must have a fate also.

THE WITCH

                 Must you?

MINISTER

    I'm wondering if perhaps my fate will be
Desertion, and joining the Philistines
Before tomorrow's battle. That is the fate
.I should like to see about. Without wishing
To give offense, however, I may point out
How tactless it would be to mention that
Before the king. Let us agree, dear lady,
That I was only thinking aloud.

THE WITCH

                        I think
Men of your sort, though they have lives and deaths,
Never have fates. Maybe because they have
Their cleverness instead, their light, dry minds
Which blow in the wind of fortune back and forth,
They can have many meanings, no one meaning.

MINISTER

    I have heard that thought before. And it is true,
I've always been a great believer

In my own comfort first, and let the great storms,
That blow the great men down, find me in bed.
One has the temperament one's born with, though.
It happens that I'm not a king, it happens
That I never wanted to be a king, and so
We live as we may. And yet I have the courage
To stare into the fire, if you will.

THE WITCH

It is no matter to me.

> (*They crouch down before the fire, the Witch doing
> her work as before. Presently, behind the fire and
> above it, at a distance and in bright light, appear
> Saul and his Commander. They are armed and dressed
> in armor, and the king wears the crown.*)

SAUL

It is over, it is done, my power gone
As blood into the ground, where my blood soon
Must follow. Now the noise of battle is drawn
Northward, away, and now we stand alone
With nothing to command. The field is won
Against us. Let not the Philistine women
Who follow the armies, finding me alive,
Abuse and torture me before they kill me.
My mind is clear, I keep a high resolve,
With nothing left of kingship but its courage,
Which I shall not need long.
Therefore, your last service.

> (*Offers his sword.*)

Come, man,
I close my eyes, I wait, let it be done
What you are sworn to do, for this is the end
Of all, as Samuel foresaid.

COMMANDER (*takes the sword*)

Lord, I cannot.
My love, my loyalty, are to your life,

297

And not your death. This hand stiffens with fear
And will not move against the king its master.

SAUL

Come, the sword, the sword. How long must courage
Endure before it wins? I wait, the king
Waits on his servant. Kill me, quickly, and then
You may yourself, or else do what you like,
Live, if you like. Ah, faithless. Give me the sword.

COMMANDER

My Lord, I cannot.

SAUL (*takes the sword from him*)
                    Then I must do all
For myself alone. Whatever I have known,
Whatever I have been, the child, the man,
And all the sights my closing eyes have seen,
Meant but this moment only, and then
The weary, painful world shall be withdrawn
And be as a stone.

                    (*He falls on his sword.*)

                    It is over, it is done.
See, Samuel, my father, David more than my son,
I make an end of time.

COMMANDER

                    My Lord, I was unable.
I stood like a stone, no matter what I vowed,
I could not think the end, and could not act.
Forgive me, Lord.

SAUL

Kill . . . in the name of mercy, kill, the sword
Is like a fire in me, and I live,
The great pain I am skewered with
Will make me live. Be quick, kill.

COMMANDER (*drawing his own sword*)
Now my Lord forgive me, but I will. I must.

(*He stabs Saul.*)

It is done. But how suddenly he stares,
As though no man were there at all, no king.
He is at peace. But I? No, no, I cannot.
And if I missed, as he did, mortality
At the single stroke, who's here to do for me
What I have done for him, open the gate
And ease the passage? No, I cannot die.
Besides, with the king's death this disaster
Is finished. Those who remain, who wants their lives?
I shall live out my time peaceably, perhaps.
But to live, to live in shifting times like these,
A man must use whatever comes to hand.
Forgive this, master. Had we any hope,

(*He takes the crown.*)

Even of dying in battle, nobly, I
Would keep my place beside you. As things are,
I go to find King David, and to him
Tender my services, with your crown. I swear,
Dear Lord, I never thought it would be thus.
You dead men are well out of it, the living
Must do what their necessity demands.

(*The scene in the fireplace fades.*)

MINISTER
So. Military honor, in the end,
Is as careful of its precious skin as any
Dry clever mind in the world. Many thanks,
Dear lady, for the lesson, but don't you think,
If destiny depends on keeping faith,
He has as little right to one as I?
These clanking heroes lord it over us,
With their lantern jaws and tiny brains, year in,
Year out. We may not be so clever, they say,
But at least we shall know how to die. And then
They don't know how to die. Disgusting fools.

299

THE WITCH

Look once again into the fire. See!


MINISTER

I know him! It is the young man David, once
The favorite, whom Saul drove into exile.

> (*In the fire, as before. King David, with soldiers.*
> *Enter to him the Commander holding the crown.*)


DAVID

Who is this man? I know his face, it is
King Saul's Commander of the Guard.


COMMANDER (*kneels, holding forth the crown*)

My Lord, David, be King in Israel!


DAVID

You tell me thus that Saul is dead?


COMMANDER

                                            He is dead.


DAVID

You come to tell me this, and hope for favor?
How did he die?


COMMANDER

After the battle broke around us, and
Those who were able fled, King Saul and I
Stood on the Mount Gilboa among the dead.
He asked for his death at my hand, but I,
Sworn to it though I was, refused to strike,
For pity, for love, for fear. He took the sword
And fell against the point, but he could not
Rid himself of his life, nor had he strength
To strike himself again. He begged his death,
And because his pain was terrible to see,
Unwillingly I finished what he had begun.

DAVID

He was to me a father and a friend,
Though of an angry and unhappy nature.
Why were you not afraid to lift your hand
Against the Lord's Anointed? and to shed
That sacred blood?

COMMANDER

It was for pity, Lord.
He would have died of the wound, after much pain.
I did it out of love.

DAVID

The crown. You bring me that too out of love?

COMMANDER

My Lord, I could not leave it to be found
By the Philistine. Now it belongs to you.
I did my duty as I saw it, and
I hope I may find favor in your eyes.

DAVID

Give me the crown.

(*He puts on the crown.*)

Ah, my father and friend,
The beauty of Israel is slain
On her high places. How are the mighty fallen!
As for this man, soldier, stand over him          (*to a soldier*)
And strike him till he die.

COMMANDER

Lord, have mercy!

DAVID

His blood be on his head. For his own mouth
Has testified against him: I have slain
The Lord's Anointed.

(*Soldiers kill the Commander.*)

301

Ye mountains of Gilboa, let there be
Upon ye neither rain nor dew, for here
The shield of Saul is vilely cast away,
As though he had not been anointed with oil.
It comes to me that I shall make a psalm
To be a requiem, when the daughters of Israel
Shall weep for Saul. . . .
Daughters of Israel, weep over Saul
Who clothed you in scarlet, in ornaments of gold.
And who is slain in the high and lonely place.
How are the mighty fallen, and the weapons of war broken.

(*The scene in the fire fades.*)

MINISTER
So that is how it ended. Strange, and sad,
And dreamy, as though it were already
An old story. After all, the man of war
Died of the war. And that, to me, is justice.
He got what he deserved, though, don't you think?
And David's indifference was admirable,
I thought, though cold. These poets!
Real people scarcely exist for them.

(*The Witch shrugs, rises, not speaking, and begins
to set a table in the other corner.*)

I wish there had been something there for me,
Something to tell me what I ought to do,
What I will do. What shall I be doing
Tomorrow at this time? How queer that is:
It would not be what I *will* do, but what
I had already done.
                    Those two in there,
They are already dead, then. Don't you think
It may be just a trifle embarrassing,
For us, I mean? How does one speak to people
Whose bodies one has seen dead in a field?

THE WITCH
I did, of all that was demanded, all

302

I could. The images came and went, came
And went as they would. The fire is almost out.
It will do you no good, you'll find, to speak
To them of what you saw.

MINISTER

You're quite certain
You can't see anything to do with me?

THE WITCH

It would be a kindness, sir, for you to fetch
A few more sticks from outside, for the fire.
It's almost out.

MINISTER

I see, you'll tell me nothing.
All right, then. We must keep these dead men warm.

(*He goes out.*)

THE WITCH (*knocks at the door of the further room*)
If my Lord please, I have something to eat,
And some wine to settle the stomach after his
Experience.

(*She listens for a moment, then withdraws from the door.*)

It's no great trouble, if you have the gift,
Seeing the future. It comes as it comes, that's all.
But wanting to! I never understood
What made them want to. I have never asked
To see my future, and I never did.
Living in time has warmth and decency,
It's like a sheep-lined coat in a cold night.

(*Saul and the Commander enter from the other room.*)

SAUL

I have to die. I have to die tomorrow.
The understanding of it, that's not it.
But to have torn open the mercy of time
And seen a corpse in a pit. . . .

303

What is this flesh, that I should give it food
Or let it sleep? There will be time to sleep.

THE WITCH

My Lord, here are both meat and wine.
Let nature's comfort work as it will,
And as it must. The strength that carries us
Never believed in death, does not believe
In death, but wants what any child wants.

COMMANDER

The woman is right, my Lord. And think that now,
Knowing the worst that is given men to know,
The hour and occasion of their end,
You have the certainty all seek, the thing
That courage and constancy train us to meet.

> (*Saul lets himself be led to the table, but sits
> staring into the fire. The Minister enters with
> an armful of wood, with which the woman builds
> the fire up.*)

MINISTER

So cold the night! It must be nearly dawn.
We should be starting back.

SAUL

My body from the wall, he said, the wall
At Beth-shan. Look at me, all of you.
I am brave, I face it, I look it in the eye
As a king should. My body hanging there,
In chains? Even on hooks. Let it happen.
The skin dries in the sun, blackens and splits,
The birds eat through the eyes, into this mind
That thinks these thoughts, and the rain, the rain
Washes the wounds, the wind blows, and the sun
Shines on this thing, this bag of blood and bones
You tell me I must feed (as I would a horse,
To carry me over a cliff), this brute of power
That once pretended to be a child, a man,

A king; that went in to women, that fathered sons,
That lusted helpless in the heat of life,
That maddened at times, and cried easily at music—

COMMANDER

This feeds the feelings, Lord, you ought to starve.

THE WITCH

Drink the wine, good sir. Past help, past tears.
See if you don't feel better after a cup of wine.

(Saul drinks unwillingly at first. During what follows,
however, he and the others, without making a particular
point of it, apply more and more to the food and drink,
which they consume while talking.)

SAUL

Now I remember how at Havilah,
After the battle, Agag the King of Amalek
Said to me, Surely the bitterness of death
Is past? Poor man, he looked me in the eye
Bravely enough, but I could smell the fear,
I heard the tremor in the voice.
I would have spared,
Because one can be sick to death of death
When the fighting is over, and besides, what use
Would one more corpse have been? But Samuel,
Taking the knife in his own hand, slaughtered
The King of Amalek before the Lord,
Our God, whose mercy and lovingkindness on Israel
Demanded blood. How long ago that is!
And did my disobedience on that day,
My disobedience treasured up in God
So many years, bring me to Endor now?
To death tomorrow? Have I lived, then,
Narrowly in the spaces of a dream,
Where motion only seemed to move? Because
We read the story as the scroll unfolds,
We think the end unwritten yet.

305

COMMANDER

       My Lord,
What can men do with time? We all must die.
And what remains is now to face it nobly,
And in the soldier's manner. For remember,
No matter what we know, it is up to us
To set a good example to the men.

MINISTER

Aha!

COMMANDER

And what does that mean?

MINISTER

O, nothing, nothing whatever. I was thinking
Of something else.

SAUL

      You tell me all men die.
A noble sentiment, I drink to it.
But neither of you has heard, as I have heard,
The moment of the sentence in advance.

COMMANDER

Respectfully, sir, but you slight my honor.
The sentence falls on me as well as you,
For I am sworn to follow where you lead,
Even to the end.

MINISTER

     Now that simply is not so.

COMMANDER

You may be unaware how dangerous
That observation is. You will think twice
Before repeating it.

THE WITCH

                    I warned you, sir,
Against the speech you are about to speak.
There's malice in it, and some danger, too.

SAUL

What he knows, let him speak it now.

MINISTER

I must regret that I may not, like you,
Indulge myself in brilliant attitudes
About what is to come. Knowledge forbids it.
I make the statement of a simple fact.
The woman showed it to me in the flames,
And it is this:
The king will die tomorrow by your hand.

SAUL

Minister, you exceed your authority.
We do not think of you among the prophets.

MINISTER

Not only that, but you will fail to follow.
Beholding the king dead, a little thought,
A tiny thought, will come between you and
That loyalty which you regard so highly.
Briefly, you are to give the crown to David.

SAUL

Can this be true?

MINISTER

I saw it where you saw the ancient rise
To speak what you were better not to hear.

SAUL

Shall I believe this? Am I sitting here
At table, drinking wine and breaking bread
With a traitor and my executioner?

307

COMMANDER

My Lord, you know my character.

MINISTER

And I, you see, I know your destiny.
I'm sorry for you both. But there it is.

COMMANDER

You must know, Minister, that you have made
An intolerable accusation, one that stains
A long life's honor. It demands your blood.

(*He draws a knife.*)

MINISTER (*backing away*)
Please understand, it is no accusation.
I have only great respect for your courage,
And was surprised, I may say even shocked,
To see what it will come to in the end.

COMMANDER

My Lord, permit me to kill this person first—

MINISTER

Stop, stop, you haven't heard how the story ends.

COMMANDER

Permit me to kill this person first, I say,
And then, because I cannot live dishonored
And under the suspicion of my king,
I beg to be put to death, sir, at once, by you.

MINISTER

It's no use, don't you see. He cannot do it.

SAUL

Be careful of saying cannot to a king.

MINISTER

Great king, not I forbid, but destiny.

If you are fated to receive your death
At this man's hand tomorrow, how can he
Be suffered to die before necessity
Is through with him? No, you are, and he is,
Held for the moment in the will of heaven,
And neither one may act until the time.

SAUL

Suppose, Commander, that I killed you now?
Not, mind you, only for my own revenge,
But for the shattering of fate, in hope
To overthrow and break the will of heaven?
And, Minister, for your part, are you sure
The same divine will is protecting you?

MINISTER

No, master, killing me will alter nothing.
Yet there is one more thing, I'm sorry to say.
For David will accept the crown from you,
Then order your immediate death—and why?
Because you shed the sacred blood of Saul.

COMMANDER (*sits down*)
My death? My lord, what have I done to you?

SAUL

Why have you told us these things? You must know
Tale-bearers, never high in favor, are
Least so when all they have to tell is ill.

MINISTER

Duty forbids my holding back. Besides,
It was the woman's fault. She showed me all.

THE WITCH

O sir, do not believe him. It was he
Who begged me for a vision of his own.
He hoped to see the image of himself,
He said, deserting to the Philistine.

SAUL

Oh so? And did he see this heart's desire?

MINISTER

No, no, my lord. That was only a joke,
A momentary thought such as crosses the mind
Of a contemptible poor creature like myself.
The destinies within the flames were silent
Concerning me. I do not matter there.
My lord, I am contemptible, I admit it.
But do not kill me.

SAUL

Why should I spare you or the woman? She
With damnable art, you with damnable malice,
Compound together to destroy my courage.
It's treason, I believe neither of you.
Could you not leave the image of a king
To stand holy and high before his trial?

COMMANDER

You're right, my lord. These are subversive acts.
Let them confess and die as they deserve.

MINISTER (*kneeling*)

Great king, I will confess myself a man
Minded to envy and malice, one of those
Who in his heart believes the world to be
A cynical joke, or else an accident
Hung emptily between the sun and moon
That fools may scratch their heads until they die
Doubting, believing, while it answers nothing.
And I confess it was envy and malice
That made me speak, though the woman warned against.
My sort of man will always want to see
The holy and high mocked at and spat upon.
We'd shape life over in our clever image.
I am, also, a coward—

COMMANDER

    We'd make a man out of you, in the army.
    But now it seems there will be no more army.

SAUL

    Your reasoning is bringing you close to death.
    I trusted you, Minister, for many years.
    And now—

MINISTER

    My wits are not enough to save my life?
    But let me speak.

SAUL (*turning away for a moment*)
                      It wearies me, all this.
    I was forgetting that nothing matters. Speak.

MINISTER

    O no, great sir, believe
    That for yourself, and not for me, the world
    Grows great with the beauty of holiness,
    Completes itself in a majestic meaning,
    Though full of terror. What we knew tonight
    Declares God's mystery behind the world,
    Dividing the waters of time to show your passage.
    Declares that earthly triumph and defeat
    Fall short of the end—
                    O Saul, because you cared
    Even in loneliness and pride, the Lord
    Rebukes you but to take you to himself,
    And punishes only as the father does
    His child, in order to forgive. While I,
    Because I did not care, have been forever
    Excluded from the story of His will,
    Which some men play in, while the others watch.

SAUL

    Well said. But you will live, and I shall die.

311

MINISTER

I do not doubt that if it pleases you
You may destroy me now. Perhaps you will,
Because some cruelty has always been
Deep in your nature; cruelty and sorrow
Together made you turn against David.
But if you say it was the will of heaven
That made you as you are, may I not say
The same will made me trivial and clever,
Both of us members of one mystery?
We cowards have our kind of courage, King;
It never lets us keep our mouths shut.

COMMANDER

I have a better way, if the king will permit.

SAUL

What does it matter to me? Either all men,
Or some men, or none at all, are subject
To God's wisdom and love that move the world.
He may say I was cruel to David, and
It was for that I lost the kingdom; then
He might say I was kind to Amalek
And lost the kingdom for my kindness; either
Or both become inscrutable toward the end.
Say what you like, Commander. The king permits.

COMMANDER

Instead of slaying this civilian now,
Though he deserves it, offer him the chance
To take the field and fight with us today,
And learn at least how men comport themselves
In time of peril.

MINISTER

                Can one forget so soon?
But yes, agreed. I'll let you put a spear
Into my hand, or whatever it is you use,
And make my debut. I am curious to see

How destiny accomplishes itself
In spite of people.

COMMANDER

Under the circumstances,
I am willing to forget the minister's
Behavior. And if the king agrees,
Let's drink to it.

SAUL

Let it be as you say.

(*They drink.*)

I am pleased to put my anger off. More wine.

THE WITCH (*pouring wine*)
It is comforting to see you friends again.
It often takes people that way, you know,
People who come to me to see their future.
They squabble among themselves and blame each other.
It's all your fault, says one, and the other says,
Had you acted otherwise than as you did—
But there, I tell myself, is just the point:
No one acts otherwise than as he does,
What might have been is hidden in what is;
That may be why the future is so harsh.
For as a general rule, I find, no one
Who doesn't fear the future wants to know it.
And yet it's strange, how quickly they forget.

MINISTER
Forget? How can they simply cancel out
What they compelled their senses to receive?

COMMANDER
This one more drink, and that will be plenty.
We shall have much hard work to do today,
A little moderate drinking before a fight,
In my experience, does no harm; one must

Know where to stop, however. My Lord the King.

> (*He raises cup, drinks.*)

Now let us drink to courage.

> (*They all drink.*)

MINISTER
    No, it won't do. I'll drink to courage, but
    I haven't got it, not that kind at least.
    It's quite ridiculous. I try to see myself
    Staggering around the field, waving a sword
    And shouting. But I'm not that kind of creature.
    Even this little bit of wine, and I
    Begin to giggle at the thought. Great men,
    The Lord made you the way you are, heroes,
    For reasons of his own. He must have had
    Some splendid reason, too, for making me
    A clever, comfortable fellow. I'll stay home.

COMMANDER
    You're under orders now, my man. You'll march
    Wherever the others march, and do as you're told.

MINISTER
    I must obey.

> (*aside*)

> But I'll carry two shields and no spear.

SAUL (*at table, eating*)
    Excellent roast. You are a rare good cook.

THE WITCH
    One learns, my Lord, one learns. My husband, while
    He lived, cared specially about good food.
    And hospitality was his first rule.

> (*All eat; the scene slowly
> begins to lighten.*)

SAUL

You know, my dear, I could have been content
To live as you do here, far from the noise
Of kingdoms and the world's contentions.
I never wanted to be a king, you know,
But came to it only by accident.
I was a farm boy, and my father sent me
After some half a dozen mules that strayed.
I went to get advice of the old man of God,
A man named Samuel, which way I should go.
And this old man—strange as a dream it is,
Just to remember—set me in the place
Of honor at his table, and put before me
The shoulder of the roast, as you have done,
Next day, in the holy place of his house,
Anointed me with oil. I was a frightened
Young fellow in those days, I hid myself
Among the baggage when the tribes assembled,
Until they found me, brought me forth, and all
The people shouted and said God save the king. . . .
Gentlemen, I've come a long road since then.


COMMANDER

My Lord, the sky is starting to light up,
The night is over, we must hasten on.


SAUL

Yes, I mustn't sit reminiscing here
While great concerns are waiting on our presence.


MINISTER (*aside*)

Praise to the Lord, the Holy One of Israel,
Who with the morning brings renewal of illusion.


SAUL

I've just remembered an old song we sang
About a man named Lamech—
        If Cain shall be avenged sevenfold,


315

Truly Lamech seventy and sevenfold—
That's how it goes. We sang it on the march.
The funny thing is, nobody ever knew
Who Lamech was, or what he did. And now
It reminds me how the women used to sing,
Dancing to music before the city gates—
Saul hath slain his thousands
And David his ten thousands.
It made me angry then, but now—no matter.
What's gone was sometimes happy, but it's gone.
And maybe I shall slay ten thousand yet.
Come, gentlemen.
And you, my dear, our thanks for what you've done.
You have been royally hospitable.

(He kisses the Witch<br>
affectionately.)

THE WITCH

Farewell, King Saul. But there is one thing more;
It's customary for some small contribution,
A token payment. . . .

SAUL

Minister, pay this woman. Be generous,
But reasonable. We'll wait for you out there.

COMMANDER

And don't imagine you can stop behind.

(Saul and the Commander leave.)

MINISTER (giving money)

They have forgotten! And they are going forth
As blind men, fateless. What was in the wine?

THE WITCH

How can you say so, sir? You drank the wine.
But in a sense, as it is written, they drink
The wine of the condemned in the house of their God.

316

MINISTER

It's true, I drank the wine, yet I remember.
The house of God, you mean, is everywhere
With those men who would have it so, while I
Must blunder through the battlefield with my
Absurd and heavy knowledge of the end.
Who would believe me? Knowing, and not believing,
A burden I must try to carry quietly.

*(He goes out.)*
*(Saul and the Commander are heard singing*
*several times, their voices growing more*
*distant:*
If Cain shall be avenged sevenfold
Truly Lamech seventy and sevenfold.)

THE WITCH

The fire dies in daylight now, and men
Wake from their dreams into the mercy of time.

# 5 Cain

*A field at the edge of a forest. Two altars, or fireplaces anyhow,*
*one blackened and smoking, the other clean stone. To the second*
*altar, enter Cain carrying vegetables.*

CAIN

    The corn is coming along,
    Tomatoes ripening up nicely, in a week
    There should be melons. The apples
    Are still green, but, then, after what happened
    It might be as well if apples were not mentioned.
    There is a good deal I don't understand
    About that story, often as I've heard it told.
    Mother doesn't like to discuss it, of course,
    And I suspect that Adam my father
    Is not entirely clear himself as to what happened,
    Though he wears a very wise expression.

                                          (*Enter Abel.*)

ABEL

    Well! My sacrifices accepted for the day, I see.
    And nothing more to be done for the moment.
    Not bad. But you, brother,
    I don't see any flames at your offering.
    It's blood and meat the Lord likes,
    Charred on the outside, red and juicy inside;
    There's something unmanly about vegetables,
    I always say. That's probably your trouble.

CAIN

    Go on, amuse yourself at my expense,
    I guess you have the right, for certainly
    God favors your offerings of meat,
    And leaves my vegetables alone. He leaves

The flowers too, that I bring
Because they are lovely, a something extra
To ornament the altar, and do Him honor
—These lilies that are blooming now.

ABEL (*laughing*)

You can't imagine the mighty God of All
Eating a lily! What God wants
Is strength. Strong men want strong meat.

CAIN

If He made All, He made the lilies too.
And He can't be like a man.

ABEL

I'm not arguing, I'm telling you,
It's simply a matter of fact.
The Lord has put His blessing on blood and meat.
Therefore He prefers me before you,
And I prosper greatly, and sit on the hillside
Watching my flocks, while you
Sweat in your vegetable patch.

CAIN

You have to kill those poor little lambs.

ABEL

Well, it's a man's work anyhow.

CAIN

It's horrible. I've heard them bleat
Before you cut the throat, and I've seen
The fear dumb in their eyes. What must it be like,
I wonder, to die?

ABEL

We can't tell, till one of us does.
I expect you'll be the first.

CAIN

Me? Why me?

ABEL

It's perfectly simple. Death is a punishment.
In dying we are punished for our sin.

CAIN

*Our* sin? I haven't sinned. What have I done?

ABEL

We have all sinned, and all will die.
But God's not respecting your offerings
Is a sign that you will be the first.

CAIN

You sound rather pleased about it.

ABEL

Do you suppose I want to be the first?
No, I am essentially a conservative person.
And I can see, looking at my lambs,
That dying's a grim business. I'm in no hurry.
It's only fit that you go first—you were born first.
Vegetarian!

CAIN

I don't understand. What have I done
That was wrong, or you that was right?
Father and Mother began the fault,
I know the story as well as you do.

ABEL

You don't accept life as it is, that's your trouble.
Things are the way they are, that's all.
They've been that way from the beginning.

CAIN

Which isn't so very long ago.

ABEL

And they will always be as they are.
Accept it, Cain. Face up to reality.

CAIN

That's easy for a winner to say.

(*Enter Adam and Eve.*)

CAIN and ABEL
Father! Mother!

(*They bow their heads.*)

ADAM

That's right, respect. It's a proper respect
As from the children to the parents
That keeps the world going round. It's a fine day,
And life is what you make it, isn't that so?
And both boys working hard, yes, that's right.
"In the sweat of thy face shalt thou eat thy bread"
Is what He said to me, but it's not so bad
When the children sweat for the father's bread.

(*He picks a tomato from Cain's
altar and eats it.*)

CAIN

Father, that is my offering to the Lord.

ADAM

Don't worry. I won't eat it all. Anyhow,
The Lord seems to prefer the flesh and fat
That Abel provides. I must say
That I agree. I'm eating this
Only to stave off hunger till mealtime.
Abel, I smell roast lamb. Good!

ABEL

Yes, the Lord God has received the essence,
And we may eat whatever is left over.

CAIN

It seems to me that everything is left except the smoke.

ABEL

Don't talk of what you don't understand.

ADAM

It is obvious, Cain, that you don't know
The first principle of sacrifice. It is
The divine effluvium of the beast that rises
To God in heaven, and does Him honor.
A spiritual essence Himself, He feeds on spirit.
The grosser parts are the leftovers of His meal,
Which we may eat, if we do so with humble hearts.

EVE

Why doesn't He eat the divine effluvium
Of Cain's vegetables?

ABEL

                     Whoever heard
Of burning vegetables? Our God
Is an eater of meat, meat, meat.

ADAM

Mother, don't mix in the relations of man with God.
Remember what happened last time.

*(There is a silence.)*

EVE

It wasn't my fault. It was only a mistake.

ADAM

A mistake to end all mistakes.

EVE

You listened to me, wise as you are.

ADAM

    It proves the wisdom of my not doing so again.
    He for God alone, and she for God in him;
    Remember that, and there won't be any trouble.

CAIN

    Sir, what really did happen last time,
    I mean in the Garden?

ABEL

    What's past is past. Cain still believes
    There's something that he doesn't understand,
    Or that you haven't told us, which would make
    Some difference to his situation.

EVE (*to Cain*)

    My poor boy, my poor, dear boy, I too
    Go over it and over it in my mind, I too,
    Though what I did is said to be so dreadful,
    Feel that the Lord's way with me
    Was very arbitrary, to say the least.

ADAM

    Woman, enough. You'll make us more trouble.

ABEL

    And as for Cain, he should have the tact
    Not to pursue a subject which so evidently
    Causes his mother pain.

                                      (*to Cain*)

                  Also, our food is ready.
  You may do as you please about that slop of yours,
  But *this family* is going to eat.

        (*Cain sits to one side, the rest to the other. Cain starts
                        eating a tomato.*)

ADAM

Not, however, before properly rendering thanks
To the Most High. Cain, have the decency
To control your appetite until Abel
Has sanctified our meal with prayer. Abel.

ABEL

Permit us, O Lord, this tender beast
Slain in Thy Holy Name, Amen.

(*All eat.*)

ADAM

Mm, good.

CAIN

Won't you let me have some? It smells good,
And I would give you all this fruit.

ADAM

Dear boy, don't let us go all over this again.
It's not that we don't care for you personally,
But we simply cannot afford to offend the Lord.
If He does not respect your offering, Cain,
It would be presumptuous in us to do so.
If He means to separate you by this sign,
We must not disobey.

ABEL

To each according to his labor, you know.

CAIN

But I haven't done anything wrong—
As far as I'm aware, that is.

ADAM

As far as you're aware, or we. Who knows
The hidden meaning of God's mysteries?
By the sign you are set off, and that's enough.

ABEL

    I'd set him further off. Suppose that God
    In His displeasure should strike Cain
    With fire from Heaven? I know that God
    Can do whatever He will, but still
    If we sit this close there might just be an accident.

CAIN (*moving a bit further away*)

    I don't want to be a danger to you, you all
    Seem to understand things so much better than I do.
    But what have I done wrong? Answer me that.

ADAM

    Ah, as to that, you would have to ask Him.

                            (*He points upward.*)

CAIN

    Did He really speak to you, Himself—then?

ADAM

    He did indeed, yes. Your father has spoken with God.

CAIN

    What does He look like?

ADAM

    Oh, you don't really see Him, you know,
    He doesn't have a form. There was a Voice.

EVE (*covering her ears*)

    Don't. Don't remind me. That Voice!

ADAM

    Mother, have more respect. We are talking
    Of divine things. Besides, who was responsible
    For His talking to us in that voice,
    And saying what He said? Remember that,
    Consider your sin, be quiet.

ABEL

    Cain thinks, because he is a gardener,
    That he would have been at home in a Garden.
    It's illogical, Cain, to suppose
    The Garden of the Lord would be anything like yours.

CAIN

    Illogical, yes. Yet if I reason it out,
    It does appear that God did once favor gardens,
    Since, after all, He put our parents there.
    And if I ask myself why He has turned against
    Garden and gardener, I will have to answer
    That what our parents did while they were there
    Was the thing that changed His mind.

ADAM

    I will not have blasphemy, Cain,
    And particularly not while we are at meat.
    As for disrespect for your father,
    I will not have that at any time. After all,
    Your mother went through much suffering
    To bring you into the world, while I
    Labored to give you food and all good things.
    For you to reward us with ingratitude
    Proves to my mind, a hidden fault in you,
    And sufficiently explains why the All-Wise
    Does not respect your offerings as Abel's;
    Some wickedness, my boy, which is bringing you to sin.

EVE

    But truly, father, it was our fault.
    It was my fault first, then it was yours.

ADAM

    We may have made an error of judgment.
    Does Cain suppose he could have done better?
    We tried our best to give you boys
    A decent life and bring you up to be honest,
    Industrious, pleasing in the sight of the Lord.

As a matter of fact, I am convinced
It was a piece of luck to have got out of that garden.
It was no place to bring up children in.
You would have had everything provided for you,
No need to learn the manly virtues,
The dignity of toil, the courage of independence.
No, Cain, hard work never hurt anybody.
What happened to us was the will of God,
Which shows He did not mean us to sit around
On our behinds in a garden all our lives,
But to get out in the world and become
The masters of it.

ABEL

                    Inventors of the knife,
The wheel, the bow.

ADAM

Sometimes I could bless that serpent!

EVE

Stop! What dreadful things you are saying.
Shame, labor, and the pains of birth
The woman knows. Those are the fruits
That grew on the forbidden tree, and I,
The first to sin, was the first to know them.
I shall be the first to know death also.

ADAM

Mother, don't excite yourself. What's done is done.
As for death, no need to talk of that, I hope,
For many years.

ABEL

The little lambs are peaceful after death,
Mother. There's only a moment of fright,
And then it's over.

CAIN

But there's that moment, that small moment.
A man might do anything, if he thought enough
How there's no way out but through that moment.
He might become wild, and run away,
Knowing there was nowhere to run, he might . . .

ABEL

Might what?

CAIN

Kill.

ABEL

He might leave off babbling in that manner,
And remember he is a man, if not a very good one.

CAIN

But if a man, even if not a very good one,
Is turned away by his God, what does he do?
Where does he go? What could he do
Worse than what is already done to him?
For there is God on the one hand,
And all the world on the other, and this man
Between them. Why should he care,
Seeing he cannot save himself?

ADAM

These are dangerous thoughts, Cain.
That man might better think
Wherein he has offended.

> (*The sky darkens. Thunder is heard, and*
> *lightning seen.*)

ABEL

Aha! he's done it now, with his talk.
Did you think He would not have heard?
Did you consider the rest of us?

328

CAIN

    I only meant to ask.

ABEL

    You are being answered.

> (*He points to the sky.*)

ADAM

    I am afraid, Cain, that Abel is right.
    I have faced up to God one time in my life,
    It was enough. The coming storm
    You brought down on yourself, and you must face
    The consequences. I am sorry for you.
    Eve, come. Come, Abel. We shall seek shelter elsewhere.

> (*They leave, and Cain stands alone. Lightning
> flashes, sounds of thunder, then a stillness.*)

CAIN

    Ah, they are right. I am going to die,
    And I deserve to die. As Abel said,
    There is no argument, the uneasy fear
    I feel in my stomach tells me I am wrong,
    Am guilty of everything, everything,
    Though I cannot say what it is. Lord!
    Lord God! Master! I am a wicked man,
    The thoughts of my heart are wicked
    And I don't know why. Punish me, Lord,
    Punish me, but do not let me die.

> (*Cain kneels.*)

THE VOICE OF GOD in silence
    Cain.
        Cain.
            Cain.

CAIN

    Here I am.

GOD

   What do you want?

CAIN

   I want to know.

GOD

   Ask.

CAIN

   Why do You respect my brother's offerings and not mine?

GOD

   That is not the question you want to ask.

CAIN

   Why do You prefer Abel to me?

GOD

   That again is not it. You must ask to the end.

                           (*A long silence.*)

CAIN

   Why are things as they are?

GOD

   I will debate it with you. Do you know
   That things are as they are?

CAIN

   But—but they *are*, they just *are*. Besides,
   My father says they are.

GOD

   Cain, I am your father.

CAIN

   Sir, as you say.

GOD

Do you want things to be other than as they are?

CAIN

I want my offering to be acceptable, Sir.
I want my offering to be preferred over Abel's.
I want to be respected, even as he is now.

GOD

Why do you trouble yourself about it, then?
The thing is easy. If you do well,
Will you not be accepted? And if you do not do well,
Look, sin lies at the door.

CAIN

Sir, I do not understand.

GOD

Cain, Cain, I am trying to tell you.
All things can be done, you must only
Do what you will. Things are as they are
Until you decide to change them,
But do not be surprised if afterward
Things are as they are again. What is to stop you
From ruling over Abel?

*(again, after a silence)*

CAIN

I do not know.

*(Thunder.)*

I do not know. I said I do not know.
He is not there and I am alone.

*(The sky clears, the light grows stronger.)*

And this is Abel's knife, which he left here
In his hurry to escape the storm he hoped would slay me.
And that storm was God.

331

And this is the knife which cuts the throats
Of acceptable sacrifices.

(*Enter Abel.*)

ABEL

You're still alive. Surely the ways of the Lord
Are past understanding. Have you seen my knife?

CAIN (*still kneeling*)
I have it here.

ABEL

Throw it to me then. I'm still uneasy
About coming close to you.

CAIN

I have spoken with God, Abel. If you want your knife,
Come over here and have it. God said things,
Abel, such as I never heard from you. He told me
About the will. Do what you will, He said.
And more than that, He said: You must
Do what you will. Abel, do you understand
That saying?

ABEL (*approaching*)
The knife, I want the knife.

CAIN

Here, then.

(*He rises, stabbing Abel, who falls.*)

My sacrifices shall be acceptable.

ABEL

My God, what have you done?

(*He dies.*)

CAIN (*standing over him*)
I have done what I willed. I have changed

The way things are, and the first man's death is done.
It was not much, I have seen some of his lambs
Die harder.

GOD (*speaking casually, conversationally, without thunder*)
Do you find it good, what you've done? Or bad?

CAIN (*as though talking to himself*)
Good? Bad? It was my will that I did.
I do not know anything of good or bad.

GOD
Do you find that you have changed
Things as they are?

CAIN (*staring at Abel*)
There is this difference, certainly.
And I have changed inside myself. I see now
That a man may be the master here.

GOD
Like that man on the ground?

CAIN
A man. Myself.

GOD
How peaceful he is, lying there.

CAIN          ·
That's true, I feel uneasy, myself.
Abel, what have you to say to me now?
Well, speak up.

GOD
He will not speak.

CAIN
He is very quiet now, considering

How much he used to talk. How lonely
Everything has become! Mother! Father!

(*He shouts.*)

GOD

They will do to you as you have done to him.

CAIN

Then I must run away.

GOD

Where will you run?

CAIN

Anywhere, to be alone.
There are no other people.

GOD

You're wrong about that. Everywhere
Men are beginning, and everywhere they believe
Themselves to be alone, and everywhere
They are making the discovery of the conditions
Under which they are as they are. One of these
Discoveries has just been made, by you.
You will be alone, but alone among many,
Alone in every crowd.

CAIN

Seeing me set apart, they will kill me.

GOD

They would. But I have set my sign
Upon your forehead, that recognizing you,
Men will be afeared. Shunning you, scorning you,
Blaming you, they may not kill you.

CAIN (*kneeling*)
Lord God! You spoke, and I did not know.

334

GOD

I send you away, Cain. You are one
Of my holy ones, discoverer of limits,
Your name is the name of one of the ways,
And you must bear it. You must bear
The everlasting fear no one can stop,
The everlasting life you do not want,
The smell of blood forever on your hand.
You are the discoverer of power, and you
Shall be honored among men that curse you,
And honored even in the moment of the curse.
From your discovery shall proceed
Great cities of men, and well defended,
And these men, your descendants, shall make
Weapons of war, and instruments of music,
Being drawn thereto by the nature of power;
But they will not be happy, and they will not know
Peace or any release from fear.

CAIN

May I not die?

GOD

Because of My sign, only you
May destroy yourself. And because of your fear,
You won't. For you have found
An idea of Me somewhat dangerous to consider,
And mankind will, I believe, honor your name
As one who has faced things as they are,
And changed them, and found them still the same.

CAIN

If I were sorry, would you raise Abel up?

GOD

No.

CAIN

Then I am not sorry. Because You have saved me

335

From everything but the necessity of being me,
I say it is Your fault. None of this need have happened.
And even my mother's temptation by the serpent in the Gar-
den
Would not have happened but for You; I see now,
Having chosen myself, what her choice must have been.

GOD

Cain, I will tell you a secret.

CAIN

I am listening.

GOD

I was the serpent in the Garden.

CAIN

I can believe that, but nobody else will.
I see it so well, that You are the master of the will
That works two ways at once, whose action
Is its own punishment, the cause
That is its own result. It will be pain to me
To reject You, but I do it, in Your own world,
Where everything that is will speak of You,
And I will be deaf.

GOD

You do not reject Me. You cannot.

CAIN

I do not expect it to be easy.

(*after a silence*)

I said: I do not expect it to be easy.
But He is gone, I feel His absence.
As, after the storm's black accent,
The light grows wide and distinct again,
So He is gone. Of all He said to me,

Only one thing remains. I send you away,
He said: Cain, I send you away.
But where is *Away?* Is it where Abel is,
My brother, as lonely and still as that?

(*Enter Adam and Eve; Cain turns away his face.*)

ADAM (*at a distance*)
Was it the thunder, Abel, the lightning?

(*Coming closer, he sees that Abel is on the ground.*)

It can't be. There has been a mistake.

EVE
Abel, my son, my lamb.

(*She runs to the corpse and throws herself down.*)

ADAM
Monster! Unnatural child! Did you do this?
Lord God, let it not go unpunished,
Let it be swiftly visited.

CAIN (*still turned away*)
Suppose it was God that struck Abel down?
Cannot the Lord do as He will do?

ADAM
Liar! I will never believe it, never.

CAIN
Well, then, it was a lie. I did it.
But had it been the other way, and I
The brother lying there, would you not have said,
As I have heard you say so many times,
What the Lord does is well done?

ADAM
Vicious boy! Have you not done enough?
Would you go on to stand against your father?

EVE

Leave off, leave off. One son and the other son,
All that I had, all that I cared to have,
One son and the other son, and from the beginning
This was the end I carried, the end we lay together
Taking our pleasure for, is now accomplished.

CAIN

I stand, it seems, alone. Neither against
Nor for father or mother or anything.

ADAM

If the Lord God will not punish, I must.

EVE

Leave off, leave off. All that we had
Is halved, and you would destroy the other half?
Abel my son and Cain my son. Old man,
It is your seed that from the beginning
Was set at odds. You ate the fruit
Of the tree of knowledge as well as I,
And sickened of it as well as I, and swelled with lust
As I swelled with the fruit of lust,
And have you yet no knowledge?

ADAM

Woman, be quiet. This is not woman's work.

EVE

Oh, fool, what else if not woman's work?
The fruit of the curse has ripened till it fell,
Can you refuse to swallow it? But you will swallow it,
I tell you, stone and all, one son and the other son.

ADAM

Cain, I am an old man, but it comes to me
That I must do to you as you did to your brother.

EVE

Fooled in the Garden, and fooled out of it!

CAIN (*turning his face to Adam, who falls back*)

Sir, you will do nothing. I am young and strong,
And I have the knife—but no, that's not it,
I do not want to stand against you, but I must.

ADAM

There is a sign, a wound, there on your brow
Between the eyes. Cain, I am afraid of you.
There is a terror written on your face.

CAIN

And I am afraid of you. That is my fear
You see written upon me, that your fear answers to.
I am forbidden to be sorry for what I did,
Forbidden to pity you, forbidden to kiss
My mother's tears, and everywhere
In everything forbidden. I feel myself filled
With this enormous power that I do not want,
This force that tells me I am to go,
To go on, always to go on, to go away
And see you both, and this place, never again.

EVE

My son, my only one, you won't go away?
I'll face the fear I see upon your face,
And you'll comfort me for what you did to me.

ADAM

And stay me in my age? Cain, I accept it,
Though I shall never understand it, this
That you have done, this final thing
In a world where nothing seemed to end,
Is somehow the Lord God's doing. I fear you,
My son, but I will learn to still my fear,
If you will stay.

CAIN

    No. I would change things if I could.
I tried to change things once, and the change
Is as you see; we cannot change things back,
Which may be the only change worth having,
So the future must be full of fear, which I
Would spare you. If this is riddling talk,
Let it go by; or, to speak plainly,
I am afraid my fear would make me kill you
If I stayed here.

EVE

                  This is the end
That we began with. Why should we not
Curse God and die?

ADAM

    Woman, be careful.

EVE

    I have been careful, full of care.
My son, my darling, why not kill us both?
It would be only what we did to you;
And that was only what was done to us.

CAIN

    Mother, Mother, I must not hear you.
You and I, we understand things alike,
And that is curse enough, maybe. But he
May have his own curse, which we
Don't understand, that is, to go on,
Into the darkness, into the light,
Having the courage not to know
That what I do to him is what he does to me,
And both of us compelled, or maybe
It is a blessing, the blindness of too much light
That comes from staring at the sun.
                           Father,
I'd bless you if I could, but I suspect

That God believes in you.
And now farewell,
If that is possible; try not to remember me.

> (*Cain goes. The scene begins to darken.*)

ADAM

Old woman, we are alone again, and the night
Beginning to come down. Do you remember
The first night outside the Garden?

EVE

We slept in the cold sparkle of the angel's sword,
Having cried ourselves asleep.

ADAM

If we went back, do you think, and stood
At the gate, and said plainly, kill us
Or take us back, do you think . . . ?

EVE

No.

ADAM

You're right, we couldn't any more go back
Than you could be my rib again, in my first sleep.
The water in the rivers running out of Eden,
Where must that water be now, do you think?

EVE

It must be elsewhere, somewhere in the world;
And yet I know those rivers glitter with water still.
Abel my son and my son Cain, all that we had is gone.
Old as we are, we come to the beginning again.

ADAM

Doing as we would, and doing as we must. . . .
The darkness is so lonely, lonelier now
Than on the first night, even, out of Eden.
Having what we've had, and knowing what we know. . . .

341

EVE

    What have we had, and what do we know?
    The years are flickering as a dream, in which
    Our sons are grown and gone away. Husband,
    Take courage, come to my arms, husband and lord.
    It is the beginning of everything.

ADAM

    Must we take the terrible night into ourselves
    And make the morning of it? Again?
    Old woman, girl, bride of the first sleep,
    In pleasure and in bitterness all ways
    I love you till it come death or daylight.

# THE BLUE SWALLOWS (1967)

*To Margaret*

# 1 Legends

THE FIRST DAY

Below the ten thousand billionth of a centimeter
Length ceases to exist. Beyond three billion light years
The nebulae would have to exceed the speed of light
In order to be, which is impossible: no universe.
The long and short of it seems to be that thought
Can make itself unthinkable, and that measurement
Of reach enough and scrupulosity will find its home
In the incommensurable. We shall not, nonetheless,
Admit to our discourse a Final Cause, but only
Groucho Marx, who said, "Closer? Any closer, lady,
And I'll be standing behind you." Now we're in the movies,
It may be said that within limits the Creation is
A going concern, imaginable because the film supplies
An image, a thin but absolute membrane whose surfaces
Divide the darkness from the light while at the same time
Uniting light and darkness, and whose linear motion,
Divided into frames, or moments, is at the same time
Continuous with itself and may be made to pace itself
Indistinguishably from the pace of time; being also
Able to be repeated, speeded up, slowed down, stopped,
And even run backwards, its model represents to us
Memory, concentration, causal sequence, analysis,
Time's irreversibility together with our doubt of this,
And a host of notions that from time long out of mind
Belong to the mind. That was the first day, and in that day
Of pure distinction, movies were without color, without sound.
Much later, words began to issue from the silence, and
The single light broke into spectral iridescence;
Meanwhile, in black and white and meddling into gray
Results, the Fall already is recorded on the film.
For "nothing in the universe can travel at the speed
Of light," they say, forgetful of the shadow's speed.

## CREATION OF ANGUISH

Whatever sleeping in the world awakes,
We are the ones who to become ourselves
Awaken it, we are the ones who reach
Forever further, where the forest and the sky
And the incessantly restless sea invite
The voice that tells them fables of themselves
Till they shall make antiphonal response,
Confirming or else violently denying:
The hurricane's correction, or the fire
At night that scribbles out a city state.

Great pain was in the world before we came.
The shriek had learned to answer to the claw
Before we came; the gasp, the sigh, the groan,
Did not need our invention. But all these
Immediacies refused to signify
Till in the morning of the mental sun
One moment shuddered under stress and broke
Irreparably into before and after,
Inventing patience, panic, doubt, despair,
And with a single thrust producing thought
Beyond the possible, building the vaults
Of debt and the high citadels of guilt,
The segregating walls of obligation,
All that imposing masonry of time
Secretly rooted at the earth's cracked hearth,
In the Vishnu schist and the Bright Angel shale,
But up aspiring past the visible sky.
So was the raw material of pain
First metamorphosed, by the human touch,
Into significance, whence every man
And every woman, every child, becomes
Communicant: Shall I get better, or die?
Will they bring the electrodes soon again?
No, tell me what you really think of me.
Hence from nose-picking to the Crucifixion

One terrible continuum extends
Binding disaster to discovery.

And so the dog first entered in the door,
Whining and cringing, till we learned from him
Something of sympathy. Before we could,
We'd learned to wait as the condemned man waits
For the first light, his darkness, in the east,
And as the hunter waits before his trap,
The theorist before his question, or
The boy before his first time with a girl.
We learned, the soldier says, to sweat it out.


## LANDSCAPE WITH FIGURES

What a dream of a landscape!
Cries Mrs Persepolis, and I
Agree, my gaze follows hers
Out to the giant recumbent
Hills in their sullen haze
Brooding some brutal thought
As it were about myself &
Mrs Persepolis, who are now
Alone in a closed garden
With various flowers and bees
And a feeble fountain that drips
On a stone in a heart-shaped
Pool with a single leopard-
Like toad immobilized all
Morning at his predatory
Meditation, making me think
Mrs Persepolis not too old
With her bright voice and
Wrinkling skin at the wrist
Patterned in sunburnt diamonds
But still a game old girl

(And I a game old guy) good
For a tumble in the August
Grass right at the center
Of the dream of a landscape

Till I see her glittering eye
Has taken this thought exactly
As the toad's tongue takes a fly
So that we laugh and the moment
Passes but Mrs Persepolis
As the bees go about their business
And we go in to have lunch
(How cold the house, the sudden
Shade! I shiver, and Mrs
Persepolis shivers too, till
Her bangles bangle) my dear
Mrs Persepolis, beautiful
Exile from childhood, girl
In your rough and wrinkled
Sack suit, couldn't you cry
Over that funny moment when
We almost fell together
Into the green sleep of the
Landscape, the hooded hills
That dream us up & down?


THE DISTANCES THEY KEEP

They are with us always, but they have the wit
To stay away. We are walking through the woods,
A sudden bush explodes into sparrows, they
Show no desire to become our friends.
So also with the pheasant underfoot
In the stubble field; and lazy lapwings rise
To give their slow, unanimous consent
They want no part of us, who dare not say,

Considering the feathers in our caps,
They are mistaken in the distances they keep.

Still, the heart goes out to them. Goes out,
But maybe it's better this way. Let them stay
Pieces of world we're not responsible for,
Who can be killed by cleverness and hate,
But, being shy enough, may yet survive our love.


## LEARNING BY DOING

They're taking down a tree at the front door,
The power saw is snarling at some nerves,
Whining at others. Now and then it grunts,
And sawdust falls like snow or a drift of seeds.

Rotten, they tell us, at the fork, and one
Big wind would bring it down. So what they do
They do, as usual, to do us good.
Whatever cannot carry its own weight
Has got to go, and so on; you expect
To hear them talking next about survival
And the values of a free society.
For in the explanations people give
On these occasions there is generally some
Mean-spirited moral point, and everyone
Privately wonders if his neighbors plan
To saw him up before he falls on them.

Maybe a hundred years in sun and shower
Dismantled in a morning and let down
Out of itself a finger at a time
And then an arm, and so down to the trunk,
Until there's nothing left to hold on to
Or snub the splintery holding rope around,
And where those big green divagations were
So loftily with shadows interleaved

349

The absent-minded blue rains in on us.
Now that they've got it sectioned on the ground
It looks as though somebody made a plain
Error in diagnosis, for the wood
Looks sweet and sound throughout. You couldn't know,
Of course, until you took it down. That's what
Experts are for, and these experts stand round
The giant pieces of tree as though expecting
An instruction booklet from the factory
Before they try to put it back together.

Anyhow, there it isn't, on the ground.
Next come the tractor and the crowbar crew
To extirpate what's left and fill the grave.
Maybe tomorrow grass seed will be sown.
There's some mean-spirited moral point in that
As well: you learn to bury your mistakes,
Though for a while at dusk the darkening air
Will be with many shadows interleaved,
And pierced with a bewilderment of birds.


## IN THE COMMERCIAL GARDENS

Everything here has a price,
But one is allowed to come and look for nothing

Through the green warm wet alleys
Set forth with flowers, leaves, and ferns,

Experiencing free of charge
The delicately allusive misremembered fragrances

And reading their Latin names,
Their American prices; and wander away

Down the rich, dark avenues
Of earth, where flowers, trees, and ornamental shrubs

350

Are given a casual going-over
By golden-liveried privately owned bees.

At the exhibit's end there is
Nothing, not so much definition as a fence,

The planted rows get smaller,
Scruffier, there seem to be more flies than bees,

And we stand in wilderness
Again. It would be easy enough to go away

Stealing a bush; but no,
We have been privileged to look for nothing,

And it is right that we return
To exit where we entered, nothing in our hands.


THE CHERRY TREE

The cherry tree, symmetrically branching
Into its green confusions, now lights up
Its many suns, that slowly into summer
Intensify from white to pink, and to bloody red.

The lives it lives are not only its own,
But the birds come also, and all day long
The leaves rattle, the branches shake and creak,
The whole tree seems to tremble where it stands.

The squirrels too come to its darkness, they flow
Heavy as waves along the bending boughs;
Inside the clattering shadow round the trunk
You hear a heterodyne hum and whine

As the economy of a minor universe
Distributes its goods (birds tearing at cherries

Are given a bonus of bugs), and everything
Keeps going until everything is gone,

And green and silent stands the tree again,
Shading the bloody stones, the rotting flesh,
In a cool circle of darkness from the sun:
Depending, at the end, from the one sun.


## A LIFE

Innocence?
In a sense.
In no sense!

Was that *it?*
Was *that* it?
*Was* that it?

That was it.


## GROWING A GHOST

From the time he knew
he groomed his hair
in a gray pompadour
and made grim his smile
fitly to represent
all that would be meant
when he arrived by growing
to that great dignity
non-denominational
but solemn all the same
and showing forth a force—
    the stone jaw
    the sharp nose

the closed lids
                    dreaming
nightmares for all
who looked their last

looking his best
the ancestral look
in evening clothes
to go underground
and have at last
in his folded hands
the peace of the world

the red clay


## EPITAPH

Crazy, girls, crazy. Don is gone.
He was bucking for second circle
Along with Dido and Semiramis
And those kids reading of Lancelot
On a rainy afternoon. Think
Of Don sobbing on that dark wind.


## THE VIEW

Under his view the wind
Blows shadows back and forth
Across the lawn beneath
The blowing leaves. And now
Into his silent room
Noon whistles, or a cry
Comes from the road where to
Is fro. Inquietude!
He walks from room to room,

From empty room to room
With the white curtains blowing.
He goes down to the kitchen
And takes from the cold tap
A glass of water pale
As glass. In the long hall
He stares into the mirror
And wills that it should break
Under his image, but
It does not break. Once more
He comes to stand before
The window and the screen,
Framing as in a graph
The view he has of flowers,
Of fields beyond the flowers,
The hanging hill, the blue
Distance that voids his vision
Though not as tears might do.
He has no tears, but knows
No one will come, there's no
Comfort, not the least
Saving discrepancy
In a view where every last thing
Is rimed with its own shadow
Exactly, and every fall
   Is once for all.


## THE HUMAN CONDITION

In this motel where I was told to wait,
The television screen is stood before
The picture window. Nothing could be more
Use to a man than knowing where he's at,
And I don't know, but pace the day in doubt
Between my looking in and looking out.

Through snow, along the snowy road, cars pass
Going both ways, and pass behind the screen

354

Where heads of heroes sometimes can be seen
And sometimes cars, that speed across the glass.
Once I saw world and thought exactly meet,
But only in a picture by Magritte.

A picture of a picture, by Magritte,
Wherein a landscape on an easel stands
Before a window opening on a land-
scape, and the pair of them a perfect fit,
Silent and mad. You know right off, the room
Before that scene was always an empty room.

And that is now the room in which I stand
Waiting, or walk, and sometimes try to sleep.
The day falls into darkness while I keep
The TV going; headlights blaze behind
Its legendary traffic, love and hate,
In this motel where I was told to wait.


THE COMPANIONS

There used to be gods in everything, and now they've gone.
A small one I remember, in a green-gray stone,
Would watch me go by with his still eyes of a toad,
And in the branch of an elm that hung across the road
Another was; he creaked at me on windless days.
Now that he's gone I think he might have wanted praise
For trying to speak my language and getting that far at least
Along on the imitation of a speaking beast.

Maybe he wanted help, maybe they all cried out
As they could, or stared helpless to enter into thought
With "read me," "answer me," or "teach me how to be
Whatever I am, and in return for teaching me
I'll tell you what I was in you, how greater far
Than I are seeking you in fountain, sun, and star."
That's but interpretation, the deep folly of man
To think that things can squeak at him more than things can.

And yet there came those voices up out of the ground
And got into my head, until articulate sound
Might speak them to themselves. We went a certain way
Together on that road, and then I turned away.

I must have done, I guess, to have grown so abstract
That all the lonely summer night's become but fact,
That when the cricket signals I no longer listen,
Nor read the glowworms' constellations when they glisten.


SARAJEVO

In the summer, when the Archduke dies
Past the year's height, after the burning wheel
Steadies and plunges down the mountainside,
The days' succession fails from one to one
Still great as kings, whose shock troops in the field
Begin to burnish their green shoots to gold.

That undeclared war always takes the field
In the summer, when the Archduke dies,
And the blind spills buried beneath the wheel
Are risen, spears bespoken through earth's side
To sacrifice their fast and turning gold
In ransom for the blood of all in one.

Now that blood will be redeemed for gold
Eagle and crown aglitter in the wheel,
In the summer, when the Archduke dies,
Europe divides and fuses, side and side,
Ranging the human filings on the field
Of force, held by the magnet, not yet one.

Still empty of its food the battle field
Waits on the harvest and the great wain's wheel,
The vessels wait at hearth and harborside.
In the summer, when the Archduke dies,

Fate and the fortune of the game are one,
The green time turns to a heavy red, to gold.

And now responsible men on either side
Acknowledge their allegiance to the One
God of battles whose name is writ in gold,
The same whose coin, that cruelly blazing wheel,
In the summer, when the Archduke dies,
Buys earth as though it were a peasant's field.

The wildly streaming past now falls to one
Plunge on the oldest number of the wheel,
The zero twice redeemed in suicide,
Last blood sport of the green civilian field
Where the old world's sun went down in gold
In the summer when the Archduke died.


## THIS, THAT & THE OTHER

*a dialogue in disregard*

This:      I stand and watch for minutes by the pond
              The snowflakes falling on the open water.
              Though I get cold, and though it tells me nothing,
              Or maybe just because it tells me nothing,
              I have to stand and watch the infinite white
              Particulate chaos of the falling snow
              Abolished in the black and waiting water.
              An instantaneous thing, time and again
              It happens, quicker than the eye can count:
              The snowflake drifting down erratically,
              Reflected for a second, suddenly
              Annihilated; no disturbance to
              The silent mirror spread beneath the sky.

That:      I hasten to attend, I take it in.
              I think I see something of what you mean:

It's just as Hermes Trismegistus said
(Or as the scholars say that Hermes said),
The things below are as the things above.
A parable of universal love,
To see the water taking in the snow
Like that, a something neither quick nor slow,
Eternal in an instant, as the All
Unchanged receives the individual.

This:   If that's the way you want it, courtesy
Must say it's yours to make of what you will.
But I was speaking only of the snow
(They say that no two snowflakes are alike,
How can they know?) touching the water's face
So gently that to meet and melt are one.
There's no more reason in it than in dreams.

That:   Then I'll interpret you this dream of yours
And make some sense of it; rather, of course,
Some mind of it, for sense is what you make,
And your provision is for me to take.
First, I observe a pretty polarity
Of black and white, and I ask, could this be
A legend of the mingling of the races?
The whites, with cold and isolated faces,
Falling, a million Lucifers, out of
Their self-made heaven into the primitive
Beginnings that for centuries they hated,
In fact into the undifferentiated?
Political and metaphysical
At once I read your little parable.

This:   Water has many forms and still is water.
The snow, the ice, the steam, the sailing cloud;
Has many ways, between the raindrop and
The great sea wave. One of the things it does
Is mirror, and there's a model for all thought.

That:     And more's to come, for mirroring reminds
          Me of Narcissus and his Echo, kinds
          One of the other, though unkind to him.
          Poor beauty pausing by the fountain's brim,
          Is he not imaged in the snowflake's last
          Moment of vanity, mirrored in the vast
          Abyss and yearning toward the steepdown gulf
          That seems to be, as it destroys, the self?

This:     Echo, reflexion, radar of all sorts,
          The beauty of the mind is mediate,
          Its beauty and its sorrow. A poet said,
          Or had a political old fool say for him,
          "By indirections find directions out."
          A thought is thinking in my head: maybe
          The mind is not a spider, but a web.

That:     The physicists are vexed between the wave
          And particle—would it not somehow save
          The appearances to think about the snow
          As particles becoming waves below,
          Exchanging not their natures but their shapes?
          And then, what's said of parity, perhaps
          That's pictured, and its overthrow as well,
          In this weakest of reactions: if, of all,
          One snowflake fell and somehow failed to drown
          But was deflected to the sky again . . .
          But there I'll stop, being compelled to see
          This isn't physics, but theology.

This:     Sleeveless speculation, someone said,
          I disremember who, and never knew
          What it could mean. For even if a sleeve
          Could speculate, the arm of action still
          Would thrust a grasping hand out at the cuff,
          Bring morsels of this world up to the mouth
          To feed these dreams of immortality
          That end in death and defecation. See,

The snow has stopped, the sun breaks out of cloud,
A golden light is drifting through the glass.

That:     A wind springs up that shatters images.

Both:     The Other is deeply meddled in this world.
          We see no more than that the fallen light
          Is wrinkled in and with the wrinkling wave.


## TO A SCHOLAR IN THE STACKS

When you began your story all its words
Had long been written down, its elements
Already so cohered in such exact
Equations that there should have seemed to be
No place to go, no entrance to the maze.
A heart less bold would have refused to start,
A mind less ignorant would have stayed home.

For Pasiphaë already had conceived
And borne her bully boy, and Daedalus
Responding had designed the darkness in
Its mystical divisions; Theseus,
Before you came, descended and returned,
By means of the thread, many and many a time.
What was there that had not been always done?

And still, when you began, only because
You did begin, the way opened before you.
The pictured walls made room, received your life;
Pasiphaë frowned, the Sea King greeted you,
And sighing Ariadne gave the thread
As always; in that celebrated scene
You were alone in being alone and new.

And now? You have gone down, you have gone in,
You have become incredibly rich and wise

360

From wandering underground. And yet you weary
And disbelieve, daring the Minotaur
Who answers in the echoes of your voice,
Holding the thread that has no other end,
Speaking her name whom you abandoned long ago.

Then out of this what revelation comes?
Sometimes in darkness and in deep despair
You will remember, Theseus, that you were
The Minotaur, the Labyrinth and the thread
Yourself; even you were that ingener
That fled the maze and flew—so long ago—
Over the sunlit sea to Sicily.


LOBSTERS

Here at the Super Duper, in a glass tank
Supplied by a rill of cold fresh water
Running down a glass washboard at one end
And siphoned off at the other, and so
Perpetually renewed, a herd of lobster
Is made available to the customer
Who may choose whichever one he wants
To carry home and drop into boiling water
And serve with a sauce of melted butter.

Meanwhile, the beauty of strangeness marks
These creatures, who move (when they do)
With a slow, vague wavering of claws,
The somnambulist's effortless clambering
As he crawls over the shell of a dream
Resembling himself. Their velvet colors,
Mud red, bruise purple, cadaver green
Speckled with black, their camouflage at home,
Make them conspicuous here in the strong
Day-imitating light, the incommensurable
Philosophers and at the same time victims

361

Herded together in the marketplace, asleep
Except for certain tentative gestures
Of their antennae, or their imperial claws
Pegged shut with a whittled stick at the wrist.
We inlanders, buying our needful food,
Pause over these slow, gigantic spiders
That spin not. We pause and are bemused,
And sometimes it happens that a mind sinks down
To the blind abyss in a swirl of sand, goes cold
And archaic in a carapace of horn,
Thinking: There's something underneath the world. . . .

The flame beneath the pot that boils the water.


## AN OLD COLONIAL IMPERIALIST

To grip through the ground with your feet;
To feel your toes curled around rocks,
Sucking up water; to stand up straight
And tall for a certain time, and after
Go off in any direction, so long as it's up;
That's what I call living: standing there.

Tons of water creeping up my stomach,
Immense strain in my many shoulders
Holding their limbs in proclamation;
When a starling lands in my hair
I know it; when the hairy woodpecker
Hits me for lice, I know where the lice are.
My patches of lichen itch for centuries,
I do not stoop to scratch; you pay
For dignity in this world.
                              Grown old,
I suffer the surgeon's pruning bill,
Cement in my cavities, healing tar
Over my incidental stumps. I go on,

Bending a little in the bigger winds,
Waving light airs away, and every fall
I drop the year's familiarity
Of used leaves with a certain contempt.


## BEYOND THE PLEASURE PRINCIPLE

It comes up out of the darkness, and it returns
Into a further darkness. After the monster,
There is the monster's mother to be dealt with,
Dimly perceived at first, or only speculated on
Between the shadows and reflexions of the tidal cave,
Among the bones and armored emptiness
Of the princes of a former time, who failed.

Our human thought arose at first in myth,
And going far enough became a myth once more;
Its pretty productions in between, those splendid
Tarnhelms and winged sandals, mirroring shields
And swords unbreakable, of guaranteed
Fatality, those endlessly winding labyrinths
In which all minotaurs might find themselves at home,
Deceived us with false views of the end, leaving
Invisible the obstinate residuum, so cloudy, cold,
Archaic, that waits beyond purpose and fulfillment.

There, toward the end, when the left-handed wish
Is satisfied as it is given up, when the hero
Endures his cancer and more obstinately than ever
Grins at the consolations of religion as at a child's
Frightened pretensions, and when his great courage
Becomes a wish to die, there appears, so obscurely,
Pathetically, out of the wounded torment and the play,
A something primitive and appealing, and still dangerous,
That crawls on bleeding hands and knees over the floor
Toward him, and whispers as if to confess: *again, again.*

## DEPARTURE OF THE SHIPS

The voyages always beginning, always ending,
Dreams of the past enacted in the future,
Autonomous, and dreamed by all and none:
Wars, oracles, sacrifices, necessary dominations
Of the driven by the driven; priestly lustrations
Of murdering hands now still in the dust as dust;
And history, the dream within a dream,
Endless, remorselessly detailed anamnesis
To justify the sufferings and the crimes
Of the unborn; the chanting, muttering, whispering
Digestion of the random in necessity,
The repetition that convicts and kills.

Wealth also, with its generations:
The circulation of the currency
Through ruble and crown, dollar and franc, blood
Of the public confidence, unlimited legend
Phantasied against original obligation
Of time unredeemable and time that grows
Impudent in the earthy vault, compounding interest
In the tidal periods of calendar and clock,
The silver of the moon and the sun's gold.

See now, the ships depart through the dark harbor
And past the breakwater rocks where the first
White-riding wave hits at the hull and washes on.
Rhythm of voyages, going out and coming back,
Beat of the sea, procession of times and seasons,
Command of variables, calculus of fluxions
*Cuius Nomen est Oriens*, keeping time
Where endless hours summon and dismiss,
The hours of adoration and revenge,
Of triumph, lamentation and despair,
Devoted hours of the iron and brazen bells
That swing in the steeple over the old Exchange,
Counting and keeping all that cannot be kept.

O star of the sea, naked and dangerous candor,
Blaze of the compass rose, our ships depart!
Iron hands of the clock meet and divide,
The white face on the tower looks to sea,
Where unaccountable sands cloudily sift
Through the salt black bitter glass that gives
Tidal ideas about time, and no tidings.

# 2 The Great Society

## THE NIGHT BEFORE CHRISTMAS

I am buying presents for everyone.
It is very late, but better late,
They say, than never. I want
Everyone to be happy, but admit
I frequently do not do enough
To implement this wish. Now
It is late, December Twenty-Fourth
Darkens, and I, with others
Scourged by the same conviction
Of an absolute delinquency,
Am walking the cold avenue
Between the lines of brilliant windows
Filled with impersonal satisfactions.
I clutch my money, I shudder with cold,
I go on attempting to buy
The happiness of others.

(An ox at a crèche looks out,
And I look in. A small doll
In the cradle has closed eyes.
You will be crucified, Baby,
I croon, before going on,
And we will buy you, Baby,
Cathedrals for Christmas.)

Lovers, relations, friends,
And business acquaintances,
I swear to express my love
Somehow. Say what you want,
Say what would make you happy,
Before I spill my money in

The dark river as it ebbs
To sea, that its hurrying current
May devalue these my dollars
In depths beyond redemption,
And in the dragon's treasury
The price of prices be forgot,
    And the potlatch of time.


## SUNDAY

He rested on the seventh day, and so
The chauffeur had the morning off, the maid
Slept late, and cook went out to morning mass.
So by and large there was nothing to do
Among the ashtrays in the living room
But breathe the greyish air left over from
Last night, and go down on your knees to read
The horrible funnies flattened on the floor.

It's still a day to conjure with, if not
Against, the blessed seventh, when we get
A chance to feel whatever He must feel,
Looking us over, seeing that we are good.
The odds are six to one He's gone away;
It's why there's so much praying on this day.


## ENTHUSIASM FOR HATS

Under their great hats the women walk
To Sunday service, all along the street
Among the secretive suburban houses
An amazement of hats, towering, askew,
Supported upon frames or cantilevered,
Held on by spikes or flying buttresses,
Hats bundled, hats bolstered, tea cozy hats

367

And hats huge that could cozy chamber pots,
Parades under the porches of the churches.

Hats must be pleasing in the sight of God.
As though they could have had no human maker
They rise in splendor, sway in independence,
Bobble and nod in glory above the heads
As manifestations from the mind itself,
Expressing the erection of pure thought
In velvet, pelt, and feather. O high hats!
As secret of significance as those
Dormers there at the peaks of private houses
Along these quiet streets, where people keep
Hidden in filth a broken relative.


## A WAY OF LIFE

It's been going on a long time.
For instance, these two guys, not saying much, who slog
Through sun and sand, fleeing the scene of their crime,
Till one turns, without a word, and smacks
His buddy flat with the flat of an axe,
Which cuts down on the dialogue
Some, but is viewed rather as normal than sad
By me, as I wait for the next ad.

It seems to me it's been quite a while
Since the last vision of blonde loveliness
Vanished, her shampoo and shower and general style
Replaced by this lean young lunk-
head parading along with a gun in his back to confess
How yestereve, being drunk
And in a state of existential despair,
He beat up his grandma and pawned her invalid chair.

But here at last is a pale beauty
Smoking a filter beside a mountain stream,

Brief interlude, before the conflict of love and duty
Gets moving again, as sheriff and posse expound,
Between jail and saloon, the American Dream
Where Justice, after considerable horsing around,
Turns out to be Mercy; when the villain is knocked off,
A kindly uncle offers syrup for my cough.

And now these clean-cut athletic types
In global hats are having a nervous debate
As they stand between their individual rocket ships
Which have landed, appropriately, on some rocks
Somewhere in Space, in an atmosphere of hate
Where one tells the other to pull up his socks
And get going, he doesn't say where; they fade,
And an angel food cake flutters in the void.

I used to leave now and again;
No more. A lot of violence in American life
These days, mobsters and cops all over the scene.
But there's a lot of love, too, mixed with the strife,
And kitchen-kindness, like a bedtime story
With rich food and a more kissable depilatory.
Still, I keep my weapons handy, sitting here
Smoking and shaving and drinking the dry beer.


MONEY

*an introductory lecture*

This morning we shall spend a few minutes
Upon the study of symbolism, which is basic
To the nature of money. I show you this nickel.
Icons and cryptograms are written all over
The nickel: one side shows a hunchbacked bison
Bending his head and curling his tail to accommodate
The circular nature of money. Over him arches
UNITED STATES OF AMERICA, and, squinched in
Between that and his rump, E PLURIBUS UNUM,

A Roman reminiscence that appears to mean
An indeterminately large number of things
All of which are the same. Under the bison
A straight line giving him a ground to stand on
Reads FIVE CENTS. And on the other side of our nickel
There is the profile of a man with long hair
And a couple of feathers in the hair; we know
Somehow that he is an American Indian, and
He wears the number nineteen-thirty-six.
Right in front of his eyes the word LIBERTY, bent
To conform with the curve of the rim, appears
To be falling out of the sky Y first; the Indian
Keeps his eyes downcast and does not notice this;
To notice it, indeed, would be shortsighted of him.
So much for the iconography of one of our nickels,
Which is now becoming a rarity and something of
A collectors' item: for as a matter of fact
There is almost nothing you can buy with a nickel,
The representative American Indian was destroyed
A hundred years or so ago, and his descendants'
Relations with liberty are maintained with reservations,
Or primitive concentration camps; while the bison,
Except for a few examples kept in cages,
Is now extinct. Something like that, I think,
Is what Keats must have meant in his celebrated
Ode on a Grecian Urn.
                Notice, in conclusion,
A number of circumstances sometimes overlooked
Even by experts: (*a*) Indian and bison,
Confined to obverse and reverse of the coin,
Can never see each other; (*b*) they are looking
In opposite directions, the bison past
The Indian's feathers, the Indian past
The bison's tail; (*c*) they are upside down
To one another; (*d*) the bison has a human face
Somewhat resembling that of Jupiter Ammon.
I hope that our studies today will have shown you
Something of the import of symbolism
With respect to the understanding of what is symbolized.

# MAKE LOVE NOT WAR

Lovers everywhere are bringing babies into the world.
Lovers with stars in their eyes are turning the stars
Into babies, lovers reading the instructions in comic books
Are turning out babies according to the instructions; this
Progression is said by demographers to be geometric and
Accelerating the rate of its acceleration. Lovers abed
Read up the demographers' reports, and accordingly produce
Babies with contact lenses and babies diapered in the flags
Of new and underdeveloped nations. Some experts contend
That bayonets are being put into the hands of babies
Not old enough to understand their use. And in the U.S.,
Treasury officials have expressed grave concern about
The unauthorized entry of stateless babies without
Passports and knowing no English: these "wetbacks,"
As they are called from the circumstance of their swimming
Into this country, are to be reported to the proper
Authority wherever they occur and put through channels
For deportation to Abysmo the equatorial paradise
Believed to be their country of origin—"where,"
According to one of our usually unformed sorcerers,
"The bounteous foison of untilled Nature alone
Will rain upon the heads of these homeless, unhappy
And helpless beings apples, melons, honey, nuts, and gum
Sufficient to preserve them in their prelapsarian state
Under the benign stare of Our Lord Et Cetera forevermore."

Meanwhile I forgot to tell you, back at the ranch,
The lovers are growing older, becoming more responsible.
Beginning with the mortal courtship of the Emerald Goddess
By Doctor Wasp—both of them twelve feet high
And insatiable; he wins her love by scientific means
And she has him immolated in a specially designed mole—
They have now settled down in an L-shaped ranch-type home
Where they are running a baby ranch and bringing up
Powerful babies able to defend their Way of Life
To the death if necessary. Of such breeding pairs
The average he owns seven and a half pair of pants,

While she generally has three girdles and a stove.
They keep a small pump-action repeater in the closet,
And it will not go off in the last act of this epic.

To sum up, it was for all the world as if one had said
Increase! Be fruitful! Multiply! Divide!
Be as the sands of the sea, the stars in the firmament,
The moral law within, the number of molecules
In the unabridged dictionary. BVD. Amen. Ahem.

AUM.

(Or, roughly, the peace that passeth understanding.)


## A NEGRO CEMETERY NEXT TO A WHITE ONE

I wouldn't much object, if I were black,
To being turned away at the iron gate
By the dark blonde angel holding up a plaque
That said White only; who would mind the wait

For those facilities? And still it's odd,
Though a natural god-given civil right,
For men to throw it in the face of God
Some ghosts are black and some darknesses white.

But since they failed to integrate the earth,
It's white of them to give what tantamounts
To it, making us all, for what that's worth,
Separate but equal where it counts.


## AT THE AIRPORT

Through the gate, where nowhere and night begin,
A hundred suddenly appear and lose
Themselves in the hot and crowded waiting room.
A hundred other herd up toward the gate,

Patiently waiting that the way be opened
To nowhere and night, while a voice recites
The intermittent litany of numbers
And the holy names of distant destinations.

None going out can be certain of getting there.
None getting there can be certain of being loved
Enough. But they are sealed in the silver tube
And lifted up to be fed and cosseted,
While their upholstered cell of warmth and light
Shatters the darkness, neither here nor there.


## PRESIDENTIAL ADDRESS TO A PARTY OF EXILES

There are too many of you.
Heaven is closed. The Age
Of Reason is full up, too.
And we have no more jobs
For Romantic Poets. Go.

I shall think of you often
In your sterilized cocoons
Stilting about in the steel wool
Or whatever, spidering
Fastidiously over the gray dust
With your grieving fingers
That want to come home. But
There are too many of you.

You might have stayed with us
In the lattice of stonework,
In the crystalline fracture
Of cemeteries, and been among
Our memories, in the chalk
Dust of a blackboard's thought
A cloudy erasure, but
So many of you . . . ? Pilots,

Man your solipsisms,
Mahomet in his coffin not
More free. Go, voyagers,
I want you to know my thought
   Goes always with you.


## TO THE GOVERNOR & LEGISLATURE
## OF MASSACHUSETTS

When I took a job teaching in Massachusetts
I didn't know and no one told me that I'd have to sign
An oath of loyalty to the Commonwealth of Massachusetts.
Now that I'm hooked, though, with a house
And a mortgage on the house, the road ahead
Is clear: I sign. But I want you gentlemen to know
That till today it never once occurred to me
To overthrow the Commonwealth of Massachusetts
By violence or subversion, or by preaching either.
But now I'm not so sure. It makes a fellow think,
Can such things be ? Can such things be in the very crib
Of our liberties, and East of the Hudson, at that?
So if the day come that I should shove the Berkshire Hills
Over the border and annex them to Vermont,
Or snap Cape Cod off at the elbow and scatter
Hyannis to Provincetown beyond the twelve-mile limit,
Proclaiming apocalypsopetls to my pupils
And with state troopers dripping from my fingertips
Squeaking "You promised, you broke your promise!"
You gentlemen just sit there with my signature
And keep on lawyer-talking like nothing had happened,
Lest I root out that wagon tongue on Bunker Hill
And fungo your Golden Dome right into Fenway Park
Like any red-celled American boy ought to done
Long ago in the first place, just to keep in practice.

## A FULL PROFESSOR

Surely there was, at first, some love of letters
To get him started on the routine climb
That brought him to this eminence in time?
But now he has become one of his betters.

He has survived, and even fattened on,
The dissertation and the discipline.
The eyes are spectacled, the hair is thin,
He is a dangerous committeeman.

An organism highly specialized,
He diets on, for daily bill of fare,
The blood of Keats, the mind of poor John Clare;
Within his range, he cannot be surprised.

Publish or perish! What a frightful chance!
It troubled him through all his early days.
But now he has the system beat both ways;
He publishes and perishes at once.


## GRACE TO BE SAID BEFORE COMMITTEE MEETINGS

The problem was to get first things
To come first, and when you had them first
To build, course after course,
In an orderly manner, the problem was,
Your tower. It wouldn't be easy,
Nobody ever said it would be easy,
But your reward would be, with first
Things first, order, the tower,
Majesty. How this would come about
Nobody ever said, and that was
The problem that so exercised
The best minds of that generation.

The last thing you get to know,
Pascal had said, is what comes first.

Of course, much had been done
Already, nobody ever said
It hadn't, but the problem was
Whether to tear it up, or build
On those shifty foundations.
So the best minds exercised
Mightily, and they decided
The past indeed had been full
Of error, nobody ever said
It wasn't, but as for them
Themselves, the answer was,
If they had been there back then,
When those things happened, that is,
They would not have happened because
They would not have let them happen,
Because they weren't the sort of guys
Who would have poisoned Socrates
Or crucified their Savior, and
By God nobody ever said they were.

A RELATION OF ART AND LIFE

Into the sacred precincts come the savage sages,
The shamans meager of body, furious of mind
From lonesome meditations near to madness,
The wizards, wardens of the kindless wonders,
And prophets, who seek to bring catastrophe
Under a copyright, and doom to its publication.
With eyeballs able to swivel in their sockets,
These are the universal joints between the All and Nothing;
Driven by dreams to the interpreters of dreams,
They are without sin, and casting their first stones.

376

Out of the desert they come, and from the mountains,
From contemplation of those still sterilities
Or the repetition of the ocean tides deriving
Each one his remedy for men, his unpriced pearl
To sell to the priesthood to be a secret saying
To say over sacrifices, to be cast in contempt
Before popular swine. The secret sayings are such
As destroy societies; to have one is to hold
A hot coal in the mouth, and what mouth would stay closed?
The sages have arrived; they are breathing fire.

First, Sexual License, all sweat and dishevel
And a scrotum stuffed like the sack of Santa Claus;
Then Drunken Disorder, big with his liquid bulk
Of unzipped incompetence and vomit and sleep.
And now comes Salutary Hatred, self-beshitten;
And Anarchy that acts, with Apathy his twin
That lets be acted; and Narcosis in his kinds,
That works the doorway to the double dream
Where pose the caterpillar and the butterfly
Their contradictions to the sunshine or the shroud.
The priesthood serenely appraises the secrets
And grades them according to order and harmony,
Establishing values, deriving from every vision
Its proper doctrine: from drunkenness a jail,
From sexual license the institution of wedlock,
From anarchy and apathy the armed services,
Industrial development from drugged sleep,
And from hatred the holy mystery of the law;
Absorbing outrage into probability,
Improving virtue from the average of vice.

Now avant garde movies are made, money is given
For receiving the sages and making them at home
In the accursed culture; with subversive civility
The bride-price is paid that the City be saved.
And the dreams of the desert are digested in art.
To reactionary mirages now the sages retire

In their neo-classical Cadillacs, miraculous
Ranches arise on the sands, and roses red and white
Bloom in the dust at the door; the sages get busy
Revising their visions comformably with fact.

While in the sacred precincts now the scribes
Already expound the Word that was without the world
An idiot star, a shining in chaos underived,
That now is marketable cosmos, and a cause
To be fought for and against, to be taught in schools
With grades, degrees, and fellowships, and gowns,
And hides, and hoods, by master ham and doctor clown;
Already in the colleges the Word that was no word
Is processed from the podium by professors in prose,
And dedicated scholars in the graduate schools
Busy to squeeze the Absurd and divide the Void
Into courses given for credit, that the generations
May batten on the bitter diet of the desert
Until the secret desire of their blood shall be
To property protected by the blue police
Whose order guards the graves beneath the vaults
Beneath the banks, whose houses now are glass
Contempting stones; in whose aquarian light, subdued,
Glow golden secretaries inaccessible on stilted heels,
And savage action paintings hanging patient on the walls.
                    *The Phi Beta Kappa poem at Harvard*
                                    *15th June, 1965*


A MODERN POET

Crossing at rush hour the Walt Whitman Bridge,
He stopped at the Walt Whitman Shopping Center
And bought a paperback copy of *Leaves of Grass.*
Fame *is* the spur, he figured; given a Ford
Foundation Fellowship, he'd buy a Ford.

## ON THE PLATFORM

Account of your what critics call Prose Style,
And all them balanced periods wherein
You imitate a thought that can't make up its mind,
People invite you, every little while,
To tell them on the one hand and the other hand
What kind of shape the world is in.

You tell'em: Bad. And they like that.
A tape recorder takes it down, puts you on ice
For future reverence. There is applause,
And you make like you are tipping your hat
And smiling go. They've got you taped because
Later they'll want to waste the same time twice.

Takes guts, to go on record time after time
Affirming all them contradictions which
Within the self belong. Sometimes in rime,
Too. They like it, they want to make you rich,
'Cause when you stand up there before the mike
You talk the way you really think, like Ike.


## CYBERNETICS

Now you are ready to build your human brain.
You have studied the plan, and taken inventory
Of all the pieces you found in the kit.
The first brain won't be inexpensive or
Compact; covering most of Central Park
With these tiny transistors, it will cost
A sum slightly in excess of the Gross
National Product for Nineteen Fifty-Nine;
But that is not a scientific problem,
For later brains will reproduce themselves
At less expense, on a far smaller scale,
Bringing down average costs in the long run.

Screwdriver ready? But before you start,
Consider, helmsman, what a brain requires.
A human brain has always needed blood,
And always got it, too, in plenty; but
That problem occupies a later stage;
Right now, some elementary decisions.

It must, of course, be absolutely free,
That's been determined, and accordingly
You will program it to program itself,
Set up its own projects and work them out,
Adjusting what it does tomorrow by
The feedback from today, and casually
Repairing yesterday's disasters with
The earliest possible editorials.
It must assure itself, by masterful
Administration of the unforeseen,
That everything works according to plan,
And that, as a General from the Pentagon
Recently told Congress, "The period
Of greatest danger lies ahead." This way
Alone it will be able to preserve
Anxiety and sloth in a see-saw balance,
Provoking the flow of both adrenalin
And phlegm (speaking electronically),
Whence its conflicting elements achieve
A fair symbiosis, something between
The flood of power and the drouth of fear:
A mediocrity, or golden mean,
Maybe at best the stoic *apatheia*.

At the same time, to be a human brain,
It has to have a limiting tradition,
Which may be simple and parochial
(A memory of Main Street in the sunlight)
But should be unequivocal as well:
"My country right or wrong," or "I believe
In free enterprise and high tariffs,"
Or "God will punish me if I suck my thumb."

Something like that. You will provide also
A rudimentary view of history:
One eyeless bust of Cicero or Caesar,
A Washington Crossing the Delaware,
The Driving of the Golden Railroad Spike;
Maybe a shot of Lenin tombed in glass.
It need not be much, but it must be there.

Maybe you want a more ambitious brain?
One that can keep all history in mind,
Revise the whole to fit one added fact,
And do this in three hundredths of a second
While making accurate predictions of
Price fluctuations for the next six months?
Perfectly possible, and well within
The technical means at hand. Only, there's this:
It runs you into much more money for
Circuits of paradox and contradiction.
Your vessels of antinomian wrath alone
Run into millions; and you can't stop there,
You've got to add at every junction point
Auxiliary systems that will handle doubt,
Switches of agony that are On and Off
At the same time, and limited-access
Blind alleys full of inefficient gods
And marvelous devils. No, you're asking the
Impossible, Dostoevsky described it:
"A Petersburg intellectual with a toothache."
Better to settle for the simpler model.
You could put a man on the moon for less.

O helmsman! in your hands how equal now
Weigh opportunity and obligation.
A chance to mate those monsters of the Book,
The lion and serpent hidden from our sight
Through centuries of shadowed speculation.
What if the Will's a baffled, mangy lion,
Or Thought's no adder but a strong constrictor?
It is their offspring that we care about,

That marvelous mirror where our modest wit
Shall show gigantic. Will he uproot cities,
Or sit indoors on a rainy day and mope?
Will he decide against us, or want love?
How shall we see him, or endure his stride
Into our future bellowing Nil Mirari
While all his circuits click, propounding new
Solutions to the riddle of the Sphinx?


## KEEPING INFORMED IN D.C.

Each morning when I break my buttered toast
Across the columns of the *Morning Post,*
I am astounded by the ways in which
Mankind has managed once again to bitch
Things up to a degree that yesterday
Had looked impossible. Not far away
From dreams of mine, I read this dream of theirs,
And think: It's true, we *are* the bankrupt heirs
Of all the ages, history *is* the bunk.
If you do not believe in all this junk,
If you're not glad things are as they are,
    You can wipe your arse on the *Evening Star.*


## THE GREAT SOCIETY, MARK X

The engine and transmission and the wheels
Are made of greed, fear, and invidiousness
Fueled by super-pep high octane money
And lubricated with hypocrisy,
Interior upholstery is all handsewn
Of the skins of children of the very poor,
Justice and mercy, charity and peace,
Are optional items at slight extra cost,
The steering gear is newsprint powered by

Expediency but not connected with
The wheels, and finally there are no brakes.

However, the rear-view mirror and the horn
Are covered by our lifetime guarantee.


## THE DREAM OF FLYING COMES OF AGE

Remember those wingovers and loops and spins?
Forbidden. Heavy, powerful, and solemn,
Our scheduled transports keep the straight and level.
It's not the joystick now, but the control column.


## GRACE TO BE SAID AT THE SUPERMARKET

That God of ours, the Great Geometer,
Does something for us here, where He hath put
(if you want to put it that way) things in shape,
Compressing the little lambs in orderly cubes,
Making the roast a decent cylinder,
Fairing the tin ellipsoid of a ham,
Getting the luncheon meat anonymous
In squares and oblongs with the edges beveled
Or rounded (streamlined, maybe, for greater speed).

Praise Him, He hath conferred aesthetic distance
Upon our appetites, and on the bloody
Mess of our birthright, our unseemly need,
Imposed significant form. Through Him the brutes
Enter the pure Euclidean kingdom of number,
Free of their bulging and blood-swollen lives
They come to us holy, in cellophane
Transparencies, in the mystical body,

That we may look unflinchingly on death
As the greatest good, like a philosopher should.

## AUGUST, 1945

Feeble Caligula! to say
You wished mankind one only neck.
The dying guards might dance that day
At Auschwitz and at Maidanek,
Seeing their bloody seed begin to swell
Where the two cities fell.

That was our deed, without us done.
Great murder in the earth was set
That day to grow, and for us won
A present freedom to regret
Necessity, that once had made us, blind,
The saviors of mankind.

The pluming shadow of that plant,
A tragic actor now grown tall
To toppling, sounds the haughty cant
And birdlike flutes of sorrow, all
That power cracked at the root and manifest
In the burnt Phoenix' nest.


## CHRISTMAS MORNING

I snuggle down under the electric blanket
Turned onto high, and sneak a look at the dawn
With one pure fire of a sinking star
Over the gray snow blanketing the lawn;

Now once again the Child is born. Downstairs
The children are early out of bed, ready
To tear the wrappings from the usual junk
Where helpless love became commodity

As knowing nothing else to do. Downstreet
The lit-up crèche before the Baptist Church

Is lapped in filthy snow, its figures stained
And leaning at a hazard in the lurch

Of headstones heaved by frost; theirs is the strength
That makes the life-size plastic toy machine-
guns on which even a moment's happiness
Depends, with all the safety of the scene—

The whitened village on the greeting card
Sent by the Bank—against the alien priest
Who drenches his white robes in gasoline
And blazes merrily in the snowy East.

# 3 Figures

## THE FLAME OF A CANDLE

Old fabulous rendering up,
Light on a shoestring, fire out of fat
Consuming oil and cup
Together, what

Miracle! the soul's splatter and flap
Aloft, enlightened lamb
That spurting through the beastly trap
Is able to say *I am*
*That I am*—

Our fathers lived on these
Desperate certainties;
Ate manna in the desert, it is said,
And are dead.

## BETWEEN THE WINDOW AND THE SCREEN

Between the window and the screen
A black fly climbed and fell
All day, then toward nightfall
Despaired and died.

Next morning there one tiny ant
Raced up and down the screen
Holding above his head
That huge black hulk.

I helped not, nor oversaw the end
Ordained to the black ant

Bearing the thin-winged heavy death
Aloft as a proud flag,

But write it out for you to read
And take what it may yield;
No harder emblem had
Achilles' shield.


## DECORATED SKULL IN A UNIVERSITY MUSEUM

Original artist, you have become
The subject of yourself, you have contained
Your own content, and in your vanity
No thought is not my own.

As when one looks at a celestial globe,
So all things here, big doll, turn inside out
With you. Instead of eyes, your spiral shells
Go spiraling standing still

In endless gaze, and your cosmetic clay
Rounds out a cosmos all disguises but
Express. *Magna cum laude*, modern poet,
You Master of Fine Arts!


## DEAD RIVER

Passive and dark, dead river,
Drifting beneath the images
Received in one sole moving eye,
Beginning nowhere, never
Arriving, ever to be done;
Reflecting back in black
The leaves, the sky, the silver sun,
Dead river, you still give
Your still moving negative

Down to the still glade
Where the beaver has made
His sill of speckled mud
And saplings silver-dry,
Deliverance of the sun,
Dead river, past which never,
Dead river, beyond which not,

While summer dries away in gold
Jeweled with bright and buzzing flies.


THE ROPE'S END

Unraveling a rope
You begin at an end.
Taking the finished work
You pick it to its bits,

Straightening out the crossed,
Deriving many from one,
Moving forward in time
And backward in idea,

Reaching to finer elements
And always thinner filaments,
From rope to cord to thread
And so on down to splinters

No longer serpentine
That break instead of coil
And that will blow away
Before a little breath,

Having attained the first
Condition, being dust,
No longer resembling rope
Or cord or thread or hair,

And following no line:
Incapable of knot or wave
Or tying things together
Or making anything secure,

Unable to bind, or whip,
Or hang till dead. All this
In the last analysis
Is crazy man's work,

Admitted, who can leave
Nothing continuous
Since Adam's fall
Unraveled all.


## PROJECTION

They were so amply beautiful, the maps,
With their blue rivers winding to the sea,
So calmly beautiful, who could have blamed
Us for believing, bowed to our drawing boards,
In one large and ultimate equivalence,
One map that challenged and replaced the world?

Our punishment? To stand here, on these ladders,
Dizzy with fear, not daring to look down,
Glue on our fingers, in our hair and eyes,
Piecing together the crackling, sticky sheets
We hope may paper yet the walls of space
With pictures any child can understand.


## IN THE BLACK MUSEUM

When all analogies are broken
The scene grows strange again. At last
There is only one of everything.

This I had seen a long time coming
In my landscape of blunt instruments,
My garden of bearded herms.

For years I had carried a traveler's word
That he had seen in Fiji "sacred stones
That had children, but the children were stones,"

And did not know till now what silent thing
That hard, two-headed saying said: one mask
To every skull, that is the end of art.

These uncertainty relations now refine
Themselves toward ever-greater accuracy,
Unreadable in any antinomian sense,

Conceding nothing to a metaphysics;
As in my dream one night a sliding door
Opened upon another sliding door;

Or as two mirrors vacuum-locked together
Exclude, along with all the world,
A light to see it by. Reflect on that.


THE RACE

So many tortoises
Unwind and wind
The clue of the wheel
On the road of the race

In each cool shadow
Under the shoulder
Of cedar and spruce
In each cool shadow
Of granite ledge
By green still pool

Under the shoulder
The failed favorite
Sprinter's asleep

He dreams of being
Wherever he is

While swish and swish
The silent families
Mounted in glass
Facing the front
Are strictly passing
Away on the slab
Of their fated freeway
Offering cokes
With cigarettes

Their eyeballs rolling
Along that road
Of the dead cats
And frightened flies

Mirages perpetual
Of asphalt pools


SIGHTSEERS

Where history was
Hordes of them come
With the black boxes
Strapped to the neck,
Borne on the breast,
Tabernacle or pyx
Priestly with symbols
In silver and black,
With numbers incised
And cryptic sayings

About the light.
These portable shrines
Covered in skins
They aim at all
Remarkable things:
*Click,* the Vatican,
*Click,* the Sphinx,
*Click,* in the Badlands,
The enormous nostrils
Of the Fathers
                    *Click*
Sometimes they dream
Of looking alive,
Of being released
To the ripple and flash
Of a fiery world
Where the dragonfly
Glitters and goes
And the gold sun sinks
In the oil black film
Of a pool, forever
Evanescent, but
No: reflexion
Has intervened, and
Again, in the box
The dark will won
That knows no now,
In the mind bowed down
Among the shadows
Of shadowy things,
Itself a shadow
Less sure than they.


THOUGHT

Thought is seldom itself
And never itself alone.

392

It is the mind turning
To images. Maybe
Idea is like the day,
Being both everywhere
And always in one place.

Leaves shaken in the wind
Rattle the light till shadows
Elide, and yet the grass
Bends to the weight of the wind
And not the shadows' weight.
The minnow-waves can mingle
In shallows at the shore
As if they were no matter,
Until they peak and break,
Taking the sunlight up
In a shatter of spray.

And mind in some such way
Passing across the world
May make its differences
At last unselfishly
The casualties of cause:
    It's likeness changes.

STYLE

Flaubert wanted to write a novel
About nothing. It was to have no subject
And be sustained upon style alone,
Like the Holy Ghost cruising above
The abyss, or like the little animals
In Disney cartoons who stand upon a branch
That breaks, but do not fall
Till they look down. He never wrote that novel,
And neither did he write another one
That would have been called *La Spirale*,

Wherein the hero's fortunes were to rise
In dreams, while his waking life disintegrated.

Even so, for these two books
We thank the master. They can be read,
With difficulty, in the spirit alone,
Are not so wholly lost as certain works
Burned at Alexandria, flooded at Florence,
And are never taught at universities.
Moreover, they are not deformed by style,
That fire that eats what it illuminates.


CELESTIAL GLOBE

This is the world
Without the world.
I hold it in my hand,
A hollow sphere
Of childlike blue
With magnitudes of stars.
There in its utter dark
The singing planets go,
And the sun, great source,
Is blazing forth his fires
Over the many-oceaned
And river-shining earth
Whereon I stand
Balancing this ball
Upon my hand.

It is the universe,
The Turning One.
As if children at the Museum
Should watch some amateur
Copying Rembrandt's painting
Of Aristotle contemplating
The skull of Homer, that

Dark fire fountaining forth
The twin poems of the war
And of the journey home—
As if the children stood
In the mind of Homer
As on the ball of the world
Where every inside's out.

It is the world
Beyond the world.
Holding it in my hand,
I wear it on my head
As a candle wears a pumpkin
At Halloween, when children
Rise as the dead; only
It has no human features,
No access to its depths
Whatever, where it keeps
In the utter dark
The candle of the sun,
The candle of the mind,
Twin fires that together
Turn all things inside out.


ONE WAY

The way a word does when
It senses on one side
A thing and on the other
A thought; at either side
It glances and goes deep
Together; like sunlight
On marble, on burnished wood,
That seems to be coming from
Within the surface and
To be one substance with it—
That is one way of doing

One's being in a world
Whose being is both thought
And thing, where neither thing
Nor thought will do alone
Till either answers other;
Two lovers in the night
Each sighing other's name
Whose alien syllables
Become synonymous
For all their mortal night
And their embodied day:
Fire in the diamond,
Diamond in the dark.

# 4 The Blue Swallows

## THE BLUE SWALLOWS

Across the millstream below the bridge
Seven blue swallows divide the air
In shapes invisible and evanescent,
Kaleidoscopic beyond the mind's
Or memory's power to keep them there.

"History is where tensions were,"
"Form is the diagram of forces."
Thus, helplessly, there on the bridge,
While gazing down upon those birds—
How strange, to be above the birds!—
Thus helplessly the mind in its brain
Weaves up relation's spindrift web,
Seeing the swallows' tails as nibs
Dipped in invisible ink, writing . . .

Poor mind, what would you have them write?
Some cabalistic history
Whose authorship you might ascribe
To God? to Nature? Ah, poor ghost,
You've capitalized your Self enough.
That villainous William of Occam
Cut out the feet from under that dream
Some seven centuries ago.
It's taken that long for the mind
To waken, yawn and stretch, to see
With opened eyes emptied of speech
The real world where the spelling mind
Imposes with its grammar book
Unreal relations on the blue
Swallows. Perhaps when you will have

Fully awakened, I shall show you
A new thing: even the water
Flowing away beneath those birds
Will fail to reflect their flying forms,
And the eyes that see become as stones
Whence never tears shall fall gain.

O swallows, swallows, poems are not
The point. Finding again the world,
That is the point, where loveliness
Adorns intelligible things
Because the mind's eye lit the sun.

THE MAY DAY DANCING

The kindergarten children first come forth
In couples dressed as little brides and grooms.
By dancing in, by dancing round and out,
They braid the Maypole with a double thread;
Keep time, keep faith, is what the music says.

The corporal piano now leads out
Successively the older boys and girls,
Grade after grade, all for the dancing paired,
All dressed in the fashion of forgotten folk;
Those nymphs and shepherds, maybe, never were.

And all the parents standing in a ring,
With cameras some, and some with only eyes,
Attend to the dancing's measurable rule
Bemused, or hypnotized, so that they see
Not seven classes of children, but only one,

One class of children seven times again
That ever enters on the dancing floor
One year advanced in their compliant skill

To patterns ever with more varied styles
Clothing the naked order of the bass.

Some here relate the May with wanton rites,
Some with the Haymarket Riots, some with nothing
Beyond the present scene and circumstance
Which by the camera's thin incisive blade
They hope to take a frozen section through,

Keeping their child with one foot on the ground
And one foot off, and with a solemn face
Or one bewildered between grin and tears,
As many times repeating time and faith
He follows the compulsions of the dance

Around the brilliant morning with the sun,
The dance that leads him out to bring him home,
The May Day dance that tramples down the grass
And raises dust, that braids a double thread
Around the pole, in the great room of the sun.


THE BREAKING OF RAINBOWS

Oil is spilling down the little stream
Below the bridge. Heavy and slow as blood,
Or with an idiot's driveling contempt:
The spectral film unfolding, spreading forth
Prismatically in a breaking of rainbows,
Reflective radiance, marble evanescence,
It shadows the secret moves the water makes,
Creeping upstream again, then prowling down,
Sometimes asleep in the dull corners, combed
As the deep grass is combed in the stream's abandon,
And sometimes tearing open silently
Its seamless fabric in momentary shapes
Unlikened and nameless as the shapes of sky

That open with the drift of cloud, and close,
High in the lonely mountains, silently.
The curve and glitter of it as it goes
The maze of its pursuit, reflect the water
In agony under the alien, brilliant skin
It struggles to throw off and finally does
Throw off, on its frivolous purgatorial fall
Down to the sea and away, dancing and singing
Perpetual intercession for this filth—
Leaping and dancing and singing, forgiving everything.


## THE BEEKEEPER SPEAKS . . .

### I

Bees aren't humble, they don't notably bumble,
They tend to run a touch Stakhanovite,
If you'll allow the lofty title to
A hedonist who works himself to death
Flying at every blossom in the orchard
In a madness of efficiency at pleasure,
Like a totalitarian Don Juan
In serious pursuit. The best of them
Will last out maybe six weeks of the season,
Doing the apple's business for his drink,
Until, exhausted, or with a broken wing,
He falls; and when he falls his fellow workers
Team up in tandem to bear him from the hive
And drop him in a field to starve to death:
There's that much nonsense to a hive of bees.

### II

The damn fool growers used to spray their trees
So early, they drove out if not knocked off
Their native hives—a typical maneuver
For people driven by the economy
Until they finish by protecting what

400

They haven't got so hard they cannot have it.
So now they have to hire hives from me,
At least around this county, anyhow,
That's how it is, five bucks a hive the season,
Some fifteen hundred hives; it brings in dough
All right, and it's a way to make a living
Still has a shade of mystery about it;
People who need you come round all respectful,
But not quite friendly, maybe a little scared:
They damn well should be, it's a mystery.

III

There's not much competition in the bee
Business, because the plain sense of it is
You can't discourage bees from stinging when
They need to, which I guess is God knows when.
I got in this game young and plenty scared,
We used to wear, back then, netting and gloves,
And get stung anyhow, right through all that.
By now I never mind, I wear my sleeves
Rolled up, no net, no nothing except bees
That when you open up the skep come out
Like steam out of a boiling kettle, but
Much louder. And they carpet you all over,
It's in the cards that some of them will sting:
Maybe a couple of dozen stings a day,
By now I hardly notice any more.


. . . AND IS SILENT

IV

Anaphylactic shock, they talk about,
The doctors. They've their language, I have mine.
I might have bothered over all that once,
Until I figured if you really were
Allergic, first you'd know about it was

401

When you were dead. And since you weren't dead,
You'd learned the human blood is subtle stuff,
Its nature is the nature of the world
Outside the human, too, it gets a knowledge,
Borne on the poisoned point, how to become
Indifferent at first, and later on
Pleased with so powerful a nourishment
As comes from nature's winged sex and source:
The bloodstream is a venom in itself,
Sometimes I think to hear it hum in me.

V

And sometimes, too, not only in the night,
Lying awake, hearing life hum away,
But at the first of summer in the field
Releasing life and death in black and gold
Bullets that shake the petals back and forth,
And not the petals only, but the boughs,
With many-winged furies bearing futures,
I have felt myself become at first a bee,
And then the single-minded hive itself,
And after that the blossoming apple tree
Inside the violation of the swarm—
Until I am the brute and fruitful earth,
Furred with the fury of the golden horde,
And hear from far upon the field of time
The wild relentless singing of the stars.


THE MUD TURTLE

Out of the earth beneath the water,
Dragging over the stubble field
Up to the hilltop in the sun
On his way from water to water,
He rests an hour in the garden,
His alien presence observed by all:
His lordly darkness decked in filth

Bearded with weed like a lady's favor,
He is a black planet, another world
Never till now appearing, even now
Not quite believably old and big,
Set in the summer morning's midst
A gloomy gemstone to the sun opposed.
Our measures of him do not matter,
He would be huge at any size;
And neither does the number of his years,
The time he comes from doesn't count.

When the boys tease him with sticks
He breaks the sticks, striking with
As great a suddenness as speed;
Fingers and toes would snap as soon,
Says one of us, and the others shudder.
Then when they turn him on his back
To see the belly heroically yellow,
He throws himself fiercely to his feet,
Brings down the whole weight of his shell,
Spreads out his claws and digs himself in
Immovably, invulnerably,
But for the front foot on the left,
Red-budded, with the toes torn off.
So over he goes again, and shows
Us where a swollen leech is fastened
Softly between plastron and shell.
Nobody wants to go close enough
To burn it loose; he can't be helped
Either, there is no help for him
As he makes it to his feet again
And drags away to the meadow's edge.
We see the tall grass open and wave
Around him, it closes, he is gone
Over the hill toward another water,
Bearing his hard and chambered hurt
Down, down, down, beneath the water,
Beneath the earth beneath. He takes
A secret wound out of the world.

## SUMMER'S ELEGY

Day after day, day after still day,
The summer has begun to pass away.
Starlings at twilight fly clustered and call,
And branches bend, and leaves begin to fall.
The meadow and the orchard grass are mown,
And the meadowlark's house is cut down.

The little lantern bugs have doused their fires,
The swallows sit in rows along the wires.
Berry and grape appear among the flowers
Tangled against the wall in secret bowers,
And cricket now begins to hum the hours
Remaining to the passion's slow procession
Down from the high place and the golden session
Wherein the sun was sacrificed for us.
A failing light, no longer numinous,
Now frames the long and solemn afternoons
Where butterflies regret their closed cocoons.
We reach the place unripe, and made to know
As with a sudden knowledge that we go
Away forever, all hope of return
Cut off, hearing the crackle of the burn-
ing blade behind us, and the terminal sound
Of apples dropping on the dry ground.


## TWO GIRLS

I saw again in a dream the other night
Something I saw in daylight years ago,
A path in the rainy woods, a shaft of light,
And two girls walking together through shadow,
Through dazzle, till I lost them on their way
In gloom embowering beyond the glade.
The bright oblivion that belongs to day
Covered their steps, nothing of them remained,

Until the darkness brought them forth again
To the rainy glitter and the silver light,
The ancient leaves that had not fallen then.
Two girls, going forever out of sight,
Talking of lovers, maybe, and of love:
Not that blind life they'd be the mothers of.


## FOR ROBERT FROST, IN THE AUTUMN, IN VERMONT

All on the mountains, as on tapestries
Reversed, their threads unreadable though clear,
The leaves turn in the volume of the year.
Your land becomes more brilliant as it dies.

The puzzled pilgrims come, car after car,
With cameras loaded for epiphanies;
For views of failure to take home and prize,
The dying tourists ride through realms of fire.

"To die is gain," a virgin's tombstone said;
That was New England, too, another age
That put a higher price on maidenhead
if brought in dead; now on your turning page
The lines blaze with a constant light, displayed
As in the maple's cold and fiery shade.


## THE SWEEPER OF WAYS

All day, a small mild Negro man with a broom
Sweeps up the leaves that fall along the paths.
He carries his head to one side, looking down
At his leaves, at his broom like a windy beard
Curled with the sweeping habit. Over him
High haughty trees, the hickory and ash,
Dispense their more leaves easily, or else

The district wind, hunting hypocrisy,
Tears at the summer's wall and throws down leaves
To witness of a truth naked and cold.

Hopeless it looks, on these harsh, hastening days
Before the end, to finish all those leaves
Against time. But the broom goes back and forth
With a tree's patience, as though naturally
Erasers would speak the language of pencils.
A thousand thoughts fall on the same blank page,
Though the wind blows them back, they go where he
Directs them, to the archives where disorder
Blazes and a pale smoke becomes the sky.
The ways I walk are splendidly free of leaves.

We meet, we smile good morning, say the weather
Whatever. On a rainy day there'll be
A few leaves stuck like emblems on the walk;
These too he brooms at till they come unstuck.
Masters, we carry our white faces by
In silent prayer, Don't hate me, on a wave-
length which his broom's antennae perfectly
Pick up, we know ourselves so many thoughts
Considered by a careful, kindly mind
Which can do nothing, and is doing that.

## SMALL MOMENT

*Isaiah 54:7*

Death is serious,
or else all things are serious
except death. A player who dies
automatically disqualifies
for the finals. If there were no death
nothing could be taken seriously,
not truth, not beauty, but that is not

406

a situation which we need to face.
Men invented the gods, but they
discovered death; therefore, although
the skull is said to grin, the flesh
is serious, and frowns, for the world
is not a stage. And the gay spirit, gone
through wisdom to absurdity,
welcomes the light that shudders in the leaves
in all weathers and at any season,
since love, the pure, unique, and useless virtue,
climbs in the stalk and concentrates this dust
until it takes the light and shines
with the fat blood of death. So men say
that flowers light the sun, and so also,
when Theseus fought Antiope,
the battlefield became the marriage bed.
When you have known how this may be
you have already lived forever,
forsaken once in the small moment,
but gathered with great mercies after.


FIRELIGHT IN SUNLIGHT

Firelight in sunlight, silver-pale
Streaming with emerald, copper, sapphire
Ribbons and rivers, banners, fountains;
They rise, they run swiftly away.

Now apple logs unlock their sunlight
In the many-windowed room to meet
New sunlight falling in silvered gold
Through the fern-ice forest of the glass
Whose tropic surface light may pierce
If not the eye. O early world,
Still Daphne of the stubborn wood
Singing Apollo's song in light,
O pulsing constancies of flame

Warping a form along the log's
Slowly disintegrating face
Crackled and etched, so quickly aged,
These are my mysteries to see
And say and celebrate with words
In orders until now reserved.

For light is in the language now,
Carbon and sullen diamond break
Out of the glossary of earth
In holy signs and scintillations,
Release their fiery emblems to
Renewal's room and morning's room
Where sun and fire once again
Phase in the figure of the dance
From far beginnings here returned,
Leapt from the maze at the forest's heart,
O moment where the lost is found!


INTERIORS

Small flame pointing, shadowing, picking out
Black lacquer, bronze, blue velvet, a tassel
That sweeps the chequered floor. God of battles,
Bless these Thy banners. Smoke and the smell of fat
Ascending to cold turbulence over us,
A cold wind crawling the stone thresholds,
And through the cry of captains in the street
The hooded women carry uprooted canes
Into the courtyard for the fire of
Their ceremony called Burning of Wands.

The icy road, a rider drawn up at the door,
Knock echoing, what he has in hand
Peremptory, urgently magnificent,
Orders, tidings, there is never time.

So warm, so clear at the line of corded velvet
The marvelous flesh, its faster rise and fall,
Sigh in the throat, the mouth fallen open,
The knees fallen open, the heavy flag of the skirt
Urgently gathered together, quick, so quick,
Black lacquer, bronze, blue velvet, gleam
Of pewter in a tarnishing light, the book
Of the body lying open at the last leaf,
Where the spirit and the bride say, Come,
As from deep mirrors on the hinted wall
Beyond these shadows, a small flame sprouts.

# GNOMES & OCCASIONS (1973)

*To William B. Ober, with gratitude and affection*

*—ludentis speciem dabit et torquebitur*

# 1

## QUAERENDO INVENIETIS

### I

I am the combination to a door
That fools and wise with equal ease undo.
Your unthought thoughts are changes still unread
In me, without whom nothing's to be said.

### II

It is a spiral way that trues my arc
Toward central silence and my unreached mark.
Singing and saying till his time be done,
The traveler does nothing. But the road goes on.

### III

Without my meaning nothing, nothing means.
I am the wave for which the worlds make way.
A term of time, and sometimes too of death,
I am the silence in the things you say.

## PRISM

It corners the sun and caroms one
Rainbow to either side, an un-
assuming virtuoso. True
That both the cue ball and the cue
Shatter on impact, but they yield
The spectrum of objects, the green field.

413

## ONE MOMENT IN ETERNITY

Before Our Lady's on Des Peres Boulevard
On a brilliant Sunday morning in December

Is drawn up, idling and breathing smoke,
A sparkling maroon and black Cadillac
Hearse having a heavy silver crucifix
In each side window and in raised relief
The name Boomgartner Funerals scrawled out
In cursive silver script across
The front doors and the back; all this

Inspected by two altar-boys, admiringly:
"Jeezus!" says one, and "Jeezus!" agrees the other.

Implacably, pretending oblivion,
The liveried black chauffeur stares ahead
Along the hood, sighting between the up-
spreading wings of a silver angel taking off.

## A MEMORY OF MY FRIEND

A Jewish atheist stubborn as Freud
(the only Father he left undestroyed),
Who when you left his house at night would nod
And say, instead of "Good night," "Go with God."

## SOLIPSISM & SOLECISM

Strange about shadows, but the sun
Has never seen a single one.
Should night be mentioned by the moon
He'd be appalled at what he's done.

## PHILOSOPHY

When sages speak of the freedom of the will,
Watch out; for they're determined once and still
To find our freedom in Necessity,
Where the will alone, and nothing else, is free.


## THE GOD OF THIS WORLD

He smiles to see His children, born to sin,
Digging those foxholes there are no atheists in.


## EXTRACT FROM MEMOIRS

Surely one of my finest days, I'd just
Invented the wheel, and in the afternoon
I stuck a bit of charcoal under the bark
And running it along a wall described
The cycloid curve. When darkness came, I sang
My hymn to the great original wheels of heaven,
And sank into a sleep peopled with gods.

When I communicated my results
To the celestial academies, sending them
Models along with my descriptions, and
Their emissaries came to ask of me
"What are the implications of the 'wheel'
For human values?" I was very lofty—
"I made the damn thing go around," I said,
"You fellows go and figure what it's for."


415

## BEING OF THREE MINDS

### I

Between identity and difference
Logicians say that likeness lies; it lies,
They say, because it can do nothing else
On a ground that's nothing but its boundaries,
Distinguishing the different from the same
By puffing out the nothing of a name.

### II

What great magician could have cast the spell
That broke the stump of Babel from the sky
And raised Jerusalem the Golden high
On mortgage money from the vaults of Hell?

Some spellers say it was the little i
That differences deify and defy.


## LINES & CIRCULARITIES

*on hearing Casals' recording of the Sixth Suite*

Deep in a time that cannot come again
Bach thought it through, this lonely and immense
Reflexion wherein our sorrows learn to dance.
And deep in the time that cannot come again
Casals recorded it. Playing it back,
And bending now over the instrument,
I watch the circling stillness of the disc,
The tracking inward of the tone-arm, enact
A mystery wherein the music shares:
How time, that comes and goes and vanishes
Never to come again, can come again.

How many silly miracles there are
That will not save us, neither will they save

416

The world, and yet they are miraculous:
The tone-arm following the spiral path
While moving inward on a shallow arc,
Making the music that companions it
Through winding ways to silence at the close;
The delicate needle that navigates these canyons
By contact with the edges, not the floor;
Black plastic that has memorized and kept
In its small striations whatever it was told
By the master's mind and hand and bow and box,
Making such definite shudderings in the air
That Bach's intent arises from the tomb . . .
The Earth, that spins around upon herself
In the simple composition of Light and Dark,
And varying her distance on the Sun
Makes up the Seasons and the Years, and Time
Itself, whereof the angels make record;
The Sun, swinging his several satellites
Around himself and slowly round the vast
Galactic rim and out to the unknown
Past Vega at the apex of his path;
And all this in the inward of the mind,
Where the great cantor sings his songs to God . . .

The music dances to its inner edge
And stops. The tone-arm lifts and cocks its head
An instant, as if listening for something
That is no longer there but might be; then
Returns to rest, as with a definite click
The whole strange business turns itself off.

## BRUEGHEL: THE TRIUMPH OF TIME

Passing a Flemish village and a burning city
possibly Babylon the Great, bringing the Spring
from Winter and any beginning to its end, there go
the actors in the ramshackle traveling show

417

that does whatever's done and then undoes it:
the horses of the sun and moon, stumbling on plate
and bullion, patiently pull the flat-bed wagon
where Cronos munches a child and the zodiac-encircled world
bears up a tree that blossoms half and withers half;
Death on a donkey follows, sloping his scythe,
and last a trumpeter angel on an elephant
is puffing the resurrection and the end of days.

Under the wheels, and under the animals' feet,
palette and book are broken with the crowns of kings
and the instruments of music, intimating to our eyes
by means of many examples the Triumph of Time,
which everything that is, with everything that isn't,
as Brueghel patiently puts it down, exemplifies.


DRUIDIC RIMES

I

The mind went forth with naked eye
To take a turn about the sky.
The number of the stars was small,
Not 'numberless' at all.

Back then, the nature of the field
Was chiefly to be unrevealed.
But when the telescope was trained
Where only darkness reigned,

Or seemed to, lights broke into being
As if to marry the eye's seeing
In the flowering of a cosmic spring
That grew like anything.

Astronomers then put their hopes
Into profounder telescopes

And for a while the universe
Answered with stars and stars,

Whole galaxies and nebulae,
As if they'd just begun to be,
Blazed in the dark of outer space
As in the mind's dark place.

## II

Now mind went forth without the eye
On waves beyond the visible sky:
Impulses from what scarce was matter
Bounced off a shallow platter

Into the realm of number pure,
The only measure made so sure
That mind was guaranteed to mind it
And always stand behind it.

Number went through the universe.
Numberless numbers in reverse
Came back in echo, pulse and blip;
It was as if the lip

Of silence learned to intimate
In integers that it might mate
Its dark selfhood to any mind
Consenting to go blind

Into the secret labyrinth
Of its own lens, and its first myth
Of sacrificing to the sky
The always naked eye.

# 2

## ZANDER ON GOD

It may not cover all theodicy
Or make him popular among the seraphim,
But "If God were true," my Zander said to me,
"He wouldn't make people not believe in Him."

## THE DEATH OF GOD

The celebrants came chanting "God is dead!"
And all as one the nations bowed the head
Thanksgiving; knowing not how shrewdly the rod
Would bite the back in the kingdom of dead God.

## POWER TO THE PEOPLE

Why are the stamps adorned with kings and presidents?
That we may lick their hinder parts and thump their heads.

## MORNING SUN

How many more this morning are there dead of
The peace I came to bring a sword instead of?

## THE POVERTY PROGRAMS

Are planned to make things better and not worse.
But by the time the billions get passed down
Someone's absconded with the integers
And let the zeroes help the poor alone.


## ON GETTING OUT OF VIETNAM

Theseus, if he did destroy the Minotaur
(it's hard to say, that may have been a myth),
Was careful not to close the labyrinth.
So After kept on looking like Before:
Back home in Athens still the elders sent
Their quota of kids to Knossos, confident
They would find something to die of, and for.


## THIRTIETH ANNIVERSARY REPORT
## OF THE CLASS OF '41

We who survived the war and took to wife
And sired the kids and made the decent living,
And piecemeal furnished forth the finished life
Not by grand theft so much as petty thieving—

Who had the routine middle-aged affair
And made our beds and had to lie in them
This way or that because the beds were there,
And turned our bile and choler in for phlegm—

Who saw grandparents, parents, to the vault
And wives and selves grow wrinkled, grey and fat
And children through their acne and revolt
And told the analyst about all that—

Are done with it. What is there to discuss?
There's nothing left for us to say of us.

## NEW WEAPONS IN THE OLD WAR

Is it for Satan's, God's, or Nature's uses
That men and women have proximity fuses?
Like teleological rockets when they meet,
Each one ignited by the other's heat.


## HISTORY OF HAIR FROM WORLD WAR II
## TO THE PRESENT

Crewcut et Ux. have raised their long-haired pup:
Samson is shorn, and Absalom's hung up.


## OF EXPERIENCE

Nature from life by piece and piece
Gently disparts us; power fails
Before desire does. It needs not sex
To illustrate what Montaigne saith,
But only what's befallen X—
Now he no longer has his teeth
He can no longer bite his nails.


## THE MOST EXPENSIVE PICTURE IN THE WORLD

We stand in line all morning long to see it,
And finally when we do come face to face
With the seamy canvas and its crackling glaze,
Where the figures hover and glow from a black smoke
Of dried and crusted oils, we are impressed—
How could we fail to be impressed? and yet
With a distinct sense of something's having failed.
The most expensive picture in the world?
Either we are edified by that, or else

Not edified at all; though someone says,
Just as we leave, a rather thoughtful thing
That might have saved the day if saying could:
"It is the most expensive picture, yes,
          But only in the world."


## ON BEING A MEMBER OF THE
## JURY FOR A POETRY PRIZE

*Jury's* the *mot juste* under our ground rules:
I may say Guilty, and I mostly do,
But sentencing's beyond me, poeticules,
As, by your poems, it's beyond most of you.


## MYSTERY STORY

Formal as minuet or sonnet,
It zeroes in on the guilty one;
But by the time I'm told who done it,
I can't remember what he done.


## ARS POETICA

*(apologies to Mr. MacLeish and Miss Moore,
but the poet who inspired this one was a
real toad with imaginary gardens in him)*

Even before his book came out
We knew there wasn't any doubt
That these was poems forevermore,
Such as the guy wrote the slogan for:
They wuz not mean, they wuz—
Big pear-shaped poems, ready to parse
In the next Creative Writing clarse.

423

Yeh, he sure fell flat on his ars
Poetica that time, palpable and mute
As an old globed fruit.


## WHAT KIND OF GUY WAS HE?

Just so you shouldn't have to ask again,
He was the kind of guy that if he said
Something and you were the kind of guy that said
You can say that again, he'd say it again.


## TO MY LEAST FAVORITE REVIEWER

When I was young, just starting at our game,
I ambitioned to be christlike, and forgive thee.
For a mortal Jew that proved too proud an aim;
Now it's my humbler hope just to outlive thee.


## TO THE POETS

Song sparrow's limited creativity,
Three eighth-notes and a trill all summer long,
The falling second of the chickadee—
It's a pretty humble business, singing song.


## EPITAPH

Of the Great World he knew not much,
But his Muse let little in language escape her.
Friends sigh and say of him, poor wretch,
He was a good writer, on paper.

# 3

## THE TAPESTRY

On this side of the tapestry
There sits the bearded king,
And round about him stand
His lords and ladies in a ring.
His hunting dogs are there,
And armed men at command.

On that side of the tapestry
The formal court is gone,
The kingdom is unknown;
Nothing but thread to see,
Knotted and rooted thread
Spelling a world unsaid.

Men do not find their ways
Through a seamless maze,
And all direction lose
In a labyrinth of clues,
A forest of loose ends
Where sewing never mends.

## A RIDDLE THE SPHINX FORGOT

What is this creature who must sweat all day
In the mill of making, in the field of fight,
And then, instead of sleeping, spend all night
To counterfeit the paper for his pay?

## SMALL MOON

Coming home on a summer night
To the empty house—it's like being
On colorless TV, on the stage set
For Return of the Grand Insomniac;
It is to watch your life as it would be
Without you: the old druggist in the darkroom
Developing someone else's negatives.


## SEPTEMBER, THE FIRST DAY OF SCHOOL

### I

My child and I hold hands on the way to school,
And when I leave him at the first-grade door
He cries a little but is brave; he does
Let go. My selfish tears remind me how
I cried before that door a life ago.
I may have had a hard time letting go.

Each fall the children must endure together
What every child also endures alone:
Learning the alphabet, the integers,
Three dozen bits and pieces of a stuff
So arbitrary, so peremptory,
That worlds invisible and visible

Bow down before it, as in Joseph's dream
The sheaves bowed down and then the stars bowed down
Before the dreaming of a little boy.
That dream got him such hatred of his brothers
As cost the greater part of life to mend,
And yet great kindness came of it in the end.

### II

A school is where they grind the grain of thought,
And grind the children who must mind the thought.

It may be those two grindings are but one,
As from the alphabet come Shakespeare's Plays,
As from the integers comes Euler's Law,
As from the whole, inseparably, the lives,

The shrunken lives that have not been set free
By law or by poetic phantasy.
But may they be. My child has disappeared
Behind the schoolroom door. And should I live
To see his coming forth, a life away,
I know my hope, but do not know its form

Nor hope to know it. May the fathers he finds
Among his teachers have a care of him
More than his father could. How that will look
I do not know, I do not need to know.
Even our tears belong to ritual.
But may great kindness come of it in the end.


## AFTER COMMENCEMENT

Across the trampled, program-littered grass
A thousand yellow chairs have broken ranks
Before the ramrod silver microphone
That stands there on the platform unaddressed
And finished with the clichés of command.

O ceremony, ceremony! Let
Expression be the mere formality
The day demands; for emptiness alone
Has generality enough to send
Yet one more generation to the world,

And platitudes become the things they are
By being uninformative and true:
The words that for the hundredth time today
Bounced off the sunlit stone into the past
Have made the silence deeper by degrees.

427

## ON BEING ASKED FOR A PEACE POEM

Here is Joe Blow the poet
Sitting before the console of the giant instrument
That mediates his spirit to the world.
He flexes his fingers nervously,
He ripples off a few scale passages
(Shall I compare thee to a summer's day?)
And resolutely readies himself to begin
His poem about the War in Vietnam.

This poem, he figures, is
A sacred obligation: all by himself,
Applying the immense leverage of art,
He is about to stop this senseless war.
So Homer stopped that dreadful thing at Troy
By giving the troops the Iliad to read instead;
So Wordsworth stopped the Revolution when
He felt that Robespierre had gone too far;
So Yevtushenko was invited in the *Times*
To keep the Arabs out of Israel
By smiting once again his mighty lyre.[1]
Joe smiles. He sees the Nobel Prize
Already, and the reading of his poem
Before the General Assembly, followed by
His lecture to the Security Council
About the Creative Process; probably
Some bright producer would put it on TV.
Poetry might suddenly be the in thing.

Only trouble was, he didn't have
A good first line, though he thought that for so great
A theme it would be right to start with O,
Something he would not normally have done,

1. "An Open Letter to Yevgeny Yevtushenko, Poet Extraordinary of Humanity,"
advt., Charles Rubinstein, *New York Times*, November 3, 1966.

O

And follow on by making some demands
Of a strenuous sort upon the Muse
Polyhymnia of Sacred Song, that Lady
With the fierce gaze and implacable small smile.


## THE WORLD AS BRUEGHEL IMAGINED IT

The world as Brueghel imagined it is riddled with the word:
Whatever's proverbial becomes pictorial; if people habitually
Go crawling up a rich man's ass, they must be seen to do so
(through an orifice widened for the passage of three abreast;
The rich man, scattering coins from a sack, pays them no heed).
If people are in the habit of turning into toads without notice,
They must be seen to do so; if the owl is said to carry
Nestlings and nest upon her back, she must be seen to do so.

The world as Brueghel imagined it is hardly easier to read
Than is the one we glibly refer to as The Real World:
The proverbs get forgotten, or their meaning leaches out,
And in the unmoving frame all motions are arrested
In an artful eternity—the hay runs after the horse
Forever—so that we can't always tell coming from going,
Or literal good from allegorical bad, or arsey-versey:
The Cross may be headed for Hell, the pruning-hook for Heaven.

But it remains, the world as Brueghel imagined it,
A plenum of meaning though we know not what the meanings
    are
In every place; and after having once experienced
The innocent and deep delight of understanding one
Or another emblem, acknowledging his just equation
Wedding the picture to the word, we take his word
In many matters wherein we have no further warrant
Than that his drawings draw enciphered thoughts from things.
So if the Ship of Fools is propped up on a pair of barrels,

Of if a man is shitting on the Beauty Shoppe's roof,
Or if Saint Anthony is somehow tempted (but to what?)
By a helmeted human jug with dagger and diarrhoea,
So that he has to turn away his halo and his head,
We get the picture, as we say, although we miss
The shrewd allusion to some ancient smart remark
That would have told us what we know and never say.

The world as Brueghel imagined it is full of decaying fish
With people in their hulls, it is centered on allegorical dames
With funny hats, who queen it over the seven deadly sins
And as many deadly virtues—the millinery architecture of Pride,
And silly Hope standing on water—: it is the world we know
And fail to know that he has seen for us and minded too,
Where from Cockaigne it's but three steps to Heaven or Hell—
Hallucinating, yes, but only what is truly here.


TWO VIEWS OF A PHILOSOPHER

*painted in oils at eighteen, he survived*
*into the age of photography, which took him*

Behold the genial boy who promised much,
And made the Will beget upon the Mind
A dark incredible scheme in double Dutch
That told of happiness for humankind

Against the odds (which were the odds he set)
That dumb would be our best intelligence
Against the dreaming fury driving it
To make its mind up never to make sense.

Behold the lapsing embers of that spark
Out at the limit of his latest year,
The curls all vanished from his shiny sconce,
His painted smile shrunk to a sepia sneer.
He lifts the last light of his learned glance
And sees it swallowed in a box of dark.

## TO D——, DEAD BY HER OWN HAND

My dear, I wonder if before the end
You ever thought about a children's game—
I'm sure you must have played it too—in which
You ran along a narrow garden wall
Pretending it to be a mountain ledge
So steep a snowy darkness fell away
On either side to deeps invisible;
And when you felt your balance being lost
You jumped because you feared to fall, and thought
For only an instant: That was when I died.

That was a life ago. And now you've gone,
Who would no longer play the grown-ups' game
Where, balanced on the ledge above the dark,
You go on running and you don't look down,
Nor ever jump because you fear to fall.


## HOPE

*(as Brueghel drew her)*

The Lady Hope should look ridiculous, and she does,
There on the storming sea, in the wind and weather
Of our mortality, where the waves leap slavering white
Against the granite of the landing stage
And the municipal jail under whose raised portcullis
Prisoners are sitting, their hands manacled to prayer.

Back further in the village a house is near burnt down,
But still the bucket brigade is climbing its ladders
Against the one remaining wall and pouring water
Into the empty blaze; while out on the wharf a fisherman
Heeds nothing but his lines, and beside him a gravid Vrouw
Unconcernedly surveys the turbulence out to sea,

431

Where in the lather and chop of the hounding waters
Ships capsize and split and go down, and the men are drowning
Though they cling while they can to splintered mast or spar;
Where even the great fish, the privileged of the Flood,
Are shipping water over the gunwales of their mouths
And may already be going down for the third time.

Yet there upon the slippery allegorical waves,
Under her tilted and towering beehive of a hat,
Hope, the beliefless lady, rides out the storm
With a shovel in one hand and a sickle in the other
Keeping her silly balance in the impossible world,
Her slippers steady on the shank of an unsinkable anchor.


## THE PAINTER DREAMING IN THE SCHOLAR'S HOUSE

*in memory of the painters Paul Klee
and Paul Terence Feeley*

I

The painter's eye follows relation out.
His work is not to paint the visible,
He says, it is to render visible.

Being a man, and not a god, he stands
Already in a world of sense, from which
He borrows, to begin with, mental things
Chiefly, the abstract elements of language:
The point, the line, the plane, the colors and
The geometric shapes. Of these he spins
Relation out, he weaves its fabric up
So that it speaks darkly, as music does
Singing the secret history of the mind.
And when in this the visible world appears,
As it does do, mountain, flower, cloud, and tree,
All haunted here and there with the human face,

432

It happens as by accident, although
The accident is of design. It is because
Language first rises from the speechless world
That the painterly intelligence
Can say correctly that he makes his world,
Not imitates the one before his eyes.
Hence the delightsome gardens, the dark shores,
The terrifying forests where nightfall
Enfolds a lost and tired traveler.

And hence the careless crowd deludes itself
By likening his hieroglyphic signs
And secret alphabets to the drawing of a child.
That likeness is significant the other side
Of what they see, for his simplicities
Are not the first ones, but the furthest ones,
Final refinements of his thought made visible.
He is the painter of the human mind
Finding and faithfully reflecting the mindfulness
That is in things, and not the things themselves.

For such a man, art is an act of faith:
Prayer the study of it, as Blake says,
And praise the practice; nor does he divide
Making from teaching, or from theory.
The three are one, and in his hours of art
There shines a happiness through darkest themes,
As though spirit and sense were not at odds.

II

The painter as an allegory of the mind
At genesis. He takes a burlap bag,
Tears it open and tacks it on a stretcher.
He paints it black because, as he has said,
Everything looks different on black.

Suppose the burlap bag to be the universe,
And black because its volume is the void

433

Before the stars were. At the painter's hand
Volume becomes one-sidedly a surface,
And all his depths are on the face of it.

Against this flat abyss, this groundless ground
Of zero thickness stretched against the cold
Dark silence of the Absolutely Not,
Material worlds arise, the colored earths
And oil of plants that imitate the light.

They imitate the light that is in thought,
For the mind relates to thinking as the eye
Relates to light. Only because the world
Already is a language can the painter speak
According to his grammar of the ground.

It is archaic speech, that has not yet
Divided out its cadences in words;
It is a language for the oldest spells
About how some thoughts rose into the mind
While others, stranger still, sleep in the world.

So grows the garden green, the sun vermilion.
He sees the rose flame up and fade and fall
And be the same rose still, the radiant in red.
He paints his language, and his language is
The theory of what the painter thinks.


II

The painter's eye attends to death and birth
Together, seeing a single energy
Momently manifest in every form,
As in the tree the growing of the tree
Exploding from the seed not more nor less
Than from the void condensing down and in,
Summoning sun and rain. He views the tree,
The great tree standing in the garden, say,
As thrusting downward its vast spread and weight,

434

Growing its green height from dark watered earth,
And as suspended weightless in the sky,
Haled forth and held up by the hair of its head.
He follows through the flowing of the forms
From the divisions of the trunk out to
The veinings of the leaf, and the leaf's fall.
His pencil meditates the many in the one
After the method in the confluence of rivers,
The running of ravines on mountainsides,
And in the deltas of the nerves; he sees
How things must be continuous with themselves
As with whole worlds that they themselves are not,
In order that they may be so transformed.
He stands where the eternity of thought
Opens upon perspective time and space;
He watches mind become incarnate; then
        He paints the tree.


IV

These thoughts have chiefly been about the painter Klee,
About how he in our hard time might stand to us
Especially whose lives concern themselves with learning
As patron of the practical intelligence of art,
And thence as model, modest and humorous in sufferings,
For all research that follows spirit where it goes.

That there should be much goodness in the world,
Much kindness and intelligence, candor and charm,
And that it all goes down in the dust after a while,
This is a subject for the steadiest meditations
Of the heart and mind, as for the tears
That clarify the eye toward charity.

So may it be to all of us, that at some times
In this bad time when faith in study seems to fail,
And when impatience in the street and still despair at home
Divide the mind to rule it, there shall some comfort come
From the remembrance of so deep and clear a life as his

Whom I have thought of, for the wholeness of his mind,
As the painter dreaming in the scholar's house,
His dream an emblem to us of the life of thought,
The same dream that then flared before intelligence
When light first went forth looking for the eye.


## MYTH & RITUAL

You come down to a time
In every poker game
Where the losers allow
They've lost, the winners begin
Sneaking into their shoes
Under the covered table;
You come down to that time,

They all go home. And hard
As it is to imagine
A fat and rowdy ghost
Pee in his empty glass
So as not to miss a hand,
That's how it happens; Paul
Is gone, and Stanley is gone,

The winners have risen with cash
And checks and promising papers
And drifted through the cold door
Forever, while the host,
Like some somnambulist
Or sleepy priest, empties
Their ashes into the dawn.

# 4

## THE CROSSING

September, and the butterflies are drifting
Across the sky again, the monarchs in
Their myriads, delicate lenses for the light
To fall through and be mandarin-transformed.

I guess they are flying southward, or anyhow
That seems to be the average of their drift,
Though what you mostly see is a random light
Meandering, a Brownian movement to the wind,

Which is one of Nature's ways of getting it done,
Whatever it may be, the rise of hills
And settling of seas, the fall of leaf
Across the shoulder of the northern world,

The snowflakes one by one that silt the field . . .
All that's preparing now behind the scene,
As the ecliptic and equator cross,
Through which the light butterflies are flying.

## LATE BUTTERFLIES

October days
Red admirals
Flutter among
Falling leaves—
Flakes of the sun
Gone glittering—

Hurrying clouds,
Milkweed seeds
Blowing along,
Birds so loud
In the red leaves,
Robin all rusty
And shabby jay—
Alas, the admirals!

Last year they spun
Their silken shrouds
And died to life,
Only in spring
To spring awake
And cruise for colors
Through the green and green.

Now there's the end
Coming, November
Coming, storms
Of ice and snow.

We see the admirals
Sail forth to seasons
We some survive
Where they will not.

Day darkens and
We take our pity
Back in the house,
The warm indoors.


## THE RENT IN THE SCREEN

*to Loren Eiseley*

Sweet mildness of the late December day
Deceives into the world a couple of hundred

Cinnamon moths, whose cryptic arrow shapes
Cling sleeping to a southward-facing wall
All through the golden afternoon, till dusk
And coming cold arouse them to their flight
Across the gulf of night and nothingness,
The falling snow, the fall, the fallen snow,
World whitened to dark ends. How brief a dream.


## THE BEAUTIFUL LAWN SPRINKLER

What gives it power makes it change its mind
At each extreme, and lean its rising rain
Down low, first one and then the other way;
In which exchange humility and pride
Reverse, forgive, arise, and die again,
Wherefore it holds at both ends of the day
The rainbow in its scattering grains of spray.


## THE PUZZLE

*to Lewis Mumford*

Two children bow their heads
Over the ruins of what is yet to be:
Sun, sky, and sand, the Pyramids, the Sphinx.

Under their fingers, under their eyes,
Before their minds, enclaves of order
Begin to appear amid the heaped debris

As they go steadily sorting and rejecting,
Turning about and matching, finding the fit
By image, color, shape, or all at once,

Rebuilding the continuum from its bits,
Until the Sphinx's head falls into place
Completing the vision of a ruined world

Divided in the crackling glaze of forms,
The seams and fissures of a kind of brain
Thinking what properties must go together

To make, accordant with mosaic law,
The real world match the mindful one, to which
The children bow their heads.


## SNOWFLAKES

Not slowly wrought, nor treasured for their form
In heaven, but by the blind self of the storm
Spun off, each driven individual
Perfected in the moment of his fall.


## THRESHOLD

When in still air and still in summertime
A leaf has had enough of this, it seems
To make up its mind to go; fine as a sage
Its drifting in detachment down the road.


## KICKS

The fishermen on Lake Michigan, sometimes,
For kicks, they spit two hunks of bait on hooks
At either end of a single length of line
And toss that up among the scavenging gulls,

Who go for it so fast that often two of them
Make the connection before it hits the water.

Hooked and hung up like that, they do a dance
That lasts only so long. The fishermen

Do that for kicks, on Lake Michigan, sometimes.


## CREATION MYTH ON A MOEBIUS BAND

This world's just mad enough to have been made
By the Being his beings into Being prayed.


## BEHAVIOR

Among our good deeds of this date:
Removed a turtle from the drive
And saved a drowning butterfly.
At evening, bowing over meat,
We call down grace on all alive.


## THE POET AS EAGLE SCOUT

I said to the stone, "Am I standing all right?"
"How's this for running?" I said to the stream.
"Is it bright enough for you?" I asked the light.
And I told my dream, "You're a damn fine dream."


## QUESTIONS

### I

Why is the universe mysterious?
Why should it be? Did someone make it so?

441

And if he did, was it as having us
In mind, and our importunate will to know?

Echo answers, the radar of the mind,
Receiving what it sends, but modified.
The breath of language goes out on the wind,
The drumming on the eardrum comes inside.

What was it drew the spirit from the stone,
Giving so much and hiding so much more?
And does the temptress of the To Be Known
Summon across a sea that has no shore?


II

Or will the whole relation end somewhere
In libraries abandoned, books decayed,
Language itself no longer in the air
And men relapsing from an eon's raid

Into the other mind? Where would it go,
Where be, the knowledge that we never had?
Would we remember what it was to know,
Be teased for a time by dreams of going mad

With nearly knowing or half-remembering
Idolatries of truth we could not keep,
Before the icy dark began to sing,
Rocking the cradle of our backward sleep?



ANALOGUE

You read the clicking keys as gibberish
Although they strike out sentences to sense.
So in the fluttering leaves, the shoaling fish,
The continuum nondenumerable and dense,
Dame Kind keeps rattling off her evidence.

442

## ABOVE

Orange translucent butterflies are cruising
Over a smoke of gnats above the trees

And over them the stiff-winged chimney swifts
Scythe at the air in alternating arcs

Among the roofs where flights of pigeons go
(slate as the roofs above and white below)

And puffs of seed go raining down the wind
While higher up a hawk turns on one wing

And higher still a silver jet climbs by
Serenely screaming with a trail of smoke

And there are sailing clouds that shift their shapes
All afternoon unseen, and last of all

Out there, a broken corner of the moon
So pale, so faint, so still, and all alone


## KNOWLEDGE

Not living for each other's sake,
Mind and the world will rarely rime;
The raindrops aiming at the lake
Are right on target every time.


## HIDE & SEEK

They move at maximum velocity,
The sun himself has never found one out.
They lie to the blind side of everything;
They've never seen the light, they never will,

Who stand to Plato for the world itself
And all that in it is, such as ourselves,
Erased like shadows when the sun goes in
And drowned like shadows when the sun goes down.

If individuals best coalesce
Under conditions of total eclipse,
Is night their vindication or their doom,
Annihilation or communion dance?

And still outside of this, beyond all this,
How could the cold and dark be absolute?
An explorer said the stars were moved by love—
Then what great light's black space the shadow of?


## BEGINNER'S GUIDE

They stand in the corner, on a shadowy shelf,
Field Books of This, Beginner's Guide to That,
Remainders of an abdicated self
That wanted knowledge of no matter what.

Of flowers, was it? Every spring he'd tear
From their hiding-places, press and memorize
A dozen pale beginners of the year
That open almost among the melting snows,

And for a month thereafter rule his realm
Of small and few and homey in such minds
As his, until full summer came to whelm
Him under the flood and number of her kinds.

Or birds? At least the flowers would stand still
For amateurs, but these flighty alightings
Would not; and as he still refused to kill
In confirmation of his rarer sightings

444

The ornithologists were not his dish,
And he made do with sedentary birds
Who watched his watching as it were their wish
To check with Peterson, pictures and words.

And even so, before he got them straight
As like as not they'd not be there at all.
On the wings and wits God gave 'em they'd migrate;
"Confusing Fall Warblers" were, each Fall, his fall.

The world would not, nor he could not, stand still.
The longest life might be too short a one
To get by heart, in all its fine detail,
Earth's billion changes swinging on the sun.

His last attempt he made upon the stars,
And was appalled, so many more of them
There were since boyhood that astronomers
Preferred a number to an ancient name.

And if, as The Beginner was advised
To do, he bought himself a telescope,
The host of stars that must be memorized
So mightily increased, he'd lose all hope.

Was it a waste, the time and the expense,
Buying the books, going into the field
To make some mind of what was only sense,
And show a profit on the year's rich yield?

Though no authority on this theme either,
He would depose upon the whole that it
Was not. The world was always being wider
And deeper and wiser than his little wit,

But it felt good to know the hundred names
And say them, in the warm room, in the winter,
Drowsing and dozing over his trying times,
Still to this world its wondering beginner.

# THE
# WESTERN
# APPROACHES
# (1975)

*To Elbert Lenrow*

# 1 The Way

According to our tradition, when a man
dies there comes to him the Angel, who
says: "Now I will tell you the secret of life
and the meaning of the universe." One man
to whom this happened said: "Take off,
grey Angel. Where were you when I needed
you?" Among all the hosts of the dead he is
the only one who does not know the secret
of life and the meaning of the universe;
whence he is held in superstitious
veneration by the rest.


FUGUE

You see them vanish in their speeding cars,
The many people hastening through the world,
And wonder what they would have done before
This time of time speed distance, random streams
Of molecules hastened by what rising heat?
Was there never a world where people just sat still?

Yet they might be all of them contemplatives
Of a timeless now, drivers and passengers
In the moving cars all facing to the front
Which is the future, which is destiny,
Which is desire and desire's end—
What are they doing but just sitting still?

And still at speed they fly away, as still
As the road paid out beneath them as it flows
Moment by moment into the mirrored past;
They spread in their wake the parading fields of food,
The windowless works where who is making what,
The grey towns where the wishes and the fears are done.

449

## LATE LATE SHOW

Movies, the Old Law. TV is the New
Wherein the dead who did our phantasies
Have stolen back into the living room
To do their thing again. Boxed in the bad
Resurrections of Hell, in a seamy air
And silver drizzle of shifting shape and shade,
Witnessed without terror and without pity,
Eternal return unrolls itself anew.

The stars and the members of unremembered casts
Are spared the selfish indifference of the selves
Kept up past bedtime by their early lives
Become our late ones, moving in a light
So swiftly scanning it can keep them up
As long as the old show stays on the road,
Addressing its advertisements for life
To us the living, while even their dead die.


## THE DOOMSDAY BOOKS

Nobody knows if the water will dry up
Before the air gives out or gets to be
Too thick to breathe in, whether we will die
Of traffic or cigarette or drug
Or bomb or plague transmitted through the air
By wingéd carriers at the speed of sound;
Inflation, famine, and fleets from outer space
Full of colonial imperialists from Mars
Are also considered among the candidates.

Meanwhile, the more lovers there are, the more
Consumers there will be, and increased food
Accelerates the fucking frequency
That multiplies the mouths over the food.

We can't win nor we can't even break even
At wearing out this world because we must.
On every front at once we reach the edge;
At least it seems that way to the middle class,
With Chicken Licken writing all these books.


## STRANGE METAMORPHOSIS OF POETS

From epigram to epic is the course
For riders of the American wingéd horse.
They change both size and sex over the years,
The voice grows deeper and the beard appears;
Running for greatness they sweat away their salt,
They start out Emily and wind up Walt.


## COSMIC COMICS

There is in space a small black hole
Through which, say our astronomers,
The whole damn thing, the universe,
Must one day fall. That will be all.

Their shrinks can't get them to recall
How this apocalyptic dream
's elaborated on a humbler theme:
The toilet bowl, the Disposall.

Let prizes from the Privy Purse
Reward the Ultimate Hygiene
For flushing all flesh from the scene.

Where Moses saw the seat of God                    *Exod. 33. 23.*
Science has seen what's just as odd,
The asshole of the universe.


451

# THE METAPHYSICAL AUTOMOBILE

I

It's abstract nouns, among the myths of mind,
Make most of the trouble. Where there used to be
Honest chimera and candid hippogriff,
Whom none did the disservice of belief,
We've Communism and Democracy,
Labor and Capital, and others of the kind;
Whole circus tents collapsed, whose shapeless terms
Cover the billow and bulge of fighting forms.

And pronouns, too. I, the erected vowel,
Stands up for a man's own lecherous will,
All right; but You already has become
Ambiguous, while We, They, Us and Them,
Four partners to a Freudian affair,
Conceal a con game and the threat of war.

II

You can't resolve a contradiction by
Getting between the warring opposites.
The idea of a car either has a dent
In its left front fender or it downright don't,
There's no third way. For on the roads of thought
You're either nominalist or realist,
The only question universals ask
Is is you is or is you ain't my baby?
And mild conceptualists, those innocent
Bystanders, stand to get hit from either side.
Accursed are the compromisers and
The sorry citizens of buffer states,
Nor fish nor flesh nor fowl nor good red herring,
And spued out by the Lamb, the great I Am.

III

In the eternal combustion engine, force
Is from the contradicting opposites,

And yet their warfare passes into play:
The pistons know that up opposes down,
Closed in their cylinders they cannot know
Around, and would not be converted by
The revelation of the wheel. So straight
Flat roads of logic lie about a globe
On which the shortest way between two points
Happens to be a curve. And so do song
And story, winding crank and widdershins,
Still get there first, and poetry remains
Eccentric and odd and riddling and right,
Eternal return of the excluded middle.


## WATCHING FOOTBALL ON TV

I

It used to be only Sunday afternoons,
But people have got more devoted now
And maybe three four times a week retire
To their gloomy living room to sit before
The polished box alive with silver light
And moving shadows, that incessantly
Gives voice, even when pausing for messages.
The colored shadows made of moving light,
The voice that ritually recites the sense
Of what they do, enter a myriad minds.
Down on the field, massed bands perform the anthem
Sung by a soprano invisible elsewhere;
Sometimes a somewhat neutral public prayer—
For in the locker rooms already both
Sides have prayed God to give them victory.

II

Totemic scarabs, exoskeletal,
Nipped in at the thorax, bulky above and below,

With turreted hard heads and jutting masks
And emblems of the lightning or the beast;
About the size of beetles in our sight,
Save for the closeup and the distant view,
Yet these are men, our representatives
More formidable than ourselves in speed and strength
And preparation, and more injured too;
Bandage and cast exhibit breakages
Incurred in wars before us played before;
Hard plaster makes a weapon of an arm,
A calf becomes a club. Now solemnly
They take up their positions in the light,
And soon their agon will begin again.

III

To all this there are rules. The players must
Remember that in the good society
Grabbing at anybody's mask will be
A personal foul and incur a penalty.
So too will pushing, tripping, interfering
In any manner with someone else's pass.
Fighting is looked on with particular
Severity; though little harm can come
To people so plated at shoulder, head and thigh,
The most conspicuous offenders are
Ejected from the game and even fined.
That's one side of the coin, the other one
Will bear the picture of a charging bull
Or some such image imprecating fear,
And for its legend have the one word: *Kill.*

IV

Priam on one side sending forth eleven
Of many sons, and Agamemnon on
The other doing much the same; is it
The Game of Troy again? the noble youth
Fiery with emulation, maneuvering
Toward power and preeminence? Well no,

It's not. Money is the name of the game
From the board room to the beers and souvenirs.
The players are mean and always want more money.
The owners are mean and always have more money
And mean to keep it while the players go
Out there to make them more; they call themselves
Sportsmen, they own, are and carry a club.
Remember this when watching the quarterback's
Suppliant hands under the center's butt.

V

We watch all afternoon, we are enthralled
To what? some drama of the body and
The intellectual soul? of strategy
In its rare triumphs and frequent pratfalls?
The lucid playbook in the memory
Wound up in a spaghetti of arms and legs
Waving above a clump of trunks and rumps
That slowly sorts itself out into men?
That happens many times. But now and then
The runner breaks into the clear and goes,
The calm parabola of a pass completes
Itself like destiny, giving delight
Not only at skill but also at the sight
Of men who imitate necessity
By more than meeting its immense demands.

VI

Passing and catching overcome the world,
The hard condition of the world, they do
Human intention honor in the world.
A football wants to wobble, that's its shape
And nature, and to make it spiral true
's a triumph in itself, to make it hit
The patterning receiver on the hands
The instant he looks back, well, that's to be
For the time being in a state of grace,
And move the viewers in their living rooms

To lost nostalgic visions of themselves
As in an earlier, other world where grim
Fate in the form of gravity may be
Not merely overcome, but overcome
Casually and with style, and that is grace.

VII

Each year brings rookies and makes veterans,
They have their dead by now, their wounded as well,
They have Immortals in a Hall of Fame,
They have the stories of the tribe, the plays
And instant replays many times replayed.
But even fame will tire of its fame,
And immortality itself will fall asleep.
It's taken many years, but yet in time,
To old men crouched before the ikon's changes,
Changes become reminders, all the games
Are blended in one vast remembered game
Of similar images simultaneous
And superposed; nothing surprises us
Nor can delight, though we see the tight end
Stagger into the end zone again again.

ROUTE TWO

Along Route Two I saw a sign
Standing out in a swamp. One line
It spoke that might epitomize
The ambition of Free Enterprise:
Save While You Spend, is what it said
Across the swamp and to the road,
Save While You Spend. As if one saw
A way to beat the Second Law
By pouring money down the drain
As long as it was one's own drain.

## OZYMANDIAS II

I met a guy I used to know, who said:
"You take your '57 Karnak, now,
The model that they called their Coop de Veal
That had the pointy rubber boobs for bumpers—
You take that car, owned by a nigger now
Likelier'n not, with half its chromium teeth
Knocked down its throat and aerial ripped off,
Side stitched with like bullets where the stripping's gone
And rust like a fungus spreading on the fenders,

Well, what I mean, that fucking car still runs,
Even the moths in the upholstery are old
But it gets around, you see one on the street
Beat-up and proud, well, Jeezus what a country,
Where even the monuments keep on the move."


## HE

Slave to a God whose sole known verb is *Flatter*!
His world a spectre and his soul a wraith
Astray in the illusion he called *Matter*,
He got religion when he lost his faith.


## TWO PAIR

More money's lost, old gamblers understand,
On two pair than on any other hand;

And in the great world that may be the cause
That we've two pairs of First and Second Laws.

The first pair tells us we may be redeemed,
But in a world, the other says, that's doomed.

In one, the First Law says: Nothing is Lost.
The other First Law adds: But we are lost.

One Second Law fulfills what spake the prophets;
The other tersely states: There are no profits.

Baffled between the Old Law and the New,
What boots it to be told both sets are true,

Or that disorder in the universe
Is perfectly legal, and always getting worse?


## NEBUCHADNEZZAR, SOLUS

Seven years I had to think it over;
Or not to think, I couldn't, but to yield.
Seven years on all fours and in clover,
Taking a nosedown closeup of the field.

I understood the weather of the season,
Endured the pain, but not the *Angst*, of heaven,
And my dumb knowledge was relieved of reason
Till I, agreed with heaven, deemed us even.

I stood, I bathed, in glory was arrayed
And formal made submission to the Will
Above, though half my soul in secret prayed
To be my animal again and still.

But I forbid all men from making ballads
About my seven years spent browsing salads.


## EINSTEIN & FREUD & JACK

*to Allen Tate on his 75th Birthday*

Death is a dead, at least that's what Freud said.
Long considering, he finally thought

Life but a detour longer or less long;
Maybe that's why the going gets so rough.

When Einstein wrote to ask him what he thought
Science might do for world peace, Freud wrote back:
Not much. And took the occasion to point out
That science too begins and ends in myth.

His myth was of the sons conspired together
To kill the father and share out his flesh,
Blood, power, women, and the primal guilt
Thereon entailed, which they must strive

Vainly to expiate by sacrifice,
Fixed on all generations since, of sons.
Exiled in London, a surviving Jew,
Freud died of cancer before the war began

That Einstein wrote to Roosevelt about
Advising the research be started that,
Come seven years of dying fathers, dying sons,
In general massacre would end the same.

Einstein. He said that if it were to do
Again, he'd sooner be a plumber. He
Died too. We live on sayings said in myths,
And die of them as well, or ill. That's that,

Of making many books there is no end,
And like it saith in the book before that one,
What God wants, don't you forget it, Jack,
Is your contrite spirit, Jack, your broken heart.


WAITING ROOMS

What great genius invented the waiting room?
Every sublime idea no doubt is simple, but
Simplicity alone is never enough.
A cube sequestered in space and filled with time,

Pure time, refined, distilled, denatured time
Without qualities, without even dust . . .
Dust in a sunbeam between Venetian blinds
Where a boy and his mother wait . . . Eternity!
But I am straying from the subject: waiting rooms.

All over the globe, in the great terminals
And the tiny rooms of disbarred abortionists,
For transport, diagnosis, or divorce . . .
Alas! Maybe this mighty and terrible theme
Is too much for me. But wait! I have an idea.

You've heard it said, of course, that anything
May instantly turn into everything
In this world secreting figures of itself
Forever and everywhere? How wonderful
That is, how horrible. Wherever you wait,
Between anticipation and regret,
Between the first desire and the second
Is but the razor of a moment, is
Not even time; and neither is motion more,
At sixty miles an hour or six hundred,
Than an illusion sent by devils to afford
Themselves illusory laughs at our expense
(we suffer, but they become no happier).

Think how even in heaven where they wait
The Resurrection, even in the graves
Of heaven with the harps, this law applies:
One waiting room will get you to the next.
Even your room, even your very own,
With the old magazines on the end tables,
The goldfish in the bowl below the window
Where the sunbeam falls between Venetian blinds . . .
And in the downstairs hall there is your mailbox,
One among many gathering paper and dust,
A waiting room in figure, summing up
Much in a little, the legendary box
Where hope only remains. You wait and see.

## CAPITALS

When a common noun becomes a Proper One
It seems to add an invisible *de* or *von*,
Gets uppity, forgets its former friends
And can't remember even what it means.

Look at intelligence. It went that way
As soon as ever it joined the CIA;
And the even dozen gods themselves turned odd
The minute they got upped in grade to God.


## CRITIC

"I am self-evident," the mirror said,
"Plain as the nose on your face; plain as your face."

I unbelieving looked behind the glass
On razor, styptic, mouthwash and Band-aid;

And it has been my life's ambition since
To elucidate the mirror by its medicines.


## NOVELISTS

Theirs is a trade for egomaniacs,
People whose parents did not love them well.
It's done by wasps and women, Jews and Blacks,
In every isolation ward in Hell.

They spend their workadays imagining
What never happened and what never will
To people who are not and whose non-being
Always depends on the next syllable.

461

It's strange, and little wonder it makes them so
Whose lives are spun out talking to themselves
In allegories of themselves that go
Down on the paper like dividing cells

That form in communes and make colonies
And do each other in by love and hate
And generally enact the ceremonies
Intended to harmonize freedom and fate

Among the creatures and in the writer's soul.
The writer's *soul*? It's as if one abyss
Primps at the other's mirror and the whole
Shebang hangs fire while the lovers kiss.

## WOLVES IN THE ZOO

They look like big dogs badly drawn, drawn wrong.
A legend on their cage tells us there is
No evidence that any of their kind
Has ever attacked man, woman, or child.

Now it turns out there were no babies dropped
In sacrifice, delaying tactics, from
Siberian sleds; now it turns out, so late,
That Little Red Ridinghood and her Gran

Were the aggressors with the slavering fangs
And tell-tale tails; now it turns out at last
That grey wolf and timber wolf are near extinct,
Done out of being by the tales we tell

Told us by Nanny in the nursery;
Young sparks we were, to set such forest fires
As blazed from story into history
And put such bounty on their wolvish heads

As brought the few survivors to our terms,
Surrendered in happy Babylon among
The peacock dusting off the path of dust,
The tiger pacing in the stripéd shade.


## THE COMMON WISDOM

Their marriage is a good one. In our eyes
What makes a marriage *good*? Well, that the tether
Fray but not break, and that they stay together.
One should be watching while the other dies.


## THE WESTERN APPROACHES

As long as we look forward, all seems free,
Uncertain, subject to the Laws of Chance,
Though strange that chance should lie subject to laws,
But looking back on life it is as if
Our Book of Changes never let us change.

Stories already told a time ago
Were waiting for us down the road, our lives
But filled them out; and dreams about the past
Show us the world is post meridian
With little future left to dream about.

Old stories none but scholars seem to tell
Among us any more, they hide the ways,
Old tales less comprehensible than life
Whence nonetheless we know the things we do
And do the things they say the fathers did.

When I was young I flew past Skerryvore
Where the Nine Maidens still grind Hamlet's meal,
The salt and granite grain of bitter earth,

But knew it not for twenty years and more.
My chances past their changes now, I know

How a long life grows ghostly towards the close
As any man dissolves in Everyman
Of whom the story, as it always did, begins
In a far country, once upon a time,
There lived a certain man and he had three sons . . .


## A MEMORY OF THE WAR

Most what I know of war is what I learned
When mine was over and they shipped me home.
I'd been a chauffeur with the RAF
And didn't know the first damn thing about
The American way of doing anything
Till they told me I was Officer of the Day
(at midnight, yet) and gave me a whopping great
Blue automatic and sat me on D Deck
At the top of a ladder leading to a hold
Where a couple hundred enlisted men were sleeping,
And said I was to sit there till relieved.
"But what's this for?" I said about the gun,
And was answered: "If this ship shows any sign
Of going down, you shoot down the first son-
ofabitch sticks his head up through this hatch."
So that is what I did, and how I learned
About the War: I sat there till relieved.


## TO THE RULERS

We read and hear about you every day,
What you decide we need, or want, or may
Be made to stand still for . . . Now let us pray.

Approaching the year One Thousand of Your Lord,
Men fixed that date for the ending of the world;
Truth and round numbers naturally in accord.

One of society's earlier ego trips,
That hinted only this to your Lordships:
A calendar implies apocalypse.

That passed. And all the reborn skeptics smiled
Over such fancies as could have beguiled
No one who was not but a simple child.

Now, as we near the next millennium,
Reality's caught up with Kingdom Come—
Why wait two dozen years to round the sum?

O Conscript Fathers, sponsors of the draft,
Prospective survivors on the little raft
That when the world sinks will be what is left,

I hear you praying, as your fingers trill
Unnervingly at night beside the pill,
The button, the hot line to the Other Will,

Your prayer, that used to be Caligula's too,
*If they all only had one neck . . .* It's so
Unnecessary and out of date. We do.


## BOY WITH BOOK OF KNOWLEDGE

He holds a volume open in his hands:
Sepia portraits of the hairy great,
The presidents and poets in their beards
Alike, simplified histories of the wars,
Conundrums, quizzes, riddles, games and poems,

465

"Immortal Poems"; at least he can't forget them,
Barbara Fritchie and the Battle Hymn,
And best of all America the Beautiful,
Whose platitudinous splendors ended with
"From sea to shining sea," and made him cry

And wish to be a poet, only to say such things,
From sea to shining sea. Could that have been
Where it began? the vast pudding of knowledge,
With poetry rare as raisins in the midst
Of those gold-lettered volumes black and green?

Mere piety to think so. But being now
As near his deathday as his birthday then,
He would acknowledge all he will not know,
The silent library brooding through the night
With all its lights continuing to burn

Insomniac, a luxury liner on what sea
Unfathomable of ignorance who could say?
And poetry, as steady, still, and rare
As the lighthouses now unmanned and obsolete
That used to mark America's dangerous shores.


AMNESTY

The memory is not good. There is something loose
Inside the head, that is threatening the brain.
The past passes, that's all, it takes the pain.
I can't remember what happened to the Jews,

I can't remember Korea or Vietnam;
Now that a decade of rut and riot is out,
Replaced by a dumber time of rot and rout,
There are days I can't remember even the Bomb

Or the Cold War, or tell one Senator
McCarthy from another, or which came first;

I've forgotten what they call *our time,* and, worst,
Forgotten what they said it all was for.

I know it's for the best, there was too much pain,
Killing those children, bombing the Iron Age
Back into the Stone Age. When you're my age
You'll have learned forgiveness over and again:

Forgiveness forgets, and I forgive the lot,
Forgive my country and the world, forgive
Especially myself, that I may live;
But what I forgive us for I have forgot.

And that the future may be bright with loss
I'm driving the children to Pike's Peak to see
The big statue of Daddy Warbucks, where he
Is shown in the act of Putting Up the Cross.


EVE

There are no more shopping days to Christmas.
Slowly we wheel our wire cages down
And back along the fluorescent aisles,
And down and back again, prowling the maze
Of goods, by many musics played upon,
The glaze of obligation in our eyes
As we take in the dozen television sets
Tuned to the same Western, and the caged birds
No one has wanted to give, and the many
Remaining goldfish desperately marked down.

Come all ye faithful, calls the music now.
We march in time, stopping to take, put back,
And sometimes take again. We buy some rolls
Of merry wrapping paper, and push the whole
Caboodle to the counter where it's counted
And added up and put in paper bags

By the girl we pay and get the right change from
With some green stamps. She smiles, and we smile back.
A dollar bill is pinned to her left tit
Somewhere about the region of the heart.


POCKETS

Are generally over or around
Erogenous zones, they seem to dive
In the direction of those

Dark places, and indeed
It is their nature to be dark
Themselves, keeping a kind

Of thieves' kitchen for the things
Sequestered from the world
For long or little while,

The keys, the handkerchiefs,
The sad and vagrant little coins
That are really only passing through.

For all they locate close to lust,
No pocket ever sees another;
There is in fact a certain sadness

To pockets, going their lonesome ways
And snuffling up their sifting storms
Of dust, tobacco bits and lint.

A pocket with a hole in it
Drops out; from shame, is that, or pride?
What is a pocket but a hole?

## HERO WITH GIRL AND GORGON

Child of the sunlight in the tower room,
When you have carried away Medusa's head,
When you have slain the dragon in the sea
And brought the maiden breathing from the rock
To be the bride, consider, wingéd man,
The things that went before and what things else
Must follow, when in the land beyond the North
The grey hags sang to you, the three grey hags
Sharing an eye and a tooth, dim-glimmering in
White darkness, sang to you their song of how
The things that were surpass the things that are . . .

As though the vision from that time reversed,
As in the glitter of the shield the sword
Cut backward in aversion from the cold
Brow's beauty and the wide unpitying gaze . . .

And now you must go onward through the world
With that great head swung by the serpents held
At lantern height before you, lighting your way
Past living images that mock or curse,
Till paralyzed to silence in the stone
They run unmoved on your undying doom.

## THE BACKWARD LOOK

As once in heaven Dante looked back down
From happiness and highest certainty
To see afar the little threshing floor
That makes us be so fierce, so we look now
And with what difference from this stony place,
Our sterile satellite with nothing to do,
Not even water in the so-called seas.

No matter the miracles that brought us here,
Consider the end. Even the immense power
Of being bored we brought with us from home
As we brought all things else, even the golf
Balls and the air. What are we doing here,
Foreshadowing the first motels in space?
"They found a desert and they left the Flag."

From earth we prayed to heaven; being now
In heaven, we reverse the former prayer:
Earth of the cemeteries and cloudy seas,
Our small blue agate in the big black bag,
Earth mother of us, where we make our death,
Earth that the old man knocked on with his staff
Beseeching, "Leve moder, let me in,"

Hold us your voyagers safe in the hand
Of mathematics, grant us safe return
To where the food is, and the fertile dung,
To generation, death, decay; to war,
Gossip and beer, and bed whether warm or cold,
As from the heaven of technology
We take our dust and rocks and start back down.

# 2 The Ground

Natura in reticulum sua genera connexit,
non in catenam: homines non possunt nisi
catenam sequi, cum non plura simul
possint sermone exponere.

Nature knits up her kinds in a network, not
in a chain; but men can follow only by
chains because their language can't handle
several things at once.

Albrecht von Haller

## THE DEPENDENCIES

This morning, between two branches of a tree
Beside the door, epeira once again
Has spun and signed his tapestry and trap.
I test his early-warning system and
It works, he scrambles forth in sable with
The yellow hieroglyph that no one knows
The meaning of. And I remember now
How yesterday at dusk the nighthawks came
Back as they do about this time each year,
Grey squadrons with the slashes white on wings
Cruising for bugs beneath the bellied cloud.
Now soon the monarchs will be drifting south,
And then the geese will go, and then one day
The little garden birds will not be here.
See how many leaves already have
Withered and turned; a few have fallen, too.
Change is continuous on the seamless web,
Yet moments come like this one, when you feel
Upon your heart a signal to attend

The definite announcement of an end
Where one thing ceases and another starts;
When like the spider waiting on the web
You know the intricate dependencies
Spreading in secret through the fabric vast
Of heaven and earth, sending their messages
Ciphered in chemistry to all the kinds,
The whisper down the bloodstream: it is time.


## FIGURES OF THOUGHT

To lay the logarithmic spiral on
Sea-shell and leaf alike, and see it fit,
To watch the same idea work itself out
In the fighter pilot's steepening, tightening turn
Onto his target, setting up the kill,
And in the flight of certain wall-eyed bugs
Who cannot see to fly straight into death
But have to cast their sidelong glance at it
And come but cranking to the candle's flame—

How secret that is, and how privileged
One feels to find the same necessity
Ciphered in forms diverse and otherwise
Without kinship—that is the beautiful
In Nature as in art, not obvious,
Not inaccessible, but just between.

It may diminish some our dry delight
To wonder if everything we are and do
Lies subject to some little law like that;
Hidden in nature, but not deeply so.

## LATE SUMMER

Look up now at what's going on aloft—
Not in high heaven, only overhead,
Yet out of reach of, unaffected by,
The noise of history and the newsboy's cry.

There grow the globes of things to come,
There fruits and futures have begun to form
Solid and shadowy along the boughs:
Acorns in neat berets, horse chestnuts huge
And shiny as shoes inside their spiny husks,
Prickly planets among the sweetgum's starry leaves.

So secretly next year secretes itself
Within this one, as far on forested slopes
The trees continue quietly making news,
Enciphering in their potencies of pulp
The matrix of much that hasn't happened yet.


## A CABINET OF SEEDS DISPLAYED

These are the original monies of the earth,
In which invested, as the spark in fire,
They will produce a green wealth toppling tall,
A trick they do by dying, by decay,
In burial becoming each his kind
To rise in glory and be magnified
A million times above the obscure grave.

Reader, these samples are exhibited
For contemplation, locked in potency
And kept from act for reverence's sake.
May they remind us while we live on earth
That all economies are primitive;
And by their reservations may they teach
Our governors, who speak of husbandry
And think the hurricane, where power lies.

473

## FLOWER ARRANGEMENTS

*for Pat*

The flowers that a friend brings twice a week
Or even oftener accumulate
In plastic cups beside me on the table.
Not only I forget to throw them out,
But also I've a curiosity,
Fading a bit myself, to watch them fade.
They do it with much delicacy and style.

Shrinking into themselves, they keep their cool
And colors many days, their drying and
Diminishing would be imperceptible
But for the instance of the followers
Arranged beside them in the order of
Their severance and exile from the earth;
In death already though they know it not.

At last the petals shrivel, fold and fall,
The colors grow pastel and pale, the stems
Go brittle and the green starts turning brown;
The fireworks are over, and life sinks
Down in or else evaporates, but where?
From time to time I throw a cup away,
Wondering where lives go when they go out.


## WALKING DOWN WESTGATE IN THE FALL

The weather's changes are the private rites
And secret celebrations of the soul
So widely now believed not to exist.
The first clear autumn day, the summer rain,
The sudden fall of winter and the dark
When Daylight Saving goes, the sunny melt
Of several February days, to these
Changes the soul with changes of its own
And overtones responds in resonance.

474

Down Westgate, in the Fall, the housewives set
Chrysanthemums in bronze or marble bowls
Forth on the stoops, defying ice and snow
With their lion's mane, sun's face ruddy glow of gold.

Things like that marry weather with the soul,
Which would have its seasons if it did exist,
And sing its songs among the falling leaves
Under the autumn rain, and celebrate
Its mass with hymns and litanies of change,
Walking down Westgate past chrysanthemums,
Consenting with the winter soon to come,
Hearing the acorns bang on the roofs of cars
And bounce and roll along the rainy street.


## GINKGOES IN FALL

They are the oldest living captive race,
Primitive gymnosperms that in the wild
Are rarely found or never, temple trees
Brought down in line unbroken from the deep
Past where the Yellow Emperor lies tombed.

Their fallen yellow fruit mimics the scent
Of human vomit, the definite statement of
An attitude, and their translucency of leaf,
Filtering a urinary yellow light,
Remarks a delicate wasting of the world,

An innuendo to be clarified
In winter when they defecate their leaves
And bear the burden of their branches up
Alone and bare, dynastic diagrams
Of their distinguished genealogies.

## AGAIN

Again, great season, sing it through again
Before we fall asleep, sing the slow change
That makes October burn out red and gold
And color bleed into the world and die,
And butterflies among the fluttering leaves
Disguise themselves until the few last leaves
Spin to the ground or to the skimming streams
That carry them along until they sink,
And through the muted land, the nevergreen
Needles and mull and duff of the forest floor,
The wind go ashen, till one afternoon
The cold snow cloud comes down the intervale
Above the river on whose slow black flood
The few first flakes come hurrying in to drown.


## THE CONSENT

Late in November, on a single night
Not even near to freezing, the ginkgo trees
That stand along the walk drop all their leaves
In one consent, and neither to rain nor to wind
But as though to time alone: the golden and green
Leaves litter the lawn today, that yesterday
Had spread aloft their fluttering fans of light.

What signal from the stars? What senses took it in?
What in those wooden motives so decided
To strike their leaves, to down their leaves,
Rebellion or surrender? and if this
Can happen thus, what race shall be exempt?
What use to learn the lessons taught by time,
If a star at any time may tell us: *Now*.

# EQUATIONS OF A VILLANELLE

The breath within us is the wind without,
In interchange unnoticed all our lives.
What if the same be true of world and thought?

Air is the ghost that comes and goes uncaught
Through the great system of lung and leaf that sieves
The breath within us and the wind without;

And utterance, or inspiration going out,
Is borne on air, on empty air it lives
To say the same is true of world and thought.

This is the spirit's seamless fabric wrought
Invisible, whose working magic gives
The breath within us to the wind without.

O great wind, blow through us despite our doubt,
Distilling all life's sweetness in the hives
Where we deny the same to world and thought,

Till death, the candle guttering to naught,
Sequesters every self as it forgives
The breath within us for the wind without;
What if the same be true of world and thought?


# A COMMON SAW

*Good king, that must approve the common saw,*
*Thou out of heaven's benediction comest*
*To the warm sun!*
King Lear, 2.2.156–8

Had God but made me a religious man
I'd have it made. The suburb where I live

Affords an ample choice of synagogues
And seven different Christianities—

I'd go to all of them, to every one
In turn, continuous performances:
Confession and yarmulka, incense, candlelight,
High, low, and broad, reform and orthodox,

Allowing God no possible way out
But my salvation—save that God did not
Make me a religious man, but left me here,
From heaven's blessing come to the warm sun,

Twined round the pinkie and pinned under the thumb
Of Dame Kind dear and beautiful and dumb


NEAR THE OLD PEOPLE'S HOME

The people on the avenue at noon,
Sharing the sparrows and the wintry sun,
The turned-off fountain with its basin drained
And cement benches etched with checkerboards,

Are old and poor, most every one of them
Wearing some decoration of his damage,
Bandage or crutch or cane; and some are blind,
Or nearly, tap-tapping along with white wands.

When they open their mouths, there are no teeth.
All the same, they keep on talking to themselves
Even while bending to hawk up spit or blood
In gutters that will be there when they are gone.

Some have the habit of getting hit by cars
Three times a year; the ambulance comes up
And away they go, mumbling even in shock
The many secret names they have for God.

## NATURE MORTE

Bees forage where the blue ajuga's grown
To make low forest of the sloping lawn,
A hummingbird on wings invisible
Kneels in the air before a lily's bell
Beneath the waving grove where light and shade
Their play among the latticed leaves have made.

Whatever the ostensive scene may be,
The painter studies its solemnity,
A stillness out of moving Nature carved,
The silence of the object unobserved.
That is what looks at us from those flat rooms
That hang in galleries like Time's own tombs.

The eye takes oriole and tanager,
A fountain's lazy splashing takes the ear,
While high above and slow across the sky
The tumbling-turreted galleon clouds go by
As Constable caught them doing long ago
Over the silent park at Wivenhoe.


## SEEING THINGS

Close as I ever came to seeing things
The way the physicists say things really are
Was out on Sudbury Marsh one summer eve
When a silhouetted tree against the sun
Seemed at my sudden glance to be afire:
A black and boiling smoke made all its shape.

Binoculars resolved the enciphered sight
To make it clear the smoke was a cloud of gnats,
Their millions doing such a steady dance
As by the motion of the many made the one
Shape constant and kept it so in both the forms
I'd thought to see, the fire and the tree.

479

Strike through the mask? you find another mask,
Mirroring mirrors by analogy
Make visible. I watched till the greater smoke
Of night engulfed the other, standing out
On the marsh amid a hundred hidden streams
Meandering down from Concord to the sea.


FIRST SNOW

*for Ian McHarg*

Always the solemnest moment of the year
Is this one, when the few first flakes
Come falling, flying, riding down the wind
And minute upon minute multiply
To being blind and blinding myriads.

It used to be said that when the sun burns down,
Being after all a mediocre star
Of the main sequence, mortal as ourselves,
One snow will seal the sleepy cities up,
Filling their deep and canyoned avenues

Forever. That will be the day. And for all
I know it may be true; at least it was
One vulgarized version of The Second Law
A century ago, and almost all
The celebrated authors did it up,

A natural: "London, Peking, Moscow, Rome,
Under their cerements of eternal snow,"
And so on; writing was a powerful stuff
Back then, and tales of entropy and The End
Could always snow the middle class. Meanwhile,
It only hisses through the whitening grass,
And rattles among the few remaining leaves.

# CHILDHOOD

*A translation of Rainer Maria Rilke's "Kindheit"*
*("Da rinnt der Schule lange Angst und Zeit . . .")*

So ran the schoolday, full of time and stress
And waiting, full of stupid public sound.
O loneliness, O time too much to spend . . .
At last let out: through streets all clean and gay,
And through the plazas where the fountains play,
And gardens where the world seemed to expand.
And through all this in one's own little dress,
Other than others in their otherness—:
O strangest time, O time too much to spend,
O loneliness.

And through all this to see so far and deep:
The men, the women; the men, women, children
All in their otherness so well wrapped up;
And here and there a house, and now a hound
(and fear becoming trust without a sound)—:
O senseless sorrow, dreadful as in sleep,
O groundless deep.

And then to games: with ball and ring and hoop
There in a garden growing twilight grey;
And sometimes brushing against a grown-up,
Blind and unheeding in the haste of play . . .
And then at dusk, with prim and proper step
To walk back home, hand in a hand's firm grip—:
O ever more uncomprehended fate,
O fear, great weight.

And hours long beside the great grey lake
Kneeling to watch one's little sailboat bear
Away and be lost among so many other there
Taller and costlier, that crossed her wake;
And then to have to think of that small, bleak
Child's face, drowning still mirrored in that lake—:
O childhood, O likeness drawn to disappear.
But where? But where?

# 3 The Mind

Poetry, Painting & Music, the three Powers
in Man of conversing with Paradise, which
the flood did not Sweep away.

William Blake


## CASTING

The waters deep, the waters dark,
Reflect the seekers, hide the sought,
Whether in water or in air to drown.
Between them curls the silver spark,
Barbed, baited, waiting, of a thought—
Which in the world is upside down,
The fish hook or the question mark?


## FICTION

The people in the elevator all
Face front, they all keep still, they all
Look up with the rapt and stupid look of saints
In paintings at the numbers that light up
By turn and turn to tell them where they are.
They are doing the dance, they are playing the game.

To get here they have gone by avenue
And street, by ordinate and abscissa, and now
By this new coordinate, up. They are three-
dimensional characters, taken from real life;
They have their fates, whether to rise or fall,
And when their numbers come up they get out.

## REFLEXION OF A NOVELIST

In time, these people all will know each other.
But me they will not know, spelling the words
Of which alone they will be put together
A certain while, though sundered afterwards.

Is happiness illusory or real?
I need not decide today, but should do soon.
Will meningitis or the automobile
Doom one or both, or should the honeymoon

End in the faced despair of their mistake?
Whichever, they cannot know me hovering there
A dimension past the space in which they speak
And do as they are told, nor be aware,
Even when bound and put upon the shelf,
How their voyeur will have exposed himself.


## THE WEATHER OF THE WORLD

Now that the cameras zero in from space
To view the earth entire, we know the whole
Of the weather of the world, the atmosphere,
As though it were a great sensorium,
The vast enfolding cortex of the globe,
Containing contradictions, tempers, moods,
Able to be serene, gloomy or mad,
Liable to huge explosions, brooding in
Depressions over several thousand miles
In length and trailing tears in floods of sorrow
That drown the counties and the towns. What power
There is in feeling! We are witness to,
Enslaved beneath, the passions of a beast
Of water and air, a shaman shifting shape
At the mercy of his moods, trying to bend,
Maybe, but under pressure like to break.

483

His mind is our mind and the world's alike,
His smiles, his rages and aridities,
Reflect us large across the continents
And improvise our inwardness upon
The desert and the sea; we suffer him
As if he were the sufferer buried in
The self and hidden in heaven's indifference;
And like us he seeks balances that are
Inherently unstable to either hand;
The id, the superego, and the god
Of this world, the apparent devil of the will
Whom God has given power over us
Or cannot or else will not bring to heel,
Our nourisher and need, our sorrow and rage,
Reacting and reflecting on our lives
In windy eloquence and rainy light
As in the brilliant stillness of the sun.


## THERE

Sacred is secret: at the confluence
Where the unclean, the holy, the forbidden,
Mingle their currents, there where mind and sense,
An inch behind the eyes, perform their hidden

And common ministry, turning a storm
Of photons into this world of trees and rocks
And stars and faces, not to forget the worm
That dieth not, back there in the black box

That listens for what's said between the ears,
The eavesdropper under the thatch, there is the place
Of power, the transformer bathed in blood
Dreaming its figures of a universe
Where all except a mirror's understood:
Disguise of devil and god, the human face.

## NIGHTMARE

When the grey stranger shows up in your dream,
Drawing his silken cord across your throat
To waken you while you die, and you hear your scream
Strangled behind you as you flee from him,

The other time, continuing yesterday,
Takes over with its watchful face aglow,
Its hands that go on scissoring away
Both worlds at once; and sweating cold you say

"I just got out in time." But that's not so,
As waking from a dark to a dark you know
That if you were for a time in mortal danger,
And are so still, it was not from a stranger.


## EXASPERATIONS OF A NOVELIST

### I

Locked in the dictionary on the table,
The people of my book, except their names,
Lie dormant, waiting for an author able
To rearrange them from their anagrams.

For that great slumber is unconscious of
Every last word that anyone can say
About them and about their doings unto love
And unto death, the tome that starts at A

And keeps in the confusion of its dream
Bible and bibliothèque before it wakes
To the last buzzing of the Z, the sum
Of follies, knowledges, wisdoms and mistakes,

Myth of the order of the alphabet,
Chaos enciphered, of all sets the set.

485

## II

Now hear this, all you people of my book,
You are a stubborn and a stiff-neck'd lot.
What is all this about your freedom? Look,
Once more, will you try to follow the plot?

Free will, in moderation, after all,
Is one thing, you can choose your suits and ties
And have what you like to eat. But when I call
For one of you to die, and no one dies,

That's serious. I'll give you a chapter more,
And that's the end: it will be suicide
For Jane and marriage among the other four—
Which way you pair your freedom shall decide.

But they go on as if they never heard
The Let There Be of my creating word.


## LEARNING THE TREES

Before you can learn the trees, you have to learn
The language of the trees. That's done indoors,
Out of a book, which now you think of it
Is one of the transformations of a tree.

The words themselves are a delight to learn,
You might be in a foreign land of terms
Like samara, capsule, drupe, legume and pome,
Where bark is papery, plated, warty or smooth.

But best of all are the words that shape the leaves—
Orbicular, cordate, cleft and reniform—
And their venation–palmate and parallel—
And tips—acute, truncate, auriculate.

Sufficiently provided, you may now
Go forth to the forests and the shady streets
To see how the chaos of experience
Answers to catalogue and category.

Confusedly. The leaves of a single tree
May differ among themselves more than they do
From other species, so you have to find,
All blandly says the book, "an average leaf."

Example, the catalpa in the book
Sprays out its leaves in whorls of three
Around the stem; the one in front of you
But rarely does, or somewhat, or almost;

Maybe it's not catalpa? Dreadful doubt.
It may be weeks before you see an elm
Fanlike in form, a spruce that pyramids,
A sweetgum spiring up in steeple shape.

Still, *pedetemtim* as Lucretius says,
Little by little, you do start to learn;
And learn as well, maybe, what language does
And how it does it, cutting across the world

Not always at the joints, competing with
Experience while cooperating with
Experience, and keeping an obstinate
Intransigence, uncanny, of its own.

Think finally about the secret will
Pretending obedience to Nature, but
Invidiously distinguishing everywhere,
Dividing up the world to conquer it,

And think also how funny knowledge is:
You may succeed in learning many trees
And calling off their names as you go by,
But their comprehensive silence stays the same.

## CONVERSING WITH PARADISE

*for Robert Jordan*

To see the world the way a painter must,
Responsive to distances, alive to light,
To changes in the colors of the day,
His mind vibrating at every frequency
He finds before him, from wind waves in wheat
Through trees that turn their leaves before the storm,
To the string-bag pattern of the pebbled waves
Over the shallows of the shelving cove
In high sunlight; and to the greater wave-
lengths of boulder and building, to the vast
Majestic measures of the mountain's poise;

And from these modulations of the light
To take the elected moment, silence it
In oils and earths beneath the moving brush,
And varnish it and put it in a frame
To seal it off as privileged from time,
And hang it for a window on the wall,
A window giving on the ever-present past;

How splendid it would be to be someone
Able to do these mortal miracles
In silence and solitude, without a word.


## PLAYING THE INVENTIONS

*Forthright instruction, wherewith lovers of the clavier, especially
those desirous of learning, are shown in a clear way not only (1) to
play two voices clearly, but also after further progress (2) to deal
correctly and well with three obbligato parts, moreover at the same
time to obtain not only good ideas, but also to carry them out well,
but most of all to achieve a cantabile style of playing, and thereby to
acquire a strong foretaste of composition. Prepared by Joh. Seb. Bach,
Capellmeister to his Serene Highness the Prince of Anhalt-Cothen.
Anno Christi 1723.*

488

I

The merest nub of a notion, nothing more
Than a scale, a shake, a broken chord, will do
For openers; originality
Is immaterial, it is not the tune
But the turns it takes you through, the winding ways
Where both sides and the roof and floor are mirrors
With some device that will reflect in time
As mirrors do in space, so that each voice
Says over what the others say, because
Consideration should precede consent;
And only being uninformative
Will be the highest reach of wisdom known
In the perfect courtesy of music, where
The question answers only to itself
And the completed round excludes the world.


II

How arbitrary it must be, the sound
That breaks the silence; yet its valency,
Though hidden still, is great for other sounds
Drawn after it into the little dance
Prefigured in its possibilities:
The tune's not much until it's taken up.
O mystery of mind, that cannot know
Except by modeling what it would know,
Repeating accident to make it fate:
This is the thread that spins the labyrinth,
The acorn opened that unfolds the oak,
Word that holds space and sequence in the seed,
That splits the silence and divides the void
In phrases that reflect upon themselves,
To be known that way and not in paraphrase.


III

It is a heartless business, happiness,
It always is. Two hundred and fifty years

Of time's wild wind that whips at the skin of that sea
Whose waves are men, two hundred and fifty years
Of a suffering multiplied as many times
As there were children born to give it form
By feeding it their bodies, minds and souls;
And still the moment of this music is,
Whether in merry or in melancholy mode,
A happiness implacable and austere,
The feeling that specifically belongs
To music when it heartlessly makes up
The order of its lovely, lonely world
Agreeing justice with surprise, the world
We play forever at while keeping time.

IV

Landowska said, to end an argument,
"Why don't you go on playing Bach your way
And let me play Bach his way?" putting down
Whoever-it-was forever; music's not
All harmony, Landowska too is dead,
Spirit acerb, though her records remain
Hermetically kept where time not much corrupts
Nor quite so quick. In our advancing age
Not only the effigy can be preserved
But the sound as well, only without the self,
As evanescent as it ever was.
At last even the inventions lock us out,
We go while they remain. The argument ends.
It's like a myth about inventing death:
We don't become immortal, but it does.

V

Ach, dear Bach, so beautiful a day!
A small breeze shakes the shadows of the leaves
Over the instrument, across your page,
Sprinklings of drops at the outer edge of spray
In patterns overpatterning your own.
And one sits here, "lover of the clavier

And desirous to learn," your backward dilettante,
Amateur, stumbling slowly through your thoughts
Where five and twenty decades of the world's
Sorrow and wrath are for a while as though
Dissolved in the clear streams of your songs
Whose currents twine, diverge, and twine again,
Seeming to think themselves about themselves
Like fountains flowering in their fall. Dear Bach,
It's a great privilege. It always is.


## THE MEASURE OF POETRY

Consider the breaking of waves on a shore. The measure
governing this movement is the product of a number of
forces, some constant or relatively constant, others which
vary somewhat, still others extremely variable or even, so
far as concerns their periodicity, accidental: the tides, the
length of travel of the waves, the angle and underwater
topography of the shore, and the winds, both the great winds
from far away and the local land and sea breezes.

The idea one gets from these waves, whether the sea is
rough or calm, is the idea of a great consistency coupled with
a great freakishness, absolute law consisting with absolute
rage. The tide, drawn mainly by the mass of the moon, is
slow and stable, a vast breathing-in-sleep, and yet, however,
eccentrically offset to the revolution of the earth by somewhat
more than an hour a day, in a long rhythmic cycle bringing
the ebb and the flood by times to every instant. The force
which generates the wave begins, perhaps, far away in
mid-ocean, but it is not *that* water which ultimately strikes
the shore; if you look at wave motion out at sea, where it is
not affected by the bottom, you notice that most of the water
going to the crest, if it is not torn off in spray up there,
slides back the way it came. It is the power, not the material,
which is transmitted. The wave begins to form, as a substantial
body with its own history and fate, when its base meets with
the slope of the shore; the resultant of the two opposed forces

produces the high and rolling form. Either the wave rises until the unstable top curls forward and smashes down, or it rises steadily until the breaker is extruded at mid-height of the wave by pressure from above and below at once; this latter sort, because it throws its force forward rather than down, is less spectacular than the other, but it reaches further up the shore. The sum of these conflicting, cooperating powers, with the prevailing wind, generates individual forms and moments of great charm too complex to be analysed except in a general way, and as unpredictable in their particularity as the rainbow which sometimes glimmers in the spray blown from the falling crest.

The measure of poetry, too, begins far from the particular conformation of the poem, far out in the sea of tradition and the mind, even in the physiological deeps, where some empty, echoing, abstract interval begins to beat; it is the angle of incidence of this measure upon the materials of the poem which produces in the first place what in the result will be called "form." This tidal, surging element has to do with the general shape of the poem, and is a prior musical imposition upon its thought—musical, in that it exists at its beginning independently of any identifiable content: it is the power, not the material, which is transmitted. The poem is a quantity of force expended, like any human action, and is therefore not altogether formless even to begin with, but limited in its cadence by the energies present at its generation.

The rise of the shore shapes the wave. The objects which are to appear in the poem, as they begin to rise beneath the empty periodicity of the pure rhythm, introduce into that rhythm a new character, somewhat obstinate, angular, critical. But in another sense, which technically may be the more useful of the two, the analogy represents the elements of speech itself. The tidal impulse from far away, the wind's generation of force without content, these are the vowels; the consonants are rock and reed and sand, and the steep or shallow slope which gives the wave its form while absorbing the shock of its force, from strength bringing forth sweetness.

The laws of this measure are simple and large, so that in the scope of their generality room may remain for moments of

freedom, moments of chaos; the complex conjunction itself
raising up iridescences and fantastic shapes, relations which
it may be that number alone could enrage into being.


## THE FOUR AGES

The first age of the world was counterpoint,
Music immediate to all the senses
Not yet exclusive in their separate realms,
Wordlessly weaving the tapestried cosmos
Reflected mosaic in the wakening mind.

That world was lost, though echoes of it stray
On every breeze and breath, fragmented and
Heard but in snatches, thenceforth understood
Only by listeners like Pythagoras,
Who held the music of the spheres was silence
Because we had been hearing it from birth,
And Shakespeare, who made his Caliban recite
Its praises in the temporary isle.

A second age. Hard consonants began
To interrupt the seamless river of sound,
Set limits, break up and define in bits
What had before been pure relationship.
Units arose, and separations; words
Entered the dancing-space and made it song.
Though the divine had gone, yet there was then
The keenest human intuition of
Its hiding from us one dimension past
What the five senses could receive or send.

In the third age, without our noticing
The music ceased to sound, and we were left
As unaccompanied and strangely alone,
Like actors suddenly naked in a dream.
Yet we had words, and yet we had the word

Of poetry, a thinner music, but
Both subtle and sublime in its lament
For all that was lost to all but memory.

The fourth age is, it always is, the last.
The sentences break ranks, the orchestra
Has left the pit, the curtain has come down
Upon the smiling actors, and the crowd
Is moving toward the exits through the aisles.
Illusion at last is over, all proclaim
The warm humanity of common prose,
Informative, pedestrian and plain,
Imperative and editorial,
Opinionated and proud to be so,
Delighted to explain, but not to praise.

This is not history, it is a myth.
It's *de rigueur* for myths to have four ages,
Nobody quite knows why, unless to match
Four seasons and four elements and four
Voices of music and four gospels and four
Cardinal points on the compass rose and four
Whatever elses happen to come in four.
These correspondences are what remain
Of the great age when all was counterpoint
And no one minded that nothing mattered or meant.


THE THOUGHT OF TREES

It is a common fancy that trees are somehow conscious and
stand as the silent or whispering witnesses of the ways in which
we bustle through the world. But it is a truth of poetical
imagination that the trees are guardians and sponsoring
godfathers of a great part of thought. Not merely that various
traditions have looked on trees as sacred figures of the cosmos,
as the source of moral distinctions, as bearing all golden things,
the apples, the bough, the fleece; but also that trees, more

than we generally allow, have formed our view of the creation and nature of things, and, ambiguously responsible for these, the mind's image of its own process. This we are told by metaphors: a family tree, the root of the matter, a trunkline, a branch of the subject, and so on.

Trees appear as the formative image behind much thought brought to the critical point of paradox—

Where order in variety we see,
And where, though all things differ, all agree,

as Pope politely says of Windsor Forest. That trees, the largest of living things, are initially contained in tiny seeds, is already a spectacularly visible legend of the mysteries of generation and death. The tree, rooted in earth and flowering in heaven, intimates obscure and powerful reflexive propositions about the two realms; that root and top strangely mirror one another deepens and complicates the human analogy. The relation of single trunk and manifold branches forms the pattern for meditation on the one and the many, cause and effect, generality and particulars; while the movement in three stages, from many roots through one trunk to many branches, is supremely the image of historical process. The tree's relation with its leaves translates the paradigm into temporal terms, speaking of individual, generation, race, of identity continuous in change, of mortal endurance threaded through mortal evanescence, of times and a time.

Trees imagine life, and our imaginations follow as they may. The growth of a tree, its synchronous living and dying, from soft shoot to implacably hard (still growing) wood; the vast liquid transactions of capillarity within the solid form; the hard bark which nevertheless, as in the elm, reminds of water in its twisting flow; the enduring image of fluid life recorded in the rivery grain of boards (a mystical saying:—"Split the stick and there is Jesus"); the generalized simplicity composed of multitudinous complexity, generalized symmetry from the chaotic scrawl of upper branches; the simultaneity of freedom and order, richness and elegance, chance and destiny—these are some of the imaginings of the trees, which out of the earth and the air have dreamed so much of the human mind.

As architectural forms reflect their material origins, the first columns having been trees, so also with the mind. And so perhaps with its conclusions? "I shall be like that tree," Swift said to Edward Young, "I shall die first at the top." Since the eighteenth century, anyhow, when cathedrals began to remind people of forests and forests of cathedrals, it has come to seem sometimes that the mind acts in a drama staged with so high a regard for *realism* that the trees on the scene are carpentered at considerable cost out of real wood. Still, dryads and dendrones, the trees are within us, having their quiet irrefutable say about what we are and may become; how they are one of the shapes of our Protean nature, Melville in a single line expresses best—

The hemlock shakes in the rafter, the oak in the
driving keel

—and it is the founding tenet of poetical imagination that such images are inexhaustibly speaking, they call to compelling, strange analogies all thought that flowers in its fact.

## DRAWING LESSONS

### I

Your pencil will do particles and waves—
We call them points and lines—and nothing else.
Today we shall explore the mystery
Of points and lines moving over the void—
We call it paper—to imitate the world.
First think a moment of the ocean wave
When it stubs its toe against the scend of the shore
And stumbles forward, somersaults and breaks.
A moment ago nothing was there but wave,
And now nothing is here but particles;
So point and line not only turn into
Each other, but each hides from the other, too.
The seed of a point grows into a tree of line,

The line unfolding generates the plane
Of the world, perspective space in light and shade.


II

The points and lines, the seashore and the sea,
The particles and waves, translate as well
Into the consonants and vowels that make
The speech that makes the world; a simple thing.
Or else a complex thing proceeding still
From simple opposites that make it seem
As if it might be understood, though this
Is probably illusion in the sense,
Delusion in the mind, making the world
Our true hallucination. Much as matter
And anti-matter are said to explode at touch,
So at the meeting-place of sea, air, shore,
Both sides explode, the ocean into spray,
The shore more slowly into boulders, rocks,
And final sand. All this repeats itself.


III

Always repeat yourself. To draw a line
's not much, but twenty-seven wavy lines
In parallel will visibly become
The sea; by tempering their distances
Apart, now near, now far away, we make
Ranges of mountains standing in their valleys;
By arbitrary obstacles of shape
That will prohibit passage to our lines,
We make a fleet of sailboats or a forest,
Depending on what shapes we have left void.
We see that repetition makes the world
The way it is, Nature repeats herself
Indefinitely in every kind, and plays
Far-ranging variations on the kinds,
Doodling inventions endlessly, as the pencil does.

## IV

We said the water and the shore explode
And then repeat; that's not quite the whole truth.
For water has the wondrous property
And power of assembling itself again
When shattered, but the shore cannot do that.
The Second Law seems to reverse itself
For water, but not for land, whose massive cliffs
Break into boulders that break into rocks
That then descend to sand and don't return.
While I've been talking, you've been drawing lines
With your pencil, illustrating what I say
Along with whatever else you illustrate:
The pencil lead's become a stub, its black
Graphite remains became the world you made,
And it will shorten when you sharpen it.

## V

The Second Law's an instrument, we're told,
Of immense power, but there's sorrow in it,
The invention of a parsimonious people
Accustomed to view creation on a budget
Cut to economy more than to delight
At splendor overflowing every vessel.
Land is the locus of form and dignity
Disguising the way down to age and death,
Shameful decay, and dust that blows away—
See, rub your drawing and it smudges into dust,
Because your pencil is a citizen
Of the middle class material world, designed
To be a minor illustrator of
What we become and what becomes of us.
The sea's a little more mysterious than that.

# DU RÊVE, DE LA MATHÉMATIQUE, ET DE LA MORT

On dreams, on mathematics, and on death.
Card-catalogues turn up such heady stuff
Sometimes as this, this rapture from the depths
Which isn't where it should be on the shelf.
For a moment, remembering Borges' poor young clerk,
I idly consider writing it myself,
Setting a record for the shortest work
The world had ever seen on three such themes
Of such import as death and math and dreams.

I think of asking that a search be made,
But give it up, my French is not so great
And right now I've got plenty on my plate
Without this title turned up by pure chance
As if designed to bait my ignorance.
And yet—? But I shall let this once-glimpsed fish
Swim through the deep of thought beyond my wish,
And resign myself to knowing nothing more
*Du rêve, de la mathématique, et de la mort.*


# TRANSLATION

*Anima quodammodo omnia,*
How lovely and exact the fit between
The language and the thing it means to say.
In English all but the sense evaporates:
*The soul is in a manner all there is.*
What's that but a poor thin mingy thing
Fit for the brain alone? Where is that world,
Where did it go, in which they said those things
And sang those things in their high halls of stone?
Vanished utterly, and we have instead
*The world is everything that is the case,*
That's flat enough to satisfy no one
After the lonely longings of plainsong:

*In paradisum deducant te angeli,*
What's that in other syllables and modes,
*Now angels lead thee into paradise?*
It still may draw a tremor and a tear
Sometimes, if only for its being gone,
That untranslatable, translated world
Of the Lady and the singers and the dead.


## SPECULATION

Prepare for death. But how can you prepare
For death? Suppose it isn't an exam,
But more like the Tavern Scene in Henry IV,
Or that other big drunk, the Symposium?

Remember, everybody will be there,
Sooner or later at first, then all at once.
Maybe the soul at death becomes a star.
Maybe the galaxies are one great dance,

Maybe. For as earth's population grows,
So does the number of the unfixed stars,
Exploding from the sempiternal Rose
Into the void of an expanding universe.

If it be so, it doesn't speak well for
The social life hereafter: faster than light
The souls avoid each other, as each star
Speeds outward, goes out, or goes out of sight.


## GYROSCOPE

This admirable gadget, when it is
Wound on a string and spun with steady force,
Maintains its balance on most any smooth

Surface, pleasantly humming as it goes.
It is whirled not on a constant course, but still
Stands in unshivering integrity
For quite some time, meaning nothing perhaps
But being something agreeable to watch,
A silver nearly silence gleaning a still-
ness out of speed, composing unity
From spin, so that its hollow spaces seem
Solids of light, until it wobbles and
Begins to whine, and then with an odd lunge
Eccentric and reckless, it skids away
And drops dead into its own skeleton.


## PLAYING SKITTLES

No matter how dull your soul, you cannot help
But fill these skittering wooden dervishes
With spirit and will as you lean over their box
To watch them skip and weave and stagger among
The dumbbell pins. You even urge them on
Their drunken courses, cursing them when they miss
With what looks like purposeful malevolence,
Although you know they are like two blind men
Shut in invisible revolving doors—

With spirit and will and, yes, with mind as well:
They seem to go where they've a mind to go,
Sometimes intent, sometimes indifferent,
Until they stutter out of energy
And tumble over and lie down and die.

Of course they know no mind, and cannot mind
Either your prayers and curses or the pins.
And yet this matter of mind's no simple matter:
If not out there, then how in the world in here?
Agelong these tops concealed the gyroscope
Whose insane energies stabilize the earth.

# TV

It would have delighted Bishop Berkeley by
Seeming to understand and demonstrate
What no one could refute by kicking stones,
The one dependency that links the mind
The senses and the world: whatever is made
The object of your vision is so made
Because another is looking at it too,
A fraction of a second earlier.

The straying lens across the battlefield,
The cameraman's quivering hand considering death,
The instant replay—all of them shopworn,
All soiled and secondhand goods of this world
Shaken in God's wavering attention just
An instant before we see it as out there.


# THE SPY

Out there, out there beyond the air,
Among the maelstroms of the burning dust,
The giant blue fires of the far away,
Beyond the eye of Palomar, out there
The witnessing astronomers go,
Lords of the Book of Zero.

Under the feet, under the solid ground,
The inaccessible burning of the earth
Makes whirlpools of the boiling rock,
Shifting the surface of the stable scene
And varying the mountains and the seas
Under the histories.

Behind the brow, a scant deep inch away,
The little nutshell mystery meditates
The spiral fire of the soul;

502

Through eyes as innocent and wide as day
It spies upon the true appearances of
Our sensible old world.


## THE OLD DAYS[1]

Remember how Daylight Saving used to end
Near Halloween, just at the fall of leaf
When all the gardens died, All Saints, All Souls,
Those solemn first few days of getting used
To the sudden darkness bringing winter down
On all the grown-ups driving home from work,
The children kicking home through drifts of leaf?

This year the hour lost will stay away,
Kept out of time in some space of its own.
Will those who die fall sixty minutes short
Of what was owed? Where is that hour now,
What is its weather, is it dark or day?


## AFTERMATH

When he had carried to term the sacred poem
That for so many years had starved him lean,
What in the world was left for him to do
In the world but wait there, in the world?

Now see him coming down Can Grande's stair
To eat Can Grande's bread, the wasted man
Who has been through Hell and seen what was to see,
And been through Heaven and seen what was to see,

---

1. Reader, the Congress crossed us up about this one,
   Which puts it with the missing hour in some gone
   Dimension of the metaphysical playpen
   Where whatever wasn't going to happen didn't happen.

And now is waiting for what is to be
Again, the second death although of bliss
Assured with his immortal girl restored—
Like Lazarus, save in his being saved.

The world is what it was: though Boniface
Is dead, so is the Savior-Emperor
(of typhoid, at Trier, all those years ago);
The world is what it always is; the Po

Is still a filthy ditch along whose banks
A populace of hogs, curs, wolves, pursues
Destruction as it did; nothing has changed,
The sacred poem is done, that heaven and earth

Had put their hands to, and like one lost he waits
Among the lost, musing sometimes on Virgil
In Limbo, and, though of bliss at last assured,
On how the Terrace of the Proud awaits

The painful penitent stooped under his stone.
Of all this, one imagines, he says nothing,
The man that mothers frighten children with:
"Be good, or he'll haul you back with him to Hell."


## THE BANQUET

*A translation of Dante Alighieri's* Convito,
*Dissertation 2, Canzone 1*

Ye intelligences, turning the third sphere,
Hear out the reasoning within my heart
Stranger than I can openly relate.
The heaven that obeys your moving art
—Such noble natures as you surely are—
I see has brought me to my present state;
So of my suffering any debate

Seems that it rightly should be told to ye:
Wherefore I pray that ye will hear my part.
I would tell the strange history of the heart,
How the sad soul there weeps bitterly
Because a spirit speaks, opposing her,
That comes upon the shining of your star.

My sorrowful heart's life often would be
A thought so sweet that it would rise in flight
Many a time to the feet of our great Sire
To see a Lady glorious in light,
Of whom it spoke so blessedly to me
That my soul spoke, and said: "I would go there."
But, putting her to flight, one does appear
Who lords it with such power over me,
My trembling heart shows outwardly its fear.
And this one made me see a Lady here,
And said: "Who would behold felicity,
Let him look in this Lady's eyes
If he fears not the agony of sighs."

Now comes the adversary, who can slay,
Against my humble thought that would give me
Word of an angel crownéd in the skies,
So that my soul cried out, and still must cry,
Saying: "Alas, how is she fled away,
The piteous one who showed my pity's guise."
Then this afflicted heart said of its eyes:
"What hour such a lady looked therein,
Why would they not believe my word of her?"
Always I said: "In such eyes as hers are
One surely stands whose glance can murder men.
It not availed me, that I saw it plain,
Against their gazing whereby I am slain."

"You are not slain, but only as though blind,
Soul in our keeping, with so great lament,"
A spirit of gentle love replied to me.
"Because, upon that Lady all intent,

The life has so been driven from your mind
That you are full of fear, and cowardly.
But she is pity and humility,
Courteous and wise in her magnificence:
Know that she is your Lady from this day!
And having undeceived your eyes you may
See such high miracles her ornaments
That you will say to Love: O my true Lord,
Behold thy handmaid, who will do thy word."

Song, I think they will be few indeed
Who well and rightly understand your sense,
So difficult your speech and intricate.
Wherefore if you should come by any chance
Among such folk so little fit to read
As that you seem not to *communicate*,
I'd have you take heart even at that rate,
My latest and dear one, saying to them:
"Look you at least how beautiful I am."


AN ENDING

After the weeks of unrelenting heat
A rainy day brings August to an end
As if in ceremony. The spirit, dry
From too much light too steadily endured,
Delights in the heavy silver water globes
That make change from the sun's imperial gold;
The mind, relieved from being always brilliant,
Goes forth a penitent in a shroud of grey
To walk the sidewalks that reflect the sky,
The line of lights diminishing down the street,
The splashed lights of the traffic going home.

## ORIGIN

I went way back and asked the old
Ones deep in the graves, the youngest dead,
How language began, and who had the cred-
it of it, gods, men, devils, elves?
And this is the answer I was told:
"We got together one day," they said,
"And talked it over among ourselves."


## PLANE

The wingéd shadow with the self within,
Image projected at infinity,
Caught in the sky-completed rainbow's eye
And haloed in the gunsight of the sun,
Cruises beneath its substance, one on one.

# Acknowledgments

Acknowledgment is made to the editors and publishers of the following periodicals and anthologies in which many of these poems have appeared: *Accent, American Poetry Review, American Scholar, Approach, Atlantic Monthly, Audience, Beloit Poetry Journal, Bennington Quarterly, Boston Review, Boston University Journal, Botteghe Oscure, Briarcliff Quarterly, Carleton Miscellany, Chicago Review, Chicago Tribune Magazine, Colorado Review, Commentary, The Dubliner, Folio* (Brandeis University), *Furioso, Gambit, Georgia Review, Halcyon, Harper's Bazaar, Harper's Magazine, Harvard Advocate, Here & Now, Hika* (Kenyon College), *Holiday, The Hollins Critic, Horizon, The Hudson Review, The Island, Kenyon Review, The London Magazine, The London Times Literary Supplement, Michigan Quarterly, The Nation, New American Review, New Poems 1944, New Republic, New World Writing, The New Yorker, The New York Times, The Noble Savage, The Northwestern Tri-Quarterly, Open Road, The Outsider, Partisan Review, The Penny Paper, Poetry, Poetry Dial, Poetry Ireland, Poetry London-New York, Polemic* (Western Reserve), *Quadrille, Quarterly Review of Literature, The Reporter, Salmagundi, The Saturday Evening Post, Saturday Review, The Sewanee Review, The Shasta Review, Shenandoah, Silo* (Bennington College), *Southern Poetry Review, Vassar Review, Vice Versa, The War Poets, Western Poetry Review, Western Review*.

The poems "Sunday at the End of Summer," "Dialogue," and "The Pond," collected in *The Salt Garden*, appeared originally in *The New Yorker*. "The Scales of the Eyes" was first printed, with a commentary by Mr. Kenneth Burke, in *The Sewanee Review* for winter 1952.

Some of the poems collected in *The Blue Swallows* first appeared in student publications of the University of Vermont and Richmond University. Others appeared in limited editions issued by the Tinker Press, Poems in Folio, the Perishable Press, and the Lowell-Adams House Printers. The following first appeared in *The New Yorker:* "The View," "The Companions," "At the Airport," "Presidential Address to a Party of Exiles," "The May Day Dancing," and "The Mud Turtle."

"The Painter Dreaming in the Scholar's House" was written for the inauguration of the Reverend C. V. Joyce, S.J., as president of Boston College, and appeared in the program on that occasion; also in a limited edition published by the Phoenix Book Shop, New York, 1968.

509

"Lines & Circularities" was written for *The New York Times Special Supplement on Records and Recordings,* March 7, 1971, at the request of Theodore Strongin.

# Index of Titles

512

515